UNDERSTANDING THE NEW GLOBAL ECONOMY

Understanding the New Global Economy: A European Perspective argues that globalisation is facing economic and political headwinds. A new global economic geography is emerging, cross-border relationships are changing, and global governance structures must come to terms with a new multipolar world.

This book clarifies the fundamental questions and trade-offs in this new global economy, and gives readers the tools to understand contemporary debates. It presents a range of possible policy options, without being prescriptive.

Following a modular structure, each chapter takes a similar approach but can also be read as a stand-alone piece. State-of-the-art academic research and historical experiences are woven throughout the book, and readers are pointed towards relevant sources of information.

This text is an accessible guide to the contemporary world economy, suited to students of international economics, political economy, globalisation, and European studies. It will also be valuable reading for researchers, professionals, and general readers interested in economics, politics, and civil society.

Harald Sander is Professor of International Economics and has been awarded the Jean Monnet Chair "Europe in the Global Economy" at TH Köln, University of Applied Sciences, Germany. He also holds a position as Professor of Economics at Maastricht School of Management.

UNDERSTANDING THE NEW GLOBAL ECONOMY

A European Perspective

Harald Sander

Routledge
Taylor & Francis Group

LONDON AND NEW YORK

First published 2022
by Routledge
2 Park Square, Milton Park, Abingdon, Oxon OX14 4RN

and by Routledge
605 Third Avenue, New York, NY 10158

Routledge is an imprint of the Taylor & Francis Group, an informa business

British Library Cataloguing-in-Publication Data
A catalogue record for this book is available from the British Library

Library of Congress Cataloging-in-Publication Data
A catalog record has been requested for this book

ISBN: 978-0-367-52373-2 (hbk)
ISBN: 978-0-367-52369-5 (pbk)
ISBN: 978-1-003-05761-1 (ebk)

DOI: 10.4324/9781003057611

Typeset in Bembo
by codeMantra

CONTENTS

PREFACE

Economic globalisation is slowing and facing political headwinds. This book argues that globalisation is not passé, but merely changing its character. A new global economy (NGE) is emerging, cross-border (inter-)dependencies are changing, and governance in the global economy has to come to terms with a new multipolar world.

The book provides an accessible executive guide to the contemporary world economy for a broad audience of all those stakeholders in business, policy, and civil society, who are deeply interested in or affected by globalisation. As the NGE is evolving fast, new issues are coming up on an almost daily basis. The basic idea of this book is therefore to clarify the fundamental questions and trade-offs, rather than offering conclusive judgements that may be outdated the very next day. Hence, the central intention is to facilitate the reader's entry into contemporary debates.

The concept for this book is inspired from my experiences as a holder of the Jean Monnet Chair on "Europe in the Global Economy" at TH Köln. When conducting summer schools and short courses on the global economy from a European perspective, I found standard textbooks often too technical for the non-specialist audience, and occasionally not close enough to current global and European affairs. Hence, the book is also designed as a text for short courses, aiming at stimulating debates among participants from Europe and the rest of the world.

In sum, the book has five distinct features:

- It is an accessible executive guide to the emerging new global economy.
- It introduces the reader to the European particularities in the new global economy.

- It features a modular structure that allows to read/study/discuss each chapter as a stand-alone. Yet, all chapter follow a similar structure, approach, and have a common thread.
- It features state-of-the-art coverage by relating to recent academic contributions, hence extending over the traditional textbook approach by directing readers to work-in-progress literature sources. Thus, the reader is guided to the ongoing research in times when knowledge is expanding fast.
- It aims at revealing relevant policy options to the reader rather than providing ready-made answers.

I hope the reader will find the book a useful daily companion for understanding and engaging with the new global economy.

Harald Sander

1

INTRODUCTION

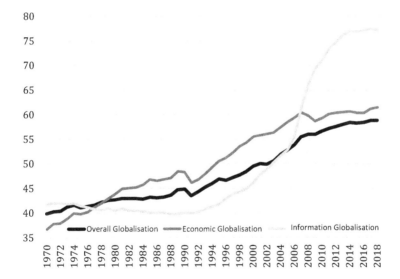

FIGURE 1.1 Development of De-facto Globalisation, KOF-Globalisation Index, 1970–2018.

Source: Own graph based on KOF Globalisation Index 2020 data. Gygli et al. (2019).

1 Towards a new global economy

Since the late 1980s, the rapid growth of cross-border economic activity, especially international trade, investment, and finance, has by far outstripped the growth of global production, a process for which the term 'globalisation' became popular in the 1990s. Economic globalisation, visualised in Figure 1.1 by a comprehensive index,[1] was at the heart of this process. However, since the

DOI: 10.4324/9781003057611-1

great financial crisis of 2008–2009, and after about 30 years of economic 'hyper-globalisation', economic cross-border activities are stalling, though they remain at a high level. Is globalisation passé? The rapid increase in the internationalisation of data and knowledge as visualised by the index of information globalisation[2] in the last two decades suggests that it is premature to announce globalisation's death. Rather, globalisation is changing its character. A **new global economy** (NGE) is emerging.

Economic globalisation in recent decades has been driven by falling transportation and communication costs and supported by a worldwide reduction of barriers to cross-border trade, investment, and finance. Production globalised, involving emerging economies deeply into the value chains of multinational enterprises. Smartphones designed in California and assembled in China, with chips, displays, receivers, etc. coming from many other countries, have become the hallmark of this globalisation, which now seems to have lost its momentum.

A slowed-down process of globalisation, however, can simply reflect that the internationalisation of economic activities has reached a level beyond which it is uneconomical to globalise further. Moreover, even if de-globalisation would happen, this is not necessarily something to worry about. After all, globalisation is at best a means to increase the 'wealth of nations', and not an end in itself. For this very reason, it is important to understand what the NGE may entail.

The first key argument for an emerging NGE relates to changes induced by **new digital technologies**. Digitalisation may impact globalisation in three major ways:

- **Robotisation**. The more robots replace workers, the less important labour costs will become for locating production in low-wage countries. Since the mid-1980s, this offshoring has been a major driver of the globalisation of production, investment, and trade, especially in manufacturing. Robotisation, thus, has the potential to reverse this trend by promoting a re-shoring of manufacturing.
- **Digitalisation of intangibles**. New technologies increasingly allow to digitalise services and make them tradable across borders. As digital delivery of services comes with basically zero transportation costs, outsourcing labour-intensive services to low-wage countries may become a key feature of the NGE. Current examples are software programming or back-office services, like booking systems for airlines.[3]
- **Digitalisation of global money and finance**. With the recent advances in digitalisation, new forms of digital finance are emerging. Even more drastic changes could emanate from digital currencies when used globally. Most prominently, Facebook is entertaining the idea of creating a private digital money, initially called Libra (now Diem), while major central banks are considering creating central bank digital currencies.

A second set of arguments posits that a NGE will emerge because the effects of the past incarnation of globalisation are undermining its sustainability in three major ways:

- **A globalisation backlash**. Globalisation has created losers, especially among low-skilled workers in advanced countries. If policies do not sufficiently pay attention to the negative side effects, anti-globalisation sentiments can emerge, ultimately undermining globalisation by lending support to a new protectionism.
- **The climate imperative**. Globalisation has promoted an unprecedented rise of economic activity in emerging economies. However, this rise is at odds with curbing climate change. To reconcile this ecological imperative with the desire for an increasing standard of living in the global South, economic growth in the NGE must become climate-neutral.
- **The emergence of a multipolar world**. The last two decades of globalisation have helped the rise of new economic superpowers. An emerging multipolar world is replacing a world order that has been economically dominated by the incumbent advanced countries. Figure 1.2 shows that China's share in world gross domestic product (GDP), measured in purchasing power parity, has already overtaken the share of the European Union (EU) in 2012, and the share of the United States of America (USA) after 2016. In a similar vein, the group of emerging economies and developing countries has jointly increased its share from 37% in 1980 to close to 58% in 2020.

As a consequence of the arguments above, this leads to a third key argument for a NGE to emerge:

- **A new governance of globalisation**. The governance of globalisation as it used to be, will have to undergo changes. Whether this will result in more global governance, a move to unilateral decision making, or a rebalancing of governance at the global, regional, and national levels, remains to be seen. Whatever the way forward, whether it supports or restrains forces of globalisation, a new governance of globalisation will impact the future of the emerging NGE.

This book takes the reader on a tour of the emerging NGE, visualised in Figure 1.3, by discussing the various ways it impacts global production, global trade, global investment, global intangibles, global money and finance, and finally governance.

The remainder of this introductory chapter familiarises the reader with the meaning (Section 2) and history of globalisation (Section 3), before outlining the major determinants of a potential evolution of the NGE (Section 4). Section 5 provides a preview of the book.

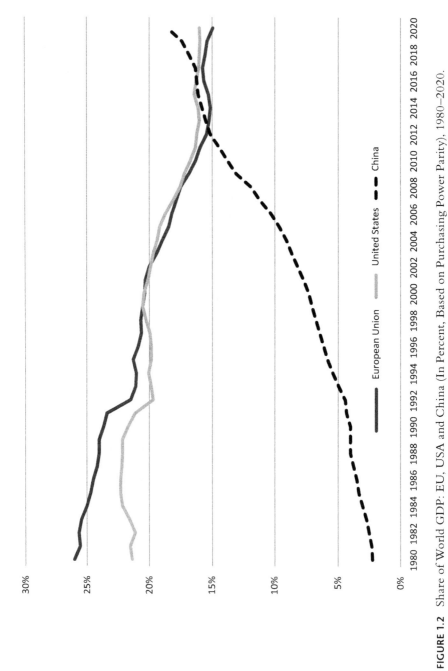

FIGURE 1.2 Share of World GDP: EU, USA and China (In Percent, Based on Purchasing Power Parity), 1980–2020.

Data source: IMF World Economic Outlook database. October 2020. 2020 data are IMF estimates.

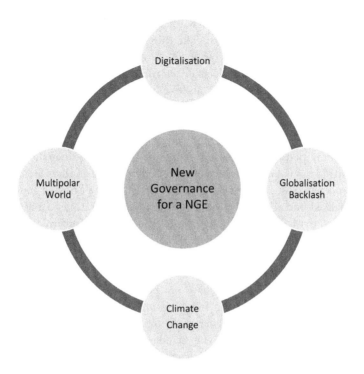

FIGURE 1.3 The Emerging New Global Economy.

2 What is globalisation?

2.1 The two meanings of globalisation

The first and most intuitive meaning of globalisation relates to the rapid increase of cross-border activities, particularly international trade, investments and finance, and increasingly information and knowledge as visualised in Figure 1.1. Economists refer to this meaning of globalisation as **economic integration**.

Why cross-border activities? The first reason is **arbitrage**: Goods are cheaper in a foreign country, profits on producing abroad are higher, higher wages and a higher standard of living attract foreign workers and migrants, financial investments elsewhere offer a higher return, more safety, or lower taxation, etc. In other words, when countries are different in terms of prices, incomes, wages, profits, interest rates, etc., these very differences invite cross-border activities. The second reason is search for **variety**: Foreign goods may be different from ours, and we like them for that very reason, some people enjoy work and the living experience abroad, and investors strive not to put 'all eggs in one basket'. Hence, even in a world that does not provide incentives for arbitrage, cross-border activities make sense and can be quite intense.

A second meaning of globalisation has been popularised by a book by Thomas Friedman (2005), *The World Is Flat*. The title suggests that in a fully globalised world, arbitrage affects every corner. As a consequence, economic activity sprawls equally over the globe. Hence, the more arbitrage is doing its job, the more globalised the world becomes, and the more equal would be the **spread of economic activity** over the globe.

Scholars of economic geography usually respond to this claim by showing a NASA map of the 'world at night', created from satellite photos (Figure 1.4). Emitted light is used as an indicator of economic activity. The map shows that the earth is indeed not flat in terms of economic activity. Rather, there are economic hotspots in a few major regions of the world. In fact, it appears that activities are both globalised and regionally concentrated at the same time, a phenomenon often referred to as global localisation, or for short "**glocalisation**".

As long as the world is not flat, there is room for arbitrage. While some emerging economies have been developing fast and started converging to advanced country per-capita income levels, many countries are still left behind. Obviously, trade in goods, investment, and finance have not been sufficient to flatten the world. In the NGE, it will be interesting to see to what extent increasing cross-border services and knowledge flows will help to flatten the world. Ultimately, in a world of persistent huge differences in living standards, this will surely push the most effective, yet most regulated arbitrage mechanism – labour migration.

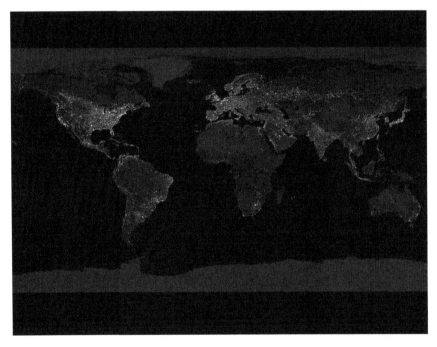

FIGURE 1.4 The Glocalisation of Global Economic Activity. Image credit: NASA/ NOAA.

2.2 The drivers of globalisation

Technological advancements, from the introduction of steam ships and railways in the 19th century to modern information and communication technologies (ICT), are key drivers of cross-border activities. However, the speed with which globalisation takes place also depends on whether policies obstruct or facilitate cross-border activities.

Figure 1.5 shows how **de-facto** economic globalisation has taken the lead in the 1980s and early 1990s, while the index of all facilitating **de-jure** liberalisation policies followed only with a time lag. However, from the early 1990s onward, it started to increase faster than de-facto globalisation. The creation of the World Trade Organisation (WTO) in 1995 has been a major step in liberalising world trade. Likewise, widespread de-regulation of trade, investment, and finance at the national level, as well as regional liberalisation efforts, such as regional and bilateral trade and investment agreements have been key in boosting cross-border activities. However, de-jure globalisation has been plateauing since the second half of the 2000s. The great financial crisis of 2008–2009 has been a major event that has led to some re-regulation of (global) finance. Moreover, in many countries an increasing public discontent with the economic outcomes of the past globalisation can be observed, and this has put a halt to liberalisation policies.

FIGURE 1.5 De-facto and De-jure Economic Globalisation, KOF-Globalisation Index, 1970–2018.

Source: Own graph based on KOF Globalisation Index 2020 data. Gygli et al. (2019).

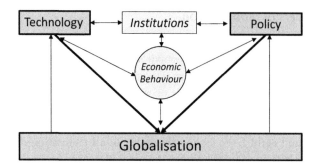

FIGURE 1.6 A Simple Model of the Drivers of Globalisation.

Our implicit theoretical framework used in this narrative is that technology and policy are the main drivers of globalisation, as illustrated by the bold arrows in Figure 1.6. They both influence trade costs in the broadest sense of the word, comprising transportation and communication costs, as well as political barriers to cross-border activities.

However, new technologies do not simply fall from heaven. Ultimately, they will only be developed and implemented when they pay off. Institutions, and the policies that back them, play a tremendous role for the direction of technological advancements.

As an example, consider Europe before the Industrial Revolution. Population was so abundant, and ordinary people were often working as serfs without citizen rights, with wages were so low that it was not profitable to develop machines to replace workers or make them more productive. A complex process of economic and political development changed this and eventually made labour-saving technologies profitable, including the steam engine that contributed greatly to reducing shipping costs and thus promoting globalisation. Institutions, such as those guaranteeing property rights, have helped to stimulate the development and investment in labour-saving technologies (see Chapter 2 for details).

To push a similar argument into the present, incentives for developing new technologies will influence whether or not they will be labour- and environmental-friendly, and how they ultimately affect globalisation.

Thus, we conclude that **institutions**, and the **economic behaviour** they incentivise, are important intermediary drivers of globalisation. This, however, is not a simple one-way street. For example, economic behaviour that results in market power will influence the intensity and direction of technological development as well, e.g. via lobbying and policy making. Moreover, the outcomes of globalisation can feed back into policies and technological developments.

In the light of this simple model, we narrate in the next section a brief history of globalisation over three historic waves of globalisation, before we apply it to an exposition of the upcoming fourth wave, the emerging NGE.

3 The first three waves of globalisation

In the pre-industrial era, the world was indeed flat. All countries had low levels of labour productivity, and therefore, low per-capita income. Some, like China and the Arab world, looked more promising than Europe in some areas by the 14th or 13th century, respectively, but transportation costs were way too high to encourage trade to arbitrage, i.e. to take advantage of differences in production costs. However, trade was still vibrant, not least along the Silk Road that connected China with Europe and the Middle East. The major trading motive was to get access to goods not available at home or – at least an exotic variety of home goods, often handcrafted in small villages. Trade was in the forms of either barter trade, or gold and other precious metals were used for international payments, though within Europe a medieval system of private banking developed to facilitate cross-border trade. However, the ruling kings and other aristocrats were not interested in encouraging trade, and basically saw it as a source of tariff revenues. Likewise, the European mercantilists of the 17th and 18th centuries viewed trade, or more precisely exports, mainly as a source of gold revenues for the Crown.

All this changed with the Industrial Revolution, which started in England around 1820, with the introduction of labour-saving technologies such as the spinning jenny and – most prominently – the steam engine. It culminated into the first wave of globalisation that emerged more than a century ago, somewhere between 1870 and World War I (WWI). While some observers argue that today the world is going through a second wave of globalisation, the development of the global economy, especially after World War II (WWII), suggests that a more granular distinction is useful. We therefore distinguish **four waves of globalisation**, which are closely related to major disruptive technological changes, recently labelled as a development from Industry 1.0 to Industry 4.0.

Industry 1.0 is related to the mechanisation of production, predominantly in manufacturing. Industry 2.0 signifies the age of mass production in 'Fordist' factories, with electricity and the combustion engine as major technological drivers. The development of information and communication technologies (ICT), and the subsequent computerisation of production, starting somewhere in the mid-1980s to early 1990s, marks the Industry 3.0 period that may or may not last until now. Recently, the label Industry 4.0 has been introduced as a catchphrase for advances in digital technologies, but in particular with respect to the robotisation of production and the rapid developments in artificial intelligence (AI).[4]

All these advances have not only shaped industrial production and the rise of nations to riches, but also the tradability and the trading cost of goods and services. As this opens possibilities for profitable arbitrage, it has also changed the political attitudes towards cross-border activities and the willingness to open up for trade and finance. Table 1.1 summarises the main developments, its enablers, and effects on cross-border activities over the four waves of globalisation.

TABLE 1.1 Four Waves of Globalisation

Globalisation Wave	0.0 *Before 1820*	1.0 *1870–WWI*	2.0 *WWII–Mid-1980s*	3.0 *Mid-1980s–?*	4.0 *Now–?*
Global production	Industry 0.0: Manual production	Industry 1.0: Manufacturing	Industry 2.0: Mass production	Industry 3.0: Global value chains	Industry 4.0: Digital & knowledge economy
Global income	• Flat world	• Great divergence I • Catching-up of advanced countries	• Great divergence II • Convergence I: newly industrialising countries (NICs) .	• Convergence II	• Multipolar world • New flat world or new divergence?
Key technologies	• Non	• Steam engine	• Electricity • Combustion engine • Containerisation	• ICT • Containerisation	• Digitalisation • Knowledge
Global trade and investment	• Variety	• Arbitrage in goods • Complementary division of labour	• Variety • Arbitrage in goods	• Arbitrage in production tasks • Surge in FDI • Variety	• Arbitrage in services • Variety
Finance	• Gold and metals • Medieval private banking	• Gold standard • Capital mobility	• Bretton-Woods system (until 1973) • Limited capital mobility, (increasing from the 1970s onward)	• Capital mobility • Globalisation of finance	• Digital currencies? • Multipolar international monetary and financial system?
Policy	• Feudal system • Mercantilism	• Free trade • Infant industry protectionism	• Liberalisation of trade and investment in advanced countries • Opening-up in NICs	• Liberalisation of trade and investment	• Multipolar global decision making? • Rise of protectionism? • Climate change policies?

The first wave of globalisation

The most important technological driving force of the first wave of globalisation were the new labour-saving technologies. The development of the steam engine, and the subsequent introduction of steamboats and railways in the 19th century brought down transportation cost drastically. But policies mattered too: entrepreneurs quickly realised new business opportunities from trading and successfully lobbied for a liberal trading order in the political sphere, especially in Britain, the technological leader at the time. Hence, trade barriers fell rapidly. However, late industrialisers, especially the USA and some continental European countries, continued to protect their infant industries against the leading British companies until they found themselves able to compete with the incumbents. The rest of the world, often colonies, however, remained un- or under-industrialised, and did not take part in this take-off. The division of labour was a complementary one, with advanced countries exporting manufactures to the developing world in exchange for primary goods, especially raw materials. The increasing gap in development between the few advanced countries and the rest of the world is known as the 'Great Divergence'.

This was also a period of globalising capital. Trade needed to be financed in a world where trustworthy global currencies were not yet in supply, at least outside the British empire. Gold (in practice often silver as well), however, was an internationally accepted means of payment. National paper monies thus had to be backed fully by gold reserves, entitling the owner of paper money to exchange it into the promised equivalent amount of gold. This **gold standard** provided the needed trust in national monies. Consequently, as gold was traded globally, so were currencies. Thus, under the gold standard capital was free to move globally.

The interwar period

WWI, and later, the great depression of 1929, contributed to a rise in nationalist sentiments, protectionism, and ultimately to a collapse of world trade. The gold standard that had helped to promote the first wave of globalisation, became a golden straitjacket when countries became short of gold reserves and eventually resorted to protectionism. As a consequence, the gold standard was abandoned and a phase of beggar-thy-neighbour currency devaluations, inward-looking protectionism, and nationalism led to global dis-integration.

The second wave of globalisation

Against this background efforts were made to rebuild an open world economy by means of creating multilateral institutions after WWII. The *General Agreement on Tariffs and Trade* (GATT) was created not only to offer a framework for trade liberalisation but also to erect a barrier against a new protectionist race to the bottom. The Bretton-Wood Institutions, the *International Monetary Fund* (IMF) and the *International Bank for Reconstruction and Development* (commonly referred to as the 'World Bank'), were created to provide stability in global finance, and financial support for, as the name says, the reconstruction of war-ridden economies, as well as for developing countries in the period of de-colonisation.

This system allowed the recovery of global trade after WWII. However, it took until the mid-1960s that especially Europe and – even later – Japan found themselves in a position to compete internationally and to agree to more substantial tariff reductions. Trade amongst advanced countries started to flourish gradually, often as so-called intra-industry trade, i.e. the exchange of similar products, like cars or clothing, that promised variety. The rise in trade was facilitated by the introduction of container ships in the late 1960s. Alongside the advances in air freight, this brought down trade costs drastically. Containerisation especially helped to boost intercontinental long-distance trade. This not only eased the classic complementary trade pattern with developing countries but, most importantly, facilitated the rise of so-called 'newly industrialising countries' (NICs), particularly in South-East Asia, to emerge as successful exporters of manufactures. However, with the exemption of the NICs from the 1970s onward, the Great Divergence between advanced and other developing countries continued.

On the finance side, in 1971 the Bretton-Woods System (BWS) was effectively abandoned. In the BWS, all currencies were fixed to the US dollar, and capital movements remained largely restricted or at least under political control. As the trust in the US dollar was lost because of high US inflation rates, exchange rates were finally allowed to fluctuate against the dollar, driven by supply and demand. This paved the way for the opening up of currency and capital markets, and deregulating finance in the subsequent decades.

The third wave of globalisation

From the mid-1980s onward, technological advancements in ICTs became the key driving technological factor behind globalisation. With the emergence of computer-aided manufacturing, production value chains could suddenly be 'sliced up'. Production of many goods no longer had to take place in a single factory. The production of parts of a product as well as the final assembling could be located wherever it is most efficient and least costly. The most prominent example is Apple's iPhone, designed in the USA and assembled in China with various intermediate inputs from many countries.

Slicing up the value chain can, of course, be done also within a country. In effect, domestic outsourcing is common too. However, given the much bigger differences between production costs and the much greater variety of specialised skills on a global scale, the globalisation of value chains often offers more efficient opportunities than pure domestic ones. This is exactly what happened from the 1990s onward: increasing possibilities for slicing-up the value chains, coupled with drastically falling information and communication costs, gave rise to what has become known as global value chains (GVCs). Arbitrage in production tasks became a major driver of globalisation in the third wave of globalisation. GVC production has been brought into being by a surge of foreign direct investments. Falling trade costs have bolstered this development. While ICTs facilitate the steering of global production networks, an overarching trend towards trade liberalisation supported the rise of GVCs, which cannot afford tariffs and other costly border obstacles.

In international finance, deregulation and liberalisation of cross-border banking and finance were high on the agenda of policy makers, not only in the advanced countries but also in emerging economies, especially those that increasingly involved themselves in GVCs.

The rise of GVCs has also helped a dramatic economic rise of some emerging countries. The great divergence that started with the Industrial Revolution, has given way, if not to a great convergence, but at least to a partial one that had started for some small NICs with the second wave of globalisation, and reached new heights, contributing greatly to the emergence of a multipolar world, in which China is the most visible new global player.

4 The emerging new global economy

A potential fourth wave of globalisation is technologically driven by the rapid development of digitalisation, especially robotisation and AI, but also by the globalisation of knowledge. Political developments, such as a globalisation backlash, the climate challenge, and the emergence of a multipolar world will further shape the approaches that countries, regions, and the global economy will ultimately have to adopt to deal with upcoming challenges.

Speaking of a potential fourth wave signals that nothing is carved in stone, and many uncertainties remain. However, we can phrase these developments in terms of globalising centrifugal and de-globalising centripetal forces to get a clearer picture of this new ambiguity.

In some areas, we are observing de-globalising **centripetal forces**:

- With robotisation and the advent of AI technologies, labour costs become less important. This may lead to re-shoring of activities, thus replacing foreign work by domestic robots.
- Increasing anti-globalisation sentiments might lead to new or higher political trade barriers.
- Global political tensions in the emerging multipolar world, such as the trade conflict between USA and China, may lead to a greater focus on regional rather than global integration.
- Policies to reduce CO_2 emission could increase the price for emissions and thus transportation costs.
- The Covid-19 pandemic has led to a debate about promoting near-shoring essential products to reduce the vulnerability. The counter-argument is to not put all eggs in one basket, hence global diversification can also help to reduce risks.

However, new globalising **centrifugal forces** are emerging, and old ones may be fostered:

- Digital delivery of service has zero trade costs. As labour costs still matter greatly in the service industry, a fourth wave of globalisation may be based on services.
- Globalisation of knowledge and the creation of global knowledge networks are further new areas of globalisation.
- Global value chains are not only established to minimise labour costs. Access to production capacities, research & development capacities or specific know how are increasingly of importance, as it could be observed from global co-operation to develop and manufacture Covid-19 vaccines.
- As countries like China upgrade their production portfolio, trade with these countries may increasingly be based on exchanging different varieties of cars, mobile phones, solar panels etc. Hence, similar to European and trans-atlantic trade, intra-industry trade may play a bigger role in trade between emerging and advanced economies.

In the area of global money and finance many issues are in flux, especially with respect to digital currencies. Likewise, it is unclear to what extent the current system, which is still dominated by the US dollar, will become a more multipolar one.

With all the uncertainties about the future of globalisation, it should be recalled that globalisation is not an end in itself. The crucial question is, therefore, what a potential fourth wave of globalisation has in store for the wealth of nations and people:

- Will income convergence of poorer countries continue, and if yes, will it work through participation in global and regional production networks, in a new globalising service industry, or – more visionary – in an emerging global knowledge economy?
- Can and will negative side-effects of globalisation be contained?
- Will we face a globalisation backlash?
- How will governance in the NGE deal with an emerging multipolar world?

5 Preview of the book

The book aims to provide the reader with an entrée into the ongoing and rapidly evolving contemporary debate on the global economy by building on both the established body of knowledge and contemporary research. To do so, the book explores how the NGE impacts the main economic activities, such as global production, trade, investment, and finance. However, the book deviates from the standard presentation of global economics in two aspects. One, a separate chapter is devoted to the globalisation of services, information, and knowledge. The second major deviation from classic texts is a single chapter on "Governance in the NGE" for two main reasons: first, there are common governance issues in all functional areas, namely what role global governance should play in a global economy, and what can be left to the discretion of nation states. Second, many regional agreements today cover several functional areas at the same time. Hence, there is often a political 'give-and-take' across these areas.

Chapter 2 (Global Production) explores the drivers of economic growth and convergence of latecomer countries, with a particular focus on the role of technology. It finishes by discussing the future of global production against the background of robotisation of production, the advent of artificial intelligence, and the challenges emanating from global climate change.

Chapter 3 (Global Trade) explores the key features of contemporary global trade through the lens of modern trade theories. It highlights the implication of global trade for income (in-)equality across and within nation states, and the role of trade policies to deal with the upcoming challenges emanating from global competition, new technologies, and climate change.

Chapter 4 (Global Investment) explores the main reasons why firms involve themselves by means of foreign direct investments (FDI) in global production and discusses the future of FDI under the conditions of the emerging NGE.

Chapter 5 (Global Intangibles) explores the increasing tradability of services, with a special emphasis on two intangibles of particular importance in the NGE, data and knowledge.

Chapter 6 (Global Money and Finance) explores the workings of global money and finance, and the impact of the design of the international monetary and financial system (IMFS) on the costs and benefits of globalising money and finance. It finishes with scrutinising the potential impact of digitalisation of money and finance on the IMFS.

Chapter 7 (Governance in the New Global Economy) analyses the role of global governance, the nation state, and regional agreements in governing cross-border activities. After a general discussion of the pros and cons of global governance, the actual and potential future governance of the global economy is discussed with a focus on the global trading system and the IMFS.

How to read this book?

The book features a modular structure. Thus, each chapter stands for itself, yet preferably read in conjunction with this introduction.

In this sense, Chapter 2 offers an executive guide to global production and economic growth. For those especially interested in global trade, Chapter 3 offers a short and comprehensive introduction to modern trade theory and trade policy. For a deeper analysis of these contemporary issues, it can easily be complemented with the shorter Chapters 4 and 5 on global investments and global intangibles, respectively. Moreover, Chapter 7 extends on trade policy issues with a coverage of the multilateral trade system and the role of regional integration schemes. For those interested in global money and finance issues, Chapter 6 offers an executive guide to the literature, while governance issues in this area are covered in Chapter 7, which, again, makes a good complementary reading.

Finally, all chapters feature "European Perspective" boxes, which apply discussed issues with respect to Europe. Jointly, they give an overview of the key features of the European economy as well as of contemporary key EU policy issues.

Notes

1 The index, regularly calculated by the Konjunkturforschungsstelle (KOF) at ETH Zurich, comprises trade in goods and services, trade partner diversity, foreign direct investment, portfolio investment, international debt and reserves, and international income payments. For details and weights of these factors, see Gygli et al. (2019).
2 The index comprises not only direct measures of data exchange, like internet bandwidth, but also indicators of the internationalisation of knowledge, like international patents and high technology exports.
3 Baldwin (2019) argues that advances in communication technologies, especially virtual and augmented reality applications, could increasingly allow "tele-migration", i.e. delivering cross-border services, ranging from supervising cleaning robots to remote surgery.
4 The term industry 4.0 appeared first in the early 2010s. Klaus Schwab of the World Economic Forum (WEF) popularised it as "Fourth Industrial Revolution" in an article published on 12 December 2015 in *Foreign Affairs* magazine. Brynjolfsson and McAfee (2014) use the label "Second Machine Age" for it.

References

Baldwin, R. (2019). *The globotics upheaval: Globalization, robotics, and the future of work.* Oxford University Press.

Brynjolfsson, E., & McAfee, A. (2014). *The second machine age.* W.W. Norton.

Friedman, T. L. (2005). *The world is flat. A brief history of the twenty-first century.* Farrar, Straus and Giroux.

Gygli, S., Haelg, F., Potrafke, N., & Sturm, J.-E. (2019). The KOF globalisation index – revisited. *Review of International Organizations, 14,* 543–574.

2

GLOBAL PRODUCTION

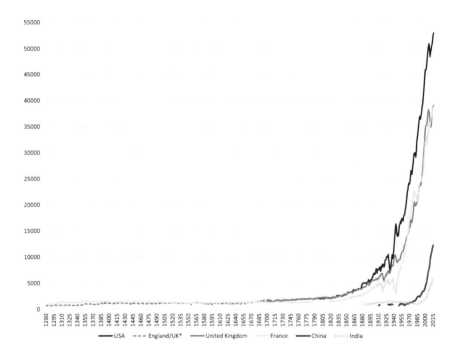

FIGURE 2.1 Real GDP Per Capita in Selected Countries in the Long Run (in 2011 US$).
Source: Real GDP per capita is obtained from the "cgdppc" data series of the Maddison Project Database, version 2018. Bolt et al. (2018). Data for England is taken from 'partial countries': England (part of United Kingdom) from 1280 to 1870, while the time series for the United Kingdom starts in 1700, hence both series overlap from 1700 to 1870 with slight differences in data.

A sustainable increase in the material standard of living was achieved by mankind only with the Industrial Revolution but was also accompanied by a 'Great Divergence', the decoupling of the dynamic economic development in the West

DOI: 10.4324/9781003057611-2

from the rest of the world. It was not until the second half of the 20th century that a few, mainly Asian countries, succeeded in catching up (see Figure 2.1). As a consequence, a multipolar world has replaced the 20th-century world order of European and American economic dominance. This chapter explores the drivers of economic growth and convergence of latecomer countries, with a particular focus on the role of technology. It finishes by discussing the future of global production against the background of robotisation of production, the advent of artificial intelligence, and the challenges emanating from global climate change, that have led to calls for changing the underlying growth model towards sustainable and inclusive growth.

1 A short history of global production

After ages of economic stagnation, the Industrial Revolution brought an unprecedented increase in material wealth to the countries of Western Europe and their Western Offshoots. The rest of the world almost completely missed it, a development that historians label the 'Great Divergence'. The divergence intensified over most of the 20th century as growth accelerated in industrial countries, with the USA taking the lead, while war-torn European countries followed only after World War II. It took the second half of the 20th century before some developing countries have started to catch up, notably some South-East Asian countries, China and, more recently, India. Figure 2.1 illustrates this process, which is narrated and explored in this section.

1.1 The Great Divergence

Until the 17th century, increases in per-capita income were at best temporary phenomena. But then things started to change. The Industrial Revolution ended a long period of economic stagnation. England was leading this process. Sustained increases in production are documented from about 1670 onward. Other continental European countries like France and Germany followed, but with a substantial time lag.

1.1.1 The industrial revolution

Why have sustained increases in per-capita income started only in Europe and not elsewhere? It is tempting to point to the development of new technologies, such as the steam engine or the spinning jenny. However, this does not answer the question why smart people had not invented them earlier, or elsewhere in the world? After all, until the 14th-century China was technologically more advanced than Europe.

The debate on the origins of the Industrial Revolution is subject to intensive and ongoing academic debates. Yet, four major and interrelated factors are most prominent in the literature: rising wages that made labour-saving technologies profitable, historical incidences, cultural change, and changes in institutions.

- **Rising wages** in Europe, particularly in England, made it profitable to replace labour by the new machines. This **labour-saving technical change** increased the productivity of the workers and ultimately allowed for higher wages.[1] In pre-industrial times, Europe was stuck in the so-called Malthusian trap. According to the "iron law of wages", formulated by Robert Malthus (1798), increases in per-capita income are at best temporary. Higher income would lead to increases in life expectancy and thus a higher level of population. With more people sharing limited land, per-capita income will then fall back to its original level.
- But why did wage rises occur in the first place? Voigtländer and Voth (2013) argue that the "three horsemen to riches", the plague, war, and urbanisation have been crucial. The plague in the early 14th century reduced Europe's population by one third. This situation was reinforced by an almost permanent state of war that European regions were in. The subsequent substantial increases in wages allowed for the development of a 'luxury market' for handcrafted goods, likes non-essential cloths produced in cities, pushing urbanisation and increases in urban wages further. Industrialisation developed thus by **chance** as a consequence of accidental events.
- **Culture**, or more precisely cultural change, is a third key factor. The cultural foundations of European growth were laid in the period of the Enlightenment between 1500 and 1700. A key feature of culture is the way in which people interact with their physical environment. According to Mokyr (2016: 7): "'Culture' affected technology both directly, by changing attitudes to the natural world, and indirectly, by creating and nurturing institutions that stimulated and supported the accumulation and diffusion of 'useful knowledge'".
- **Changes in institutions** are the fourth key factor. Supporters of this hypothesis point to the fact that the creation of the Commonwealth in 1649 and the Glorious Revolution of 1688 coincide with the rise of England. The argument is that these new institutions protected investors from arbitrary expropriation, while a constitutional long-term commitment to property rights allowed for and promoted long-term investments. It is, however, not straightforward that 'enlightened' sovereigns are willing to give up their powers. Rather, the institutional change was repeatedly an outcome of a power struggle between incumbent rulers and upcoming powerful classes. Acemoglu, Johnson and Robinson (2005) point to the catalysing role of Atlantic trade with the Americas, Asia, and West Africa. While in countries like Spain and Portugal, this trade remained in the hands of the sovereigns, countries like England and Holland allowed merchants to engage in this highly profitable trade. The new British and Dutch bourgeoisie eventually

became powerful enough to demand institutional change that effectively constrained the power of the sovereigns and protected property rights. This paved the way for the frontrunner role of England which, in turn, provided a role model for other European countries as well as for the USA, which adopted its constitution in 1786.

Arguably, these four factors mutually reinforced each other, supplemented by other technological and societal developments that followed and contributed to the rise to riches. One important element was the **agricultural revolution**. However, it was not only the development of new technologies such as fertilisers that increased agricultural productivity, but also societal innovations. For example, in England, the ancient system of joint farming was replaced by farming privately-owned enclosures and providing incentives for farmers to increase productivity.[2] The role of the **printing press** was the second factor that cannot be underestimated in spreading both, knowledge and literacy throughout Europe, thus helping to improve productivity.[3]

In sum, we identified a few **fundamental factors** as key drivers of the unprecedented rise of Europe. Their role will also help us to understand growth in the 20th and 21st centuries more deeply.

1.1.2 The golden age of western countries

The Industrial Revolution soon spread from England to the European continent, and most notably to the United States. These catching-up processes are all unique in themselves, but they also share some common features. Allen (2011: 41–42) argues that continental Europe's

> standard development strategy, which built on Napoleon's institutional revolution, had four imperatives:
>
> - create a large national market by abolishing internal tariffs and improving transportation;
> - erect an external tariff to protect 'infant industries' from British competition;
> - create banks to stabilise the currency and provide business with capital; and, finally
> - establish mass education to speed the adoption and invention of technology.

After independence from Britain in 1776, the economy of the United States developed swiftly on almost the same pillars as in Europe, but with a few important differences:

- The US market was huge and growing driven by four key factors:
    - no internal tariffs;

- huge immigration inflows;
- the high purchasing power of the southern states that were engaged in growing cotton on highly profitable slave plantations;
- high external tariffs, which protected the internal market until World War I (WWI).
- The abundance of free land allowed a high output per worker. This attracted people, who were leaving the urban areas to start a farm and, thus, contributed to labour scarcity and high wages in the cities. This induced investments in labour-saving technologies, which in turn, increased the output per worker.

After WWI, the USA took over the leading role from Britain in the global order, and a transition was made from Pax Britannica to Pax Americana. While Pax Britannica was characterised by industrialisation plus colonialism, the economic base of American world power was industrial mass-production.

The formative innovations were the internal combustion engine and electricity. The former changed the mobility of a whole nation, the latter introduced the networked household. Both innovations led to a huge wave of complementary public infrastructure investments, like roads and telephone lines, and an outburst of private consumption, be it cars, TVs, refrigerators, and more. According to Robert Gordon (2016), the period from 1920 to 1970 became the golden age of growth for the USA. The growth stood out not only in terms of increases in per-capita income, but also because they were strongly driven by increases in production efficiency, as will be discussed in Section 2.

Europe – and later Japan – entered the mass-production age only after World War II (WWII). War-devastated countries like Germany experienced an economic miracle of fast growth and rising standards of living, mainly based on a rapidly growing manufacturing industry. Public infrastructure contributed to the catch-up growth, as did investments in mass education, often directed to the needs of the industry. With the notable exception of Japan, catching-up remained largely a European affair. The great divergence continued as long as developing countries remained locked in the complementary division of labour.

1.2 From the Great Divergence to great convergence?

It was only in the late 20th century that the catching-up process of some laggard countries started. First, a small group of so-called 'newly industrializing countries' (NICs) – South Korea, Taiwan, Hong Kong, and Singapore, started to grow rapidly, leading to what the World Bank (1993) has labelled the 'East Asian Miracle'. Later, other emerging economies followed. The key element was the fast development of a manufacturing sector. While South-East Asian countries were successful in developing their new industries into successful exporters – often concentrating on garments, simple electronics, and steel – other emerging

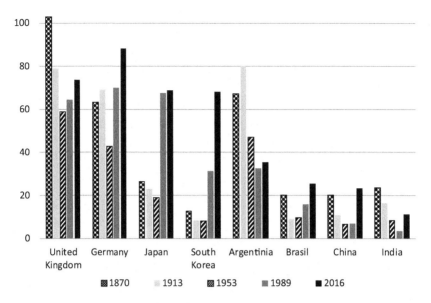

FIGURE 2.2 Real Per Capita GDP of Selected Countries (USA = 100).
Source: Own calculations. Real GDP per capita is measured in 2011 US$, provided by the
"cgdppc" data of the Maddison Project Database, version 2018. Bolt et al. (2018).

economies, notably in Latin America, often failed to do so. South-East Asia
increased its share in global manufacturing dramatically, partly at the expense of
the former socialist countries of the Soviet Bloc, which lost ground way before
their collapse in 1989 (Figure 2.2).

Especially from the 1990s onward, the catching-up process of emerging
economies has intensified dramatically and lifted many people in the developing
world out of poverty, notably in China (Lakner & Milanovic, 2013). The most
successful emerging economies became those which involved themselves deeply
in the global value chain production.

As discussed in Chapter 1, the information and communication technology
(ICT) revolution of the 1980s and 1990s allowed to slice up the value chain
and to locate the various tasks of value chain production in countries where the
production costs were the lowest, supported by drastically falling transportation
and communication costs. The iPhone is the best-known showcase, as being
"dreamed-up in California and assembled in China". Countries in transition to a
market economy, mainly in Central and Eastern Europe, also profited from participating in such production networks, which are often concentrated regionally.
The European automotive industry is a case in point, as well as regional production networks with heavily interlinked values chains along the US-Mexico
border. Performing tasks in increasingly globalised and regionalised value chains
and engaging in **trade in tasks** has given rise to what Baldwin (2016) has called
the "great convergence", the narrowing of the gap between emerging and advanced countries.

However, up to date, the great convergence is still limited to a small number of emerging countries and countries in transition, while many countries, especially in Africa are still left behind. Will these countries be able to repeat the experience of the successful forerunners? The next section takes a closer look at this issue from a theoretical and empirical point of view.

2 Understanding economic growth

2.1 The fundamental and proximate sources of growth

The history of global production suggests going beyond the obvious and visible factors of growth, such as investments in new technologies, to fully understand economic take-offs, catch-up processes, and ultimately the reasons for differences in the material standard of living of countries.

Figure 2.3 illustrates the potential causes behind it. To start with the economic outcomes on the right-hand side of the figure, it is clear that the current differences in per-capita income are basically the result of past economic growth of per-capita income.

Scholars of economic growth differentiate between proximate and fundamental factors. The **proximate factors** are the input factors in the production process: capital, labour, and technology. The logic is straightforward: the more capital and labour is used to produce goods and services, the more will be produced. Further, the more productively these factors are utilised, the higher will be the output. We will discuss later that what is short-handedly, here, called 'technology', is the result of a complex interaction between new technologies and their efficient use.

Investments into physical and human capital as well as introducing and adopting new technologies are crucial, but they do not fall from heaven. Rather, they must pay off. Hence, incentives are crucial and government policies play an important role in providing them. For example, patent protection is important for private companies to undertake research and development. Likewise, a carbon emission tax can induce investments in climate friendly technologies. However, not just policies matter and as we have learned from the Industrial Revolution, **fundamental factors** are often behind the provision of such incentives. Unique historical events – **chance** – such as the decrease of the European population after the Black Death, can trigger rising wages and labour-saving investments.

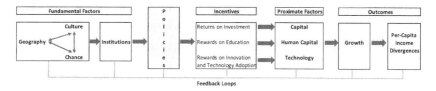

FIGURE 2.3   Fundamental and Proximate Sources of Economic Growth and Prosperity.

At the same time, and maybe related, a **change in culture** can occur. Both events, often depending on the **geography** of the country at hand, can lead to a change in **institutions**, often driven by a changing societal distribution of power.

Researchers differ in the weight they attach to these four fundamental factors. For example, in their book *Why Nations Fail*, Acemoglu and Robinson (2012) have argued that countries' economic rise and fall is not so much based on culture, geography, or chance but predominantly on the quality of their institutions. One may, however, argue that the emergence of growth-supportive institutions, itself, is a result of the interaction of the former three forces. In Figure 2.3, we have therefore separated these factors from institutions, to highlight that the latter play a more direct role in influencing pro-growth policies, but yet are evolving in interaction with the other fundamentals.

That said, it should also be clear that there are numerous feedbacks present, often making it difficult for researchers to identify the true impact of each of these factors. For example, a rising standard of living may, and often will lead to cultural change. Conversely, a low growth experience over a long time, can induce structural reforms that ultimately change institutions for the better. Moreover, the massive increase in production over the last 200 years has impacted so heavily on nature that its effect on geography via climate change and rising ocean levels has modified nature to an extent that scientists have proposed a new geological age, called the 'Anthropocene', in which even geography cannot be assumed to be exogenously given. In the following section, we explore the role of fundamental and proximate sources of growth in more detail.

2.2 Fundamental factors

The deeper we dig to uncover the fundamental roots of growth, the more difficult it becomes to firmly establish their relevance. As can be seen from Figure 2.3, the chain of causality from potentially fundamental factors to a higher standard of living is long, and reserve causality is likely. Hence, the impact of these factors and their relative importance is subject to considerable scientific debates. Without taking positions here, the major arguments with respect to the four factors are briefly discussed.

2.2.1 The importance of chance and path dependence

It may surprise some that chance is labelled a fundamental factor. But as we have seen from the pre-history of the industrial revolution, the plague outbreak in Europe in the 14th century arguably gave rise to rising wages and finally making investments in machines profitable. Similar arguments can be made about the great depression of 1929. The subsequent 'New Deal' in the USA was not only about mitigating negative social consequences of the depression, but it also helped in creating mass markets for industrial goods, thus giving the US industry a competitive edge.

If such major events change the development path of economies, there is no simple way back. Economists speak of *path dependency*: once embarked on a different trajectory, it may continue to determine the behaviour and performance of the economy.

2.2.2 Geography

Geography impacts income and growth through two major channels, location and resources. **Location** can hold back or promote growth in various ways:

- Being **landlocked** can lead to less growth when it limits trade by high trading costs.
- Being **closely located to high-income countries** can make a country an attractive location for outsourcing production. The Mexican *maquiladora* industry at the border with the USA as well as the Central European countries are cases in point.
- Being located in **tropical regions** is often associated with a higher incidence of tropical diseases and lower productivity growth. However, from a certain development level onwards, a tropical location must not be a disadvantage in times of air-conditioning, as the example of Singapore shows.

Turning to **resources**, natural resources can form the base of a country's wealth. However, they can also constitute a growth trap:

- **Colonialism** has often targeted resource-rich countries and installed institutions that prevented industrial development.
- In weak states, often civil wars on **controlling resources** hold back development.
- An abundance of resources can hold back industrialisation by what has become known as the 'Dutch disease': In the 1960s, the Netherlands discovered and started exploiting offshore natural gas, which resulted in a relocation of resources and a contraction of the manufacturing sector.

2.2.3 Culture

It is a widely held belief that culture matters greatly for economic performance. In fact, many travellers return from foreign countries with a strong opinion on the cultural roots of the economic success or failure of the visited country – more often than not related to some casual observations on labour efforts. However, there is a risk of a misleading 'observer bias'. For example, Europeans have a higher preference for leisure than Americans. Working less hours results in lower per-capita income but not necessarily in a lower productivity. Likewise, an observed low 'labour effort' is often related to a lack of complementary resources. In other words, culture is often blamed or praised, while the true roots of economic performance lie elsewhere. Moreover, as there is no consensus measure of what constitutes culture, the role of culture in growth is difficult to identify. We therefore concentrate here on reviewing briefly the key research contributions on the role of culture in promoting (productivity) growth.

Culture, understood as the way people interact with each other, reflects a complex set of values and norms, and this set typically differs across countries, regions, or social groups. Measuring these cultural traits is a major challenge in itself, let alone linking it to economic performance. A few approaches shall be highlighted:

- The German sociologist Max Weber has linked growth to a "protestant ethic", which treasures hard work and high savings. More recently, several studies reject a simple direct link between the ethic and economic performance by pointing to the role of a human capital channel in promoting literacy after Luther's translation of the Bible.[4]
- Several modern attempts of quantifying culture include the four different cultural dimensions proposed by Hofstede (2001). Other studies use a measure of social trust, e.g. how much people trust each other, as a proxy for culture. Gorodnichenko and Roland (2011) argue that of Hofstede's original cultural dimensions only *individualism* has a causal effect on measures of long-run growth by impacting favourably on innovation, while Zak and Knack (2001) provide evidence for a positive effect of trust on growth.

The problem with all these cultural measures is threefold[5]:

- Cultural traits are not always independent of economic outcomes. For example, being poor can lead to low social trust.
- If culture does not change over time, the culture hypothesis has difficulties explaining sudden growth miracles, such as those in South-East Asia.
- Cultural traits are both driven by, and drive the institutional developments within a society. For example, social trust may be higher when good institutions, such as rule of law, exist. On the other hand, an individualist society may be more eager to develop such institutions. It may thus be more appropriate to think of cultural traits as complements to institutional factors, rather than as independent determinants.

Finally, from our discussion of the Industrial Revolution, the reader may recall that Mokyr (2016) has highlighted a second meaning of culture, namely the way people interact with their physical environment. The Enlightenment *changed* the attitudes of people towards the natural world, with a view to exploit it to their own advantage. Hence, in Europe a culture of openness towards new ideas developed gradually over time and allowed for technological progress, which often had to overcome societal resistance against these changes from those who profited from the status quo ante. In this sense, it may be **cultural change**, rather than culture per se that matters most.

2.2.4 Institutions

Acemoglu and Robinson (2012) argue that countries' rise and fall is based on the quality of their institutions. But what kind of institutions are relevant for growth?

- **Contracting institutions** facilitate contracting between regular citizens or private entities, such as between lenders and borrowers, companies, or companies and households. They comprise all elements concerning contract enforcement, such as commercial laws, courts, and other arbitration mechanisms.
- **Property rights institutions** typically protect citizens against the power of the state or other privileged groups, for example, by protecting investors and innovators from expropriation.

Most research results point to the importance of property rights institutions (Acemoglu, 2009). This does not mean that contracting institutions do not matter, but their effectiveness depends on the inability of the civil society to create mechanism of contract enforcement, e.g. by reputation or mutual trust.

Taking the argument further, Acemoglu and Robinson (2012) also differentiate between inclusive and extractive institutions.

- **Extractive institutions** are typically in the hands of a few, who use these institutions for their benefit (Acemoglu & Robinson, 2012: 430). The historical example is feudal Europe, where the elite had no interest in technological progress as long as they could extract value from their serfs.
- By contrast, **inclusive institutions** restrain the power of the elite by a broader distribution of power through democratic institutions.

In empirical growth studies, *governance indicators*, such as indices for property rights, the rule of law, and democratic rule are often found both, statistically significant and of high economic relevance, pointing to the important role of institutions. European integration is also an important example of how institutions impact on economic performance (see European Perspectives 2.1).

EUROPEAN PERSPECTIVE 2.1

The growth effects of the European integration

As a member of the European Union (EU), countries have to adopt the whole body of EU laws and regulations, the *Acquis Communautaire*. Is EU membership economically beneficial? Unfortunately, it is not easy to quantify the growth effects of EU membership. To start, one could look at the development of per-capita income after joining the EU. Figure EP 2.1 illustrates that countries often experienced a convergence process to leading incumbents

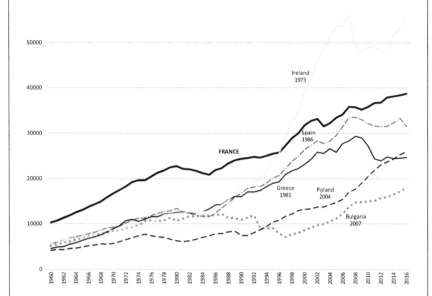

FIGURE EP 2.1 EU Accession and Convergence.

Data source: Real GDP per capita is obtained from the "cgdppc" data series of the Maddison Project Database, version 2018. Bolt et al. (2018).

(using France as benchmark) after accession to the EU (accession year is indicated below the county name), with Greece as a notable exception. However, the key problem in quantifying the benefits from membership is that we do not know how countries would have developed without membership. We simply miss the counterfactual.

One way to solve the problem is to unravel what EU membership means in detail and then to evaluate how the situation would look like in the absence of these features. Boltho and Eichengreen (2008) take this into account and conclude that in their most conservative estimate, the gross domestic product (GDP) is about 5% higher with EU membership.

Campos, Coricelli and Moretti (2019) create "synthetic countries" as counterfactuals. These artificial countries are constructed from a weighted average of selected non-EU member countries in such a way that the synthetic country's economic development has been closely following that of the new member country before EU accession. If a new member country grows faster after accession than its synthetic counterpart, then a positive growth effect is established. The authors conclude that on average, per-capita income would be some 10% lower without EU integration in the first ten years after accession. However, the effects are not uniform. While the three small Baltic states appear to have profited the most, the UK had benefited like the average but more than the Nordic countries. Greece is – as already visible from simple GDP data – the only country with a negative membership effect.

2.2.5 Final thoughts on fundamental factors

Fundamental factors play an important role in providing incentives to work, invest, and innovate. While the evidence supports that institutions and their quality matter for growth and development, they are not a panacea to solve all growth problems. Moreover, they develop in interaction with both, other fundamental factors and economic development. Thus, institutions may not be supportive for growth the same way at every stage of development. For example, more competition can be supportive for innovation in advanced countries, but it could have detrimental effects on catching-up in latecomer countries. Moreover, developing good institutions takes time and goes along with human capital development.

In sum, to explain why countries rise to riches requires us to go into the very details of a particular growth process, and the interaction of these fundamental factors. The ongoing research on the Industrial Revolution illustrates the value of such an approach. Likewise, covering all bases and their interaction is key to understanding recent growth miracles, for example in Asian NICs and China. The lesson is that rather than relying on simplistic one-for-all growth recipes, country-specific circumstances matter for igniting economic take-offs.

2.3 The proximate sources of growth

Labour, capital, and technology are the proximate factors contributing to growth, and can thus explain per-capita income differences across countries. Knowing the relative importance of each of these factors is extremely useful information for policymakers. For example, if technological growth is found to be low by international standards, policies that promote new technologies or enable a country to use technologies more efficiently are crucial.

2.3.1 Quantifying the proximate sources of growth

Nowadays we have for most countries fairly good data on the input of labour and physical capital into the production of goods and services. However, what is not directly observable is 'technology', or more precisely, the overall efficiency with which we use the inputs of labour and capital. To understand how economists identify the contribution of each factor of production, and ultimately the contribution of technology, we have to be a bit technical.

2.3.1.1 Methodology

Consider cooking as a simple example of a production process. To prepare meals in a restaurant, we employ capital (K), say two pans, and labour (L), say one cook. With these resources we produce an output (Y) of two dishes within a given time, say per hour. When we double the number of pans and cooks and the output also doubles, economists speak of **constant returns to scale**. However, if we only double the number of pans, we may obtain less than a doubling of meals, maybe they increase only from two to three because the chef cannot handle four pans simultaneously with the same attention. Likewise, adding a cook without increasing the number of pans will also lead to less than a doubling of output. This feature is known as **diminishing returns** to factors of production. Finally, if our cook with his two pans produces three dishes instead of two, we would attribute this increase in production to an increase in productivity, or more specifically an increase in **total factor productivity** (TFP).[6] The term reflects that the increase in production results from an improvement in efficiency in combining capital with labour. We thus quantify technology as the part of production that cannot be explained by the accumulable factors of production, capital and labour. TFP is therefore also known as the 'Solow residual', named after Nobel laureate Robert Solow.

We can describe this behaviour by a so-called production function[7]:

$$Y = AK^a L^{(1-a)} \tag{2.1}$$

K and L are the accumulable factors of production, capital and labour. They contribute to production according to the parameters 'a' and '(1-a)', which reflect the income share of capital and labour, respectively. As total production is distributed completely to these factors, the shares add up to one. Finally, 'A' measures TFP.

The simplest way to quantify the growth contribution of the proximate factors is the so-called 'Solow-decomposition'. Converting (2.1) into growth rates (g), i.e. percentage rates of change, paves the way for '**growth accounting**'. The growth of output (g_Y) is then driven by growth rates of the proximate input factors capital (g_K), labour (g_L), and total factor productivity (g_A):

$$g_Y = (1-a)g_L + ag_K + g_A \tag{2.2}$$

The interpretation of (2.2) is straightforward. Consider, for example, that labour and capital inputs are both growing at a rate of 3% per annum and TFP remains constant ($g_A = 0$). Assume – not unrealistically – that the capital share in income is 30% (a = 0.3) and, thus, the labour share is 70% (1 − a = 0.7). Output, then, is also growing at 3%. This reflects constant returns to scale.

If, however, only capital input grows by 3%, then output increases by $0.3 \times 3\% = 0.9\%$. Likewise, if only labour input grows by 3%, output increases by $0.7 \times 3\% = 2.1\%$. Percentage output increases are lower than the percentage increase of the input of a single factor of production. Hence, we have diminishing returns to each accumulable factor.

Finally, assume that both factors are growing at 3%. We would then calculate the growth contribution of capital as 0.9% and labour as 2.1%. Hence, an output increase of 3% can be fully explained by putting in more capital and labour. However, if output would then increase by 4%, we have a 1%–point increase in output that cannot be explained by factor accumulation. We thus attribute this increase in production to an increase in TFP. Equation (2.2) is the base of the growth accounting exercise, which has become a standard tool for diagnosing the economic growth performance of countries.

Equation (2.2) accounts for **extensive growth**, i.e. the increase in total production. Since the ultimate objective of growth and development is to increase the standard of living, we should also look at **intensive growth**, defined as the growth rate of per-capita income. Even more insightful is to focus directly on labour productivity growth, understood as the increase of output per unit of labour, e.g. per working hour. By deducting the growth rate of labour input g_L from both sides of equation (2.2), we gain a key insight into the sources of labour productivity growth ($g_{Y/L}$, defined as g_Y minus g_L).

$$g_{Y/L} = ag_{K/L} + g_{TFP} \qquad (2.3)$$

Equation (2.3) shows that there are two ways to increase labour productivity: equipping workers with more capital, the so-called capital deepening ($g_{K/L}$, defined as g_K minus g_L), and TFP growth.

Capital deepening is key to industrialisation and growth. Equipping workers with more and more capital is what distinguishes an industrial country from a pre-industrial one. However, capital deepening cannot go on indefinitely as there are diminishing returns to capital, and thus, limits to increasing the capital–labour ratio ($a < 1$). To reconsult our initial example, at some point, more pans for the same number of cooks will not be economical anymore. The contribution of capital deepening ($g_{K/L}$) will eventually fall towards zero, and finally only TFP growth is the ultimate source of growth. This key insight makes it important to know more about the sources of growth, and what role in particular TFP plays (see European Perspective 2.2).

EUROPEAN PERSPECTIVE 2.2

Europe's productivity catch-up

In most advanced European countries, per-capita income does not match the US level, even when measured in purchasing power parities. However, the reason is not that these EU countries have a lower labour productivity. As the graph (left) in Figure EP 2.2 shows, the so-called core EU countries like Germany and France, especially have been catching up rapidly with the US after WWII in terms of production per working hour, the most relevant productivity measure. Why, then, do they have a lower per-capita income? The main answer is that Europeans prefer more leisure time, longer holidays, and less working hours per week. This is at least partly a voluntary choice.

But this may not be the full story. Some countries like Italy failed to keep the momentum of catching-up and fell behind because of stagnating labour productivity growth since the 1980s, not least because of a stagnating economy in general.

The right-hand-side figure shows that European catching-up has also been a success story in increasing TFP, and thus converging to the US efficiency level. But it also sends a signal of caution, as some core European countries could recently not keep pace with US TFP development anymore. A potential reason behind this failure might be a lagging behind in IT-related industries and IT-applications (see European Perspective 2.3), as well as the Euro crisis after 2010.

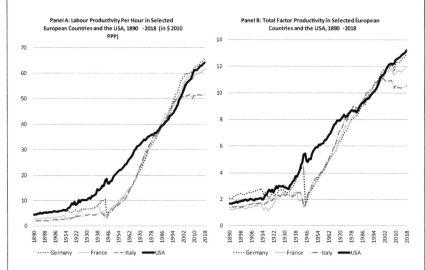

FIGURE EP 2.2 Europe's Productivity Catch-Up.

Source: Own figures based on data obtained from Bergeaud, A., Cette, G., and Lecat, R. (2016). Long Term Productivity Database, Version 2.3. http://www.longtermprodcutivity.com.

A growth accounting analysis of economic miracles of Asian NICs by Alwyn Young (1994, 1995) can perfectly illustrate the usefulness of growth accounting. Young found that the fast growth in these countries between the mid-1960s and 1990, was predominantly driven by factor accumulation: high investments ratios, massive investment in human capital, and mobilisation of labour force. The contribution of TFP was found in most cases to be reasonable, but not stellar. However, for Singapore, the contribution of TFP to the quite remarkable average annual growth rate of 8.7% over the whole period from 1966 to 1990 was close to zero. Why should Singaporeans care about these results? The message from the analysis was that the city state's growth model was eventually not sustainable.

The main reason why Young did not find any TFP growth was that Singapore switched from one industry to another (mostly with the help of foreign investments) instead of getting smarter in one industry over time. If at some point there is no industry left to switch to, growth will only be sustainable when

Singaporeans learn to learn and get smarter on the job. Ultimately, the Singapore government bought the argument. Promoting smartness and TFP became central in the country's economic strategy.

2.3.1.2 The role of human capital

But have Singaporeans not become much smarter over the last 25 years? The answer is that Young has made an adjustment for labour quality, and thus controlled for the effect of education. Contemporary growth accounting allows for differences in the quality of labour, often proxied by average years of schooling. This human capital (HC) is then measured as the product of the quantity of labour (L) and the human capital per worker (H). The production function (2.1) can then be rewritten as:

$$Y = AK^a (LH)^{(1-a)} \tag{2.1a}$$

With this modification our growth accounting equations are now given as:

$$g_Y = (1-a)(g_L + g_H) + a g_K + g_{TFP} \tag{2.2a}$$
$$g_{Y/L} = a g_{K/L} + (1-a) g_H + g_{TFP}. \tag{2.3a}$$

Equation (2.3a) highlights that labour productivity growth is driven by equipping workers with more capital – **capital deepening**, educating people – **human capital accumulation**, and getting smarter – **TFP growth**.

2.3.2 Accounting for growth: evidence from two centuries

Equipped with these basics of growth accounting, we now review the history of modern global production. Table 2.1 reports results from various growth accounting studies. We focus on **intensive growth**, preferably measured by output per working hour, the most precise measure of labour productivity, though some studies use output per worker or even per-capita income. Hence, we rely on growth accounting as defined in equation (2.3), preferably in the version (2.3a), which includes a measure of labour quality, whenever available.

Starting with the United Kingdom in the early phase of the Industrial Revolution from 1780 to 1860, we observe three major features. First, labour productivity growth was rather modest and below modern standards. Second, the modern sector (e.g. cotton, iron, shipbuilding, railways etc.) contributed mostly. Third, TFP growth and not capital deepening was key to labour productivity increases, and predominantly occurred in the new manufacturing industries.[8]

The catching-up processes of European countries and the United States during the first wave of globalization around 1900, show the typical mix of 1/3 coming from capital deepening and 2/3 from technological catch-up. By contrast, in Spain, the growth mix relied more on capital deepening, and the country was left behind by other European countries. The US overtook Great Britain after

TABLE 2.1 Accounting for Growth since 1780

		Labour Productivity Growth	Contribution to Labour Productivity Growth			Source
			Capital Deepening	*Human Capital*	*TFP Growth*	
Industrial revolution in the UK	United Kingdom 1780–1860	0.6	0.2	na	0.4	Crafts and O'Rourke (2014)
	Of which 'Modern Sector'	*0.5*	*0.1*	*na*	*0.3*	Crafts and O'Rourke (2014)
Catch-up growth in Europe and European Off-shoots around 1900	United Kingdom 1899–1913	0.5	0.4	na	0.1	Crafts and O'Rourke (2014)
	Germany 1891–1911	1.8	0.6	na	1.2	Crafts and O'Rourke (2014)
	Sweden 1890–1913	2.8	0.9	na	1.8	Crafts and O'Rourke (2014)
	Spain 1884–1920	1.0	0.7	na	0.3	Crafts and O'Rourke (2014)
	United States 1890–1905	1.9	0.5	na	1.4	Crafts and O'Rourke (2014)
The US golden age	1890–1920	1.5	0.7	0.3	0.5	Gordon (2016)
	1920–1970	2.8	0.5	0.3	1.9	Gordon (2016)
	1970–2014	1.6	0.7	0.3	0.7	Gordon (2016)
Advanced economies	1980s	2.0	0.9	0.4	0.8	Dieppe (2020)
	1990s	1.7	0.4	0.3	0.4	Dieppe (2020)
	2003–2008	1.5	0.7	0.3	0.6	Dieppe (2020)
	2013–2018	0.8	0.1	0.2	0.4	Dieppe (2020)

The rise of Asian NICs	'Tale of Two Cities'	Hong Kong 1966–1991	4.7	2.1	0.2	2.3	Young (1995), own calculations
		Singapore 1966–1990	4.2	3.6	0.6	0.0	Young (1995), own calculations
	China	1990s	8.1	2.8	0.9	4.4	Dieppe (2020)
		2003–2008	10.2	4.7	0.4	5.2	Dieppe (2020)
		2013–2018	6.6	3.1	0.7	2.8	Dieppe (2020)
	India	1993–2004	4.6	1.8	0.4	2.3	Dieppe (2020), own calculations
		2003–2008	7.1	2.9	0.9	3.3	Dieppe (2020), own calculations
		2013–2018	5.6	1.5	0.9	3.2	Dieppe (2020), own calculations
Shifts in Europe	Core advanced Europe	France 1990–2007	1.3	0.6	0.3	0.4	Dieppe (2020), own calculations
		2010–2018	0.8	0.4	0.4	0.0	Dieppe (2020), own calculations
		Germany 1990–2007	1.8	0.8	0.3	0.8	Dieppe (2020), own calculations
		2010–2018	1.1	0.1	0.1	1.0	Dieppe (2020), own calculations
		UK 1990–2007	2.0	0.9	0.7	0.5	Dieppe (2020), own calculations
		2010–2018	0.7	0.1	0.1	0.7	Dieppe (2020), own calculations
		Italy 1990–2007	0.8	0.7	0.5	−0.4	Dieppe (2020), own calculations
		2010–2018	0.1	0.1	0.3	−0.4	Dieppe (2020), own calculations
	The rise of Central and Eastern European countries	2003–2008	3.6	1.7	0.4	1.5	Dieppe (2020)
		2013–2018	2.6	0.9	0.4	1.3	Dieppe (2020)

(Continued)

			Labour Productivity Growth	Contribution to Labour Productivity Growth			Source
				Capital Deepening	Human Capital	TFP Growth	
Developing economies in major regions	East Asia and Pacific	2003–2008	8.5	3.9	0.4	4.3	Dieppe (2020)
		2013–2018	6.0	2.8	0.6	2.6	Dieppe (2020)
	Europe and Central Asia	2003–2008	5.1	2.7	0.4	2.1	Dieppe (2020)
		2013–2018	1.6	0.5	0.4	0.8	Dieppe (2020)
	Latin America and the Caribbean	2003–2008	1.7	0.7	0.6	0.4	Dieppe (2020)
		2013–2018	0.4	0.6	0.7	-1.0	Dieppe (2020)
	Middle East and North Africa	2003–2008	1.2	2.2	0.5	-1.6	Dieppe (2020)
		2013–2018	-0.7	-1.4	0.4	0.3	Dieppe (2020)
	South Asia	2003–2008	6.7	2.8	0.6	3.3	Dieppe (2020)
		2013–2018	5.3	1.5	0.8	3.0	Dieppe (2020)
	Sub-Saharan Africa	2003–2008	2.7	0.5	0.7	1.4	Dieppe (2020)
		2013–2018	0.7	1.2	0.3	-0.8	Dieppe (2020)

Notes: Labour productivity growth is defined as GDP per worker at 2010 market prices exchange rates, when the source is Dieppe (2020). Gordon (2016) measures labour productivity as output per hour. Crafts & O'Rourke (2014) have not made explicit allowance for human capital and working hours. For UK 1780–1860 data, "a" is set at 0.4, for calculating catch-up growth at 0.35 for all reported countries. Labour productivity growth based on Young (1995) is calculated as output growth minus raw labour growth as reported by Young (1995). The growth rate of human capital is calculated as the difference between the weighted and the raw labour growth rate. Data reported as Dieppe (2020) are directly taken from the source. Own calculations from Dieppe (2020) are based on the accompanying Global Productivity Database available at the publications website https://www.worldbank.org/en/research/publication/global-productivity, retrieved on 15 August 2020. For a detailed list of countries for the country groupings see Dieppe (2020). Not available data are denoted as "na".

the turn of the century, first modestly, but with the arrival of mass-production and new general purpose technologies (GPTs), like electricity and the internal combustion engine, labour productivity soared. The US 'golden age' from 1920 to 1970 can largely be attributed to the rise of industrial manufacturing, which went hand-in-hand with a historically thus-far unmatched record TFP growth.

Turning to emerging economies, the general observation is that productivity growth has been falling recently, which is still an unresolved issue.[9] However, the cases of China and India are of particular interest. China has become the world's leading manufacturing production country, mainly by participating in global value chain production, such as assembling iPhones. This allowed China to achieve for several years dramatic TFP growth rates of 4%–5% per annum. By contrast, India, which concentrates much more on services and service exports, especially in the IT sector, shows more moderate TFP growth rates. This may reflect the fact that efficiency increases in manufacturing can be more easily obtained than in services, especially when manufacturing is concentrated on simpler routines like assembling. However, it is remarkable that more recently, the TFP growth of India accelerated, probably indicating productivity growth in modern IT-related service industries.

Central and Eastern European Countries (CEECs) maintained relatively high TFP growth rates in their catch-up process, but also feature a high contribution of capital deepening, especially in the period 2003–2008, possibly reflecting a boost of foreign direct investment (FDI) after the EU accession of several CEECs in 2004.

Finally, for advanced countries, we also observe a general slowdown of productivity growth. This has raised concerns whether new ICT technologies are really capable of producing growth miracles similar to the GPTs in the second industrial revolution (Gordon, 2016). Moreover, the problem to extract productivity advanced from new technologies appears to be more pronounced in Europe than in the US (see European Perspectives 2.3).

EUROPEAN PERSPECTIVE 2.3

Information technology and productivity growth in Europe

From the mid-1990s until the great financial crisis, European labour productivity growth fell below US productivity growth. As the period coincides with the arrival of ICTs, a European backwardness in ICT is a potential culprit.

ICT influences labour productivity in two major ways: by equipping workers with ICT capital, and by increasing efficiency, thus leading to a higher TFP. Van Ark, O'Mahony and Timmer (2008) show that both factors have contributed to the growth of productivity per working hour between 1995 and 2004 in the USA and the EU-15, the 15 members of the European Union before the enlargement in 2004. However, the 1.5% point higher US productivity growth is largely explained by a TFP growth of 1.5% points in the US, as compared to 0.5% points in EU-15. The authors conclude that Europe may have some issues with productivity growth in the service sector, and here in particular with effectively using ICTs.

A recent study by Gordon and Sayed (2020) confirms this view by decomposing the role of ICTs further. It finds that the surge in US productivity growth between 1995 and 2005 was up to nearly 50% driven by productivity increases in **ICT-using service industries**, notably in the wholesale and retail trade industry, e.g. by the transition to the 'big box' retail format. For the ten European countries investigated, the authors actually find a negative productivity effect emanating from this industry. The study concludes that a lower productivity response to ICT investment accounts for 83% of the European productivity gap vis-à-vis the US, while only 17% of the gap is attributed to ICT–capital deepening.

Both studies are remarkably similar in their conclusion regarding enabling European countries to use ICT more efficiently: both point to deeper roots in labour market organisation and the lack of a truly integrated single market to benefit from scale economies.

2.4 Growth theory and the economics of convergence

How can countries catch up economically, and ultimately converge to the forerunners? Modern growth theory can help understanding the economics of convergence. Robert Solow is the father of the modern growth theory, which is also labelled neoclassical growth theory, because it builds on the major features of the neoclassical production function discussed before, namely diminishing returns to each accumulable factor of production and constant returns to scale. To be sure, production can rise faster than the inputs of these factors, but this increase is then attributed to a rise in TFP, which is not explained within the Solow growth model. For this reason, it is called an **exogenous growth** model. By contrast, in the 1990s **endogenous growth** models have been developed that aim at explaining technical progress within the growth model, particularly as being introduced with new capital investments. In this case constant returns to capital and increasing returns to scale can be obtained. Both models differ in their predictions on convergence. While the Solow model predicts convergence based on several conditions – the so-called **conditional convergence**, the endogenous growth model allows for divergence because a country that continues to invest in ever better capital could ultimately grow faster forever.

2.4.1 The Solow growth model in a nutshell

Solow's core idea is the so-called **steady state**. In the long run, he argues, capital deepening cannot go forever if capital suffers from diminishing returns.

As a consequence, in the long run there is a point when the growth rate of capital (g_K) will not exceed the growth rate of labour (g_L) anymore. As a condition for reaching this steady state, the supply of new capital must be equal to the demand for capital to keep the capital–labour ratio constant. The latter is determined by the need to equip every new unit of labour (additional worker, more working hours) with the same capital. Hence, g_K will equal g_L, and capital deepening will be zero ($g_{K/L} = 0$). In the steady state, output growth is then only driven by labour and technology. Equation (2.2) is then reduced to the steady state condition:

$$g_Y = g_L + g_{TFP} \tag{2.2b}$$

From this, it is immediately clear that in the steady state output per worker can only continue to increase with TFP growth. In the steady state, Equation (2.3) reduces thus to

$$g_{Y/L} = g_{TFP} \tag{2.3b}$$

This logic is behind the previously discussed debate on the Singaporean growth model. Ultimately only increasing smartness matters for increasing productivity and thus the standard of living.

2.4.2 Convergence and catch-up growth

The Solow model helps in understanding per-capita income convergence across countries by pointing to two major drivers, capital deepening and technological catch-up.

Imagine a country that operates at the technology frontier. Production per working hour is given by the upper curve in Figure 2.4. It shows that a higher capital-per-worker ratio will lead to more output per working hour but with decreasing returns until eventually output per hour will not increase anymore.

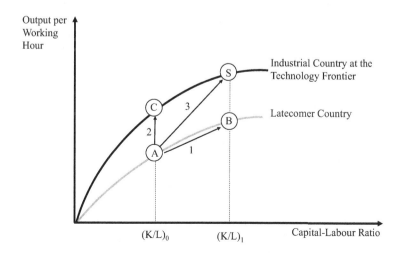

FIGURE 2.4 Catch-Up Growth in the Solow Model.

Solow's steady state is here simply indicated by point S on the production function at a steady state capital–labour ratio of $(K/L)_1$. How do we arrive at this
point? Left of this point, e.g. at $(K/L)_0$, the capital–labour ratio is so low that
the invested savings exceed the required investments to replace old, depreciated
capital. As a consequence, capital deepening takes place. A capital–labour ratio
higher than $(K/L)_1$, however, cannot be sustained as the productivity increases
from capital deepening are too small to generate enough savings to keep the
capital–labour ratio above that level.[10]

Consider now the case of a latecomer country with a less efficient technology. Production per working hour is lower than in the advanced country at
any capital–labour ratio. Hence, its curve is below the one for the advanced
country. Additionally, the steady state capital–labour ratio is only $(K/L)_0$.
Hence, the output per working hour of our latecomer country is also lower,
indicated by point A on the production function. How can the latecomer
country converge?

- First, it can take path 1 of capital-deepening without technological catching-
  up, for example by increasing its savings ratio. There may then be temporary
  catch-up growth, but at point B the latecomer country falls short of catching
  up fully.
- Second, the country can try to catch up technologically (path 2) and move
  to point C. However, without capital-deepening, convergence remains
  incomplete.
- Third, and as a consequence, full convergence requires both, technological
  catch-up and capital-deepening (path 3).

Economists use **development accounting** to estimate where countries stand
relative to the country at the frontier, for which usually the US serves as the
proxy. Weil (2013) describes the approach, and based on his dataset one can
make an insightful comparison between India and China in 2009.[11] In India, the
combined measure of capital and human capital per worker stood at 34% of the
US level, and TFP at 31%. As development accounting is based on the production
function (2.1a), we arrive at an output per worker of just 10% of the US level
by multiplying both shares ($0.34 \times 0.31 = 0.1$). China achieved at the same time
16% of the US output per worker, but mainly based on the accumulable factor of
production (49%) rather than TFP (33%).

Convergence of income per-capita or per working hour requires that countries with an initially lower income grow faster than the countries with a higher
per-capita income.[12] However, empirically there is little evidence for **unconditional convergence**.

What can be found instead is **conditional convergence**. Poorer countries
grow faster than rich ones, if and only if their economies share key features with
their rich cousins. This is the result of a widely discussed seminal article by Mankiw, Romer and Weil (1992). In simple words, income per capita of a relatively
poorer country will converge to that of the leading country if it has

- the same savings (and thus investment) rate,
- the same (lower) population growth rate,
- the same level of human capital, and
- the same level of technology.

In a way, especially the successful Asian latecomer countries, seem to have very much followed this blueprint. The features include high investment rates, often supported by foreign direct investment, but also by means of public savings to finance infrastructure investments; expansion of secondary and tertiary education; in some cases, a strict population policy like China's one child policy; and, most importantly, by employing strategies for catching-up in technology.

2.4.3 Evidence on convergence: what do we know?

The empirical study of convergence is a thriving field for a simple reason: it may help countries identifying the crucial factors for catching up and ultimately 'making a miracle'. Durlauf, Johnson and Temple (2005) have reviewed econometric growth studies and listed **145 conditioning factors**, others than those highlighted in the Solow growth model, which were all found to be of significant influence. They range from indicators of (good) governance and institutions, over openness of the economy and financial development, to variables measuring cultural and geographical particularities.[13] Many of these variables are somehow linked to the fundamental factors of growth discussed before.

A recent study by the World Bank (Dieppe, 2020) re-examines convergence in terms of productivity per working hour, the most relevant concept of convergence. The results can be briefly summarised:

- There is little to no evidence for unconditional convergence, except for the last two decades, where some evidence was found that the productivity gap for the average country is closing, but at such a low rate that it would take 140 years to close half of the initial productivity gap.
- There is stronger evidence for conditional convergence. The authors report a convergence rate of 1.3% per annum over all decades investigated, and a rate of 1.5% over the last decade. The latter implies that – if this rate can be sustained – the productivity gap to the frontier will be halved in 50 years.
- The authors find some evidence for unconditional convergence **within convergence clubs** at different stages of development, which share important economic characteristics. Especially, members of the clubs at a lower level of development are converging to a common lower level.
- In the last two decades, where some unconditional convergence is found, it is concentrated within a convergence club of advanced countries. However, next to the classic advanced countries, the group also comprises the first generation of Asian NICs, several Asian emerging economies, such as China, India, Malaysia, and Vietnam, some CEECs that joined the EU, Turkey, only Chile and Panama from Latin America, but no African country.

With respect to the latter results, an argument made by Rodrik (2013) can shed light on this. Rodrik points to a **crucial role of manufacturing** for convergence. In his view, a structural shift out of traditional low-productivity activities into modern ones have been key to most fast growth episodes, such as in East Asian countries or China. The main reason is that manufacturing exhibits strong economies of scale, which can be obtained relatively easily through learning-by-doing, even in the presence of low skills and weak institutions.

Rodrik shows that unconditional convergence of labour productivity is a key feature of manufacturing. The average estimate for a convergence rate is reported at 2.9% per year – a much faster rate than the one found in the World Bank study for conditional convergence.

The crucial issue, however, is that the manufacturing sector needs to become large enough to dominate diminishing returns in other sectors, namely traditional agriculture and services. If not, countries may not experience unconditional convergence. If yes, this could explain why some countries have been experiencing fast growth and convergence. They have been able to develop a huge manufacturing sector. Not surprisingly, China, the country with the fastest convergence rate, did so by becoming the world centre of manufacturing, commanding a share of 28.4% of world manufacturing production in 2018.[14]

3 Technology and growth

Both theory and empirical studies highlight the role of technology for sustained economic growth. Improvements in technology, as measured by TFP, do not simply mean the introduction of new technologies but also the ability to use all resources efficiently. This section looks deeper at both these sides of TFP growth.

3.1 Technology versus efficiency

Increasing TFP is about extracting more value out of the accumulable factors of production. Two factors are key. Recall our earlier example of cooking. A cook can become more efficient by employing a **new technology**. This must not always be a technological breakthrough; it could also be a different pan or a new technique of cutting onions without tears. Second, the cooking process can be performed with a **higher efficiency**.

The TFP level achieved is the combination of both factors. If your level of technology is, say 80% of the best technology at the frontier, and your efficiency level is 60% of the best practices level, then you achieve (0.8 times 0.6) 48% of the TFP level of the most productive economy.

Which factor is the most important for explaining a low TFP? Research at the industry level shows that most modern industries adopt technologies that are not too far from the technological frontier. A clothing factory in Bangladesh may not employ the most sophisticated sewing machines available, but at least ones that have been the state-of-the-art a few years ago. The main reason is that because modern machines and technologies can cross borders, it is not very likely that there are very long-lasting persistent technology gaps, especially when capital is brought in by multinational companies.

Hence, low efficiency goes a long way in explaining low TFP levels. Weil (2013: 290–292) provides an illustrative calculation for India. Assume that the US is at the technological frontier and it pushes forward by about 0.5% point per year. If then, India is 10 years behind the US, it would still achieve about 95% of the US technology level. If it is 50 years behind the US, it would still achieve 76%. Weil has calculated India's TFP to be at 31% of the US level in 2009. In the case of a ten-year technological gap, the Indian efficiency level would then stand at 33% of the US-level ($0.95 \times 0.33 = 0.31$), and for an unlikely 50-year technological backwardness at 41% ($0.76 \times 0.41 = 0.31$).Hence, the main culprit is low efficiency.

3.2 Technological progress: innovation and imitation

Technological progress is often described as a **process of creative destruction**. Innovators create new products or new production processes. By doing so they will enjoy a temporary monopoly position until imitators will challenge it, and the initially high profits will be melted away by competition, thus giving incentives to new innovations.

This process is therefore a double-edged sword. If imitation is too fast, competition will reduce monopoly profits so rapidly that the incentives to innovate are too low. On the other hand, if imitation is too slow, the innovator enjoys a monopoly position and has no incentive to innovate any further. Moreover, monopoly prices can be charged, and the innovation does not sufficiently benefit the consumer.

The key task of technology policy is therefore to support an imitation process that is neither too fast nor too slow. To allow temporary monopoly positions, a key policy instrument are intellectual property rights which protect the innovation from being copied, e.g. by means of patents. However, it is important that the patent protection is not too long and that competition policies make sure that after some time new entrants can enter the market. In the following, we look at this process from a country perspective.

3.2.1 Innovating at the frontier

A country at the technological frontier has to rely on pushing the frontier outward. Most studies estimate that the frontier can be pushed outward by between some 0.5% and 1% per annum (Weil, 2013).

For countries to innovate at the frontier, an innovation-supportive environment is crucial. This environment, the so-called innovation system, on the one hand, refers to policies that favour innovation, such as a property rights protection or competition policies. On the other hand, a good innovation system is also characterised by an efficient interaction between basic research at universities, government-funded research, and applied Research and Development (R&D) in the private sector. This includes the whole gamut of basic research in government-funded universities and research laboratories, applied research, often publicly co-funded, and put into practice in companies where learning-by-doing plays a huge role (Stiglitz & Greenwald, 2014). Moreover, as Mazzucato (2013) has argued forcefully, for many high-tech companies, e.g. digital superstar firms or the pharmaceutical industry, government-funded research often laid the base for their business model.

3.2.2 Technology catch-up

A country below the technological frontier can increase TFP by imitation. In a way, the farther away a country is from best practices, the faster it may be able to catch up. This is what has been called the 'advantage of backwardness'. However, as we have seen before, there is little evidence for such an unconditional advantage.

In fact, the ability to catch-up technologically depends crucially on the ability of latecomer countries to learn, also dubbed as the 'absorptive capacity' of a country (Cohen & Levinthal, 1989). Hence, the required environment conducive for catching-up is different from that for countries at the frontier. In the words of Aghion and Jaravel (2015: 536):

> While institutions or policies such as property right protection, contractual enforcement, the rule of law and macroeconomic stability are conducive to both frontier innovation and imitation, there are other institutional or policy features that tend to be more favourable to the former than to the latter. Thus, more product market competition and more free entry encourage innovation in sectors or countries that are closer to the technological frontier but can have detrimental effects on innovations in laggard sectors or countries.

3.3 Knowledge and growth

Both developing new technologies and using them efficiently require knowledge. To develop new technologies and pushing the technology frontier, innovators build on the stock of acquired knowledge, while imitators learn from experience and their exposure to this experience.

3.3.1 The special character of knowledge

To understand these processes, it is important to identify two key characteristics of knowledge, which give it the character of a **public good**. First, knowledge is different from other goods because it is **non-rival**. This means that if you use it everybody else can still use it. The classical example by Nobel laureate Paul Romer (1990) is the Pythagorean theorem. Once you know it, it helps constructing buildings everywhere. Likewise, a formula for a new drug to cure contagious diseases can in principle be used by every laboratory in the world to produce the drug. The latter point brings us to the second crucial feature of knowledge: **non-excludability**. In principle, nobody can be excluded from using the Pythagorean theorem. Hence, knowledge spreads, and if this knowledge spreads globally, the whole world benefits from it. The combination of both features makes knowledge a special factor of production: it has non-diminishing returns.

However, in reality creation and diffusion of knowledge is not without frictions. New knowledge often renders old knowledge obsolete and incentives to innovate may not be sufficient to invest privately in knowledge creation when it can be used freely by others as well. This gives rise to policy as well as corporate strategies to restrict knowledge diffusion by patents and other regulations, or secrecy.[15]

3.3.2 The role of learning and diversification

Producing even seemingly simple goods such as toothpaste in an industrial process, requires a lot of knowledge and experience. It is not just about how to develop the recipe to make the paste from various ingrediencies but also to produce the tube and finally fill the toothpaste into it. This is a complex process, which requires a lot of specialised knowledge in various areas. By contrast, 'producing' gold by 'gold panning' is an extremely simple production process that requires little knowledge and can be learned fast.

Countries with low levels of knowledge tend to concentrate on producing only few goods, often based on natural resources. More often than not this focus is a legacy of colonialism. However, the jump to more complex products is only possible when it goes hand-in-hand with developing and broadening the knowledge base by means of both, formal education and learning-by-doing.

Hausmann et al. (2013) argue that diversifying the economy, and thus moving to more economic complexity, is a key factor to obtain higher growth. By economic complexity they mean both, to diversify, i.e. to produce more different goods, and to produce products with a higher degree of complexity. Both processes typically go hand-in-hand. If a country expands its production possibilities over time, learning takes place and countries can move up the ladder to produce more and more complex goods.

Especially, participation in global value chains can allow countries to start as a supplier of rather simple tasks, such as assembling electronic goods. With learning over time, the countries may later embark on producing more and more inputs rather than importing them. This is exactly what China has been doing: starting as an assembler of the iPhone but now producing many inputs within the country.

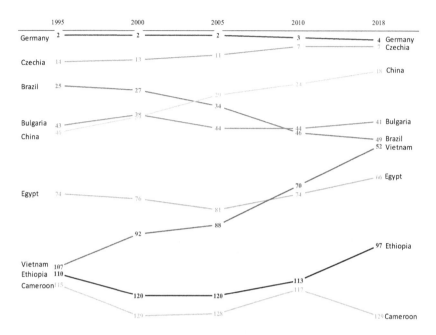

FIGURE 2.5 Economic Complexity Ranking of Selected Countries, 1995–2018.
Data source: Atlas of economic complexity, http://atlas.cid.harvard.edu/rankings.

Figure 2.5 shows how selected countries perform in terms of economic complexity. The global country ranking shows that advanced countries like Germany typically lead the complexity ranking. Fast-growing Asian countries like China and Vietnam have managed to increase their economic complexity over time. Likewise, some African countries also have made progress, though at a lower level, as exemplified here by Egypt and Ethiopia, though reductions in complexity can be observed as well, as illustrated by the case of Cameroon. In CEECs, the development is mixed as shown by the two differing cases of the Czech Republic and Bulgaria. Some countries, like the Czech Republic, have been able to increase their complexity fast, especially by integrating themselves into European production networks, e.g. in the automotive and electronics industry.

Empirical evidence shows that countries with higher economic complexity tend to grow faster (Hausmann et al., 2013) and achieve higher productivity growth rates (Dieppe, 2020). Hence, these results suggest that diversifying production and exports can be an important strategy for a country to increase productivity levels, and eventually converge to the technological leaders.

4 Growth policies

Policy measures can be classified as growth policies, whenever a relationship to the proximate and fundamental factors of growth can be established. Providing incentives to invest in physical and human capital are typically viewed as key growth policies. Likewise, supporting basic R&D as well as technology adoption and learning-by-doing are part and parcel of growth strategies.

4.1 Understanding growth policies: static and dynamic effects

The common understanding of a growth policy is that of a policy that lifts an economy into a higher growth path. Our discussion of the Solow growth model has shown that this leads to two separable effects:

- First, growth policy should deliver immediate effects on per-capita output, or more precisely, labour productivity. Hence, it can be viewed as pushing the production function upward, meaning that at any given level of capital-deepening more output per working hour can be produced. This immediate, **static efficiency effect** is illustrated in Panel A of Figure 2.6 by the move from A to B.
- Second, higher productivity allows for more savings and thus, investments. Consequently, the capital–output ratio will increase to $(K/L)_1$, by creating additional **dynamic growth effects** as indicated by the move from B to C. As a consequence, the economy would grow fast on its trajectory from A to C. However, once it arrives at C, growth will return to its normal rate, determined by the exogenous growth rate of technology.

Studies assessing the likely effects of growth policies differ not only in the effectiveness they assign to different policies, but also by the underlying growth model. Studies that rely on the Solow model will typically report the estimated static efficiency effect (from A to B). As an example, imagine an economy with an initial GDP of 1,000. If an investment incentive raises the GDP to 1,050, then a static productivity growth effect of 5% can be calculated. Some studies also estimate the expected dynamic effects of that policy emanating from capital-deepening (from B to C). This will result in a temporarily higher growth rate. Including this effect may lead to an estimated increase to 1,100 after several years. Clearly, when including the dynamic growth effects, the numbers are typically higher but beset with more uncertainties about their presence and size.

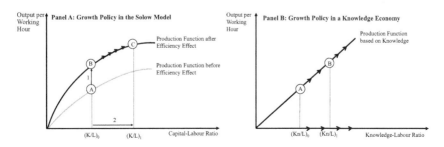

FIGURE 2.6 Static and Dynamic Effects of Growth Policy.

Finally, some studies are based on growth models that assume ceaseless growth. As discussed before, knowledge is a special factor of production as it exhibits non-diminishing returns. Hence, there is simply no equivalent to the steady-state capital–labour ratio of the Solow model as there is no such thing as too much knowledge per person. Hence, as investment in knowledge has constant returns in such a way that it can lead to ceaseless growth. This is illustrated in Panel B in Figure 2.6.[16] Studies that use such underlying growth models, estimate and predict permanent increases in the annual growth rate. The numbers reported typically appear small, but the total effect can indeed be large as time elapses. For example, if a policy is estimated to have a 'growth bonus' of raising the long-run growth rate by 1.5% per year, the productivity of our economy will exceed 1,100 already after seven years, and after ten years, it will stand at 1,160.5. It is therefore important to understand what kind of predictions are being reported in growth policy studies to give full justice to it. A good example are the growth estimates that were made for the European Single Market project (see European Perspective 2.4).

EUROPEAN PERSPECTIVE 2.4

The European single market as a growth policy

Establishing a common or single market has been at the heart of European integration policy, and finally resulted in the Single European Act, signed in 1986, that aimed at establishing the "four freedoms" of the *European Single Market Project* (SMP) by 1992, the free movement of goods, services, labour, and capital.

The SMP has been proposed as a growth project. A key EU study on the effects of the single market has been carried out. The so-called Cecchini Report focuses on the static effects of trade integration and estimates "the costs of non-Europe" between 4.25% and 6.5% of GDP (Cecchini, Catinat & Jacquemin, 1988). In terms of Figure 2.8, this relates to an upward shift of the production function and ignores dynamic effects. By contrast, Baldwin (1989) has estimated a 0.2%–0.9% point increase in the long-run growth rate as a result of the SMP.

Nowadays, the original Cecchini estimates are widely considered as too optimistic (Mariniello, Sapir & Terzi, 2015). One reason is the rising share of the service sector where tradability is limited, and hence fewer positive effects from market integration can be expected. Another issue is that regulatory barriers and public procurement rules were less quickly adjusted than envisioned. Up to the present day, the completion of the single market therefore remains an important European policy issue.

4.2 Growth policy concept

Arguably, the simplest growth concept is no concept, and policy makers basically could pursue only policies that 'work'. But how to agree on 'what works'? Our discussion in this chapter has shown that policy effects often depend on the circumstances. Infant industry protection had a better track record in the 19th century than in today's environment of global value chain trade; whether countries can benefit from foreign direct investment (FDI) and technology transfer depends crucially on the absorptive capacity of the country; and openness to cross-border finance has a mixed record, depending on the state of economic and financial development. However, not all 'recipes for growth' take country and time-specifics into account.

The most prominent version of a one-for-all recipe was the so-called **Washington Consensus**, which especially informed the policy recommendations of the International Monetary Fund (IMF) and the World Bank in the 1990s and 2000s. In this, the concept of 'letting the market work' is key. There is little room for state interventions other than to provide the institutional framework, such as the rule of law and guaranteeing property rights, and to correct for obvious market failures, such as monopoly power. Williamson (1994) has put together the famous ten-point 'laundry list' of recommended policy reforms: (1) fiscal discipline, (2) redirection of public expenditure towards health education and infrastructure, (3) tax reform (includes broadening the tax base and cutting marginal tax rates), (4) unified and competitive exchange rates, (5) secure property rights, (6) deregulation, (7) trade liberalisation, (8) privatisation, (9) elimination of barriers towards direct foreign investment, and (10) financial liberalisation. Especially points (6)–(10) have led to fierce debates on whether all these policies are always appropriate. After the great financial crisis (GFC), deregulation policies have been criticised heavily, and have often given way to more subtle approaches that take country-specifics into account.

A popular alternative country-specific approach, proposed by Hausmann, Velasco and Rodrik (2008), is **Growth Diagnostics** (GD). The starting point of GD is that each country is held back by its own binding constraint(s), which can also change over time. It can thus be viewed as a tool to identify country- and time-specific growth constraints. Hence, it is essentially a heuristic instrument for prioritising policies by tailoring them to the specific situation of a country. As such, rather than imposing a uniform policy reform agenda, GD can serve as an instrument for policy dialogue, especially when the political reform capital is limited.

Finally, there is now a clear trend towards evidence-based growth policies,[17] which take into account the country- and time-specifics of the country.

4.3 Openness and growth

A key recommendation of the Washington Consensus has been to open up economies. This has spurred intensive research and debates on the role of openness for growth. A key pro-openness argument highlights that exchange is a major way to acquire foreign knowledge. While it is obvious that countries which completely isolate themselves from the rest of the world – like North Korea today, China in the 15th century, or the socialist countries of the Soviet Bloc before 1990 – have been left behind. Do we have clear evidence of what the impact of openness and cross-border activities is on economic growth? The key point is that it depends on the type of openness.

The consensus among most economists today is that **openness to trade and FDI** has a positive impact on growth, per-capita income, and productivity. The key link to growth is that they are expected to increase economic efficiency in two major ways:

- trade openness increases competition, thus eliminating inefficient domestic suppliers, while efficient ones will survive and – if need be – are forced to increase efficiency;
- openness to trade and especially to FDI leads to growth-inducing knowledge spillovers.

However, the size, direction, and economic significance of these effects depend on country- and time-specific circumstances. With respect to the country-specifics, it makes a difference whether a country increases its trade by expanding traditional exports, or by shifting from traditional products to exporting more complex manufactures. The latter allow fast learning effects, hence leading to significant economy-wide productivity gains.

With respect to time-specifics, Eichengreen (2019) reminds us that studies on protectionism in the 19th century find that protecting manufacturing more than the traditional sector led to faster growth. Among other reasons why openness to trade today works better than in the past, is that openness to trade is nowadays key to attracting FDI. This is especially the case when these investments involve the country in a global or regional value chain that requires open borders to import intermediate inputs. Such foreign investments allow fast learning effects and are very different from earlier FDI which was largely directed towards extracting raw materials.

Empirical studies regularly report positive growth and productivity effects of trade openness, openness to FDI, and especially from participation in global value chains, such as most recently, Dieppe (2020). The effects reported are sizeable but averaged. The benefits may thus differ across countries. Countries with limited potential to become part of global values chains, low economic complexity, and low absorptive capacity, especially, may benefit much less from trade and FDI openness than others.

Openness to foreign finance was another key element of the Washington Consensus. Finance was not only seen as a panacea for spurring growth in advanced countries but also for emerging economies as it allows countries to increase investment beyond the narrow limits of their domestic savings.

International finance in the forms of portfolio investment and cross-border banking had a good track record of spurring growth in the 19th century.

As Schularick and Steger (2010) show, these positive effects worked via relaxing investment constraints for financing infrastructure such as railways etc. in developing countries. Thus, it helped in releasing capital for financing other domestic activities. For the present time, however, the authors were unable to establish a positive effect of financial globalisation on growth, neither directly by alleviating finance constraints nor by any positive effects of cross-border finance on efficiency as measured by TFP.

Finally, the GFC has shown that underregulated international banking and finance can increase the vulnerability of countries to events beyond their control, and lead to long-lasting recessions. In sum, cross-border finance is a mixed blessing for growth of both advanced and developing economies.

Migration is arguably the most powerful mechanisms to increase global production. It is well documented that people who move from a poor, low productivity environment to rich countries, are quick in reaching similar productivity levels as their peers in the new home country. Likewise, emigration is often a relief to low productivity countries. Migration from poor European countries to the US in the 19th and early 20th centuries has been an economic success story for both sides. The effects on the native population of an immigrant country are more complex, yet standard conventional wisdom argues that it will experience an "immigration surplus" (Borjas, 1995).

Simply judged by its global welfare effects, migration by far dwarfs the welfare effects of global trade, investment, and finance. Yet, migration remains the most regulated cross-border activity. However, the push and pull factors that drive economic migration are still the huge differences in income and productivity across countries. As long as convergence is not yet a 'great convergence', large-scale migration remains an issue.

5 The future of global production

What will shape the future development of global production? We discuss three core issues. First, the quest for a rising standard of living in many still underdeveloped and poor countries must be reconciled with the need to limit climate change. Greening growth will therefore play a key role in making global production sustainable. Second, new technologies will make their impact felt, for good or bad, and societies have to deal with them. And finally, it is increasingly becoming clear that all major countries and regions are taking a more active policy stance in dealing with and directing these changes. In other words, industrial policies are back on the global policy agenda.

5.1 Sustainable growth

Economic growth uses scarce resources. Especially the impact of carbon dioxide emissions will ultimately put a limit on economic growth. Hence, making growth sustainable requires decoupling growth from resource use.

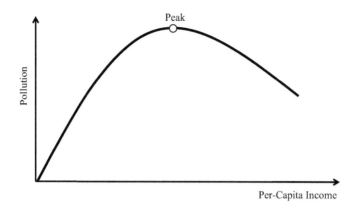

FIGURE 2.7 The Environmental Kuznets Curve (EKC).

The so-called **Environmental Kuznets Curve** (EKC) visualises a widely held view on the relation between pollution and per-capita income.[18] Typically pollution increases with rising income, but beyond a certain income level, pollution starts to decrease (Figure 2.7). However, decoupling depends on the pollutant. For example, for many high-income countries there is evidence for a decoupling with respect to smog-contributing nitrogen oxides (NO_X) and acid-rain-causing sulphur dioxide (SO_2) emissions. Hence, these countries are operating on the right-hand side of the peak, while many developing economies are still found to operate on the left-hand side of the EKC.[19] For greenhouse gases, especially carbon dioxide (CO_2), decoupling is mostly not visible yet.

Why do countries decouple after surpassing a certain income level? The wish to decouple depends, among others, especially on:

- the spatial closeness of negative effects,
- the time distance to the effect, and
- the costs of avoiding negative effects.

For example, emissions of NO_X contribute to smog, which is directly felt where the substances are emitted. However, while the desire for clean air increases with rising per-capita income, this does not necessarily mean that individuals will stop or decrease polluting. The reasons are what economists call **external effects**: each single polluter, for example the driver of a diesel-engine car has no incentive (other than ethical behaviour) to emit less, as he cannot directly be charged by those who suffer from the pollution for the decreased quality of the air they breathe. The classic solution to this market failure is government intervention, such as regulation of emissions, or price-based incentives, such as a gasoline tax. As such, decoupling also depends on the government responding to popular will (Frankel, 2009). Regarding acid rain, the situation is more complicated as the effect is often felt in other jurisdictions. For example, if French SO_2 emissions contribute to *Waldsterben* in Germany, international

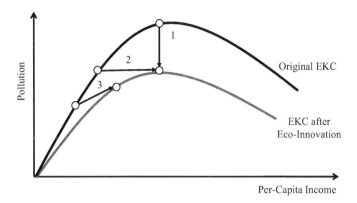

FIGURE 2.8   The EKC and Eco-Innovation.

cooperation is required, including a discussion on the distribution of abatement costs.

Carbon dioxide emissions are an extreme case, as they relate to all three aspects, thus explaining why decoupling is lagging behind. The impact of one country's CO_2 emissions may be felt only in the future in faraway countries by a higher incidence of devastating climate events, such as rising sea levels, floods, or storms. Yet, the cost of fast decarbonising for the economy today can be very high. And finally, given the global character of the problem, it requires a globally coordinated policy response.[20]

By now, it has increasingly become clear that global climate change needs to be addressed at the global level, as envisioned in the Paris Climate Agreement. Countries are increasingly committing themselves to aim at, first, decoupling carbon dioxide emissions from economic growth, and ultimately climate neutrality.

Without stopping growth, effective decoupling requires **eco-innovations**. The concept comprises not only technological innovation, e.g. photovoltaic cells, but also social or societal innovations, such as more home-office usage or shared mobility (OECD, 2011). Eco-innovations are best understood as innovations that push the EKC downward as illustrated in Figure 2.8. They may thus allow to (1) pollute less at any given level of per-capita income, (2) to increase the standard of living without increasing pollution, or, especially for the case of poorer countries, (3) at least a relative decoupling.

Unfortunately, eco-innovations do not simply take place as the outcome of market processes because they often do not pay off. Some may get adopted because of secondary benefits, such as fuel-efficient cars, yet most face multiple market failures. Most importantly, eco-innovations are facing a **double market failure**, which potentially holds them back[21]:

- **External environment effects** require governments to intervene via regulation or price incentives to make the adoption of eco-innovations pay off. Otherwise, the adoption rate would not be sufficient.

- **Research and Development (R&D) market failures** have their root in the public good nature of knowledge. If all can use newly created knowledge for free, the incentive to innovate is low. Creating and protecting intellectual property rights is a way to reward innovation, but it makes eco-innovations more expensive and will thus limit their diffusion. Moreover, many eco-innovations are characterised by **network externalities**, i.e., their adoption depends on a critical number of adopters. Obvious examples are fuelling stations for electric cars. Again, it is clear that public intervention is needed to overcome these obstacles.

What makes the issue so pertinent is that it may be necessary to address both the market failures simultaneously to trigger eco-innovations. Moreover, even when the double market failure is addressed properly, diffusion of eco-innovation may still be limited, as adoption might be held back by habit persistence. Especially for developing countries, the necessary infrastructure, the absorptive capacity, and access to new green technologies are often key limiting factors.

In sum, for making global production and growth sustainable, eco-innovations will be indispensable. Hence, policy makers need to reduce the obstacles that hold back eco-innovations at the local, national, regional, and global levels.

5.2 The role of new technologies in the NGE

Digitalisation, robotisation, and the advent of artificial intelligence (AI) are considered key elements of change in the new global economy (NGE). What are their likely impacts on productivity, the workplace, and globalisation?

5.2.1 New technologies and productivity

What is the impact of digitalisation on growth and productivity? Growth accounting finds it difficult to detect productivity effects of the ICT revolution. In fact, the recent evidence still points to low labour productivity growth almost everywhere. Gordon (2016) posits that ICT simply does not have the same potential of unlocking complementary investment, as we know from the cases of electricity and the combustion engine. Hence, he argues that the productivity effects of the new technologies are at best temporary. Brynjolfsson, Rock and Syverson (2021) challenge this view and argue that the new modern technologies are also general purpose technologies (GPTs). In this view, the new GPTs enable and require significant complementary investments, however, these are often intangibles, like the invention and implementation of new business processes and business models. Moreover, people need time to learn to use the new technologies efficiently. For example, it is argued that it took a whole generation to adjust factory layouts to fully harvest the benefits from electrification. Hence, the argument goes that in the early years of introducing a new GPT, the value of these intangibles is often underestimated, while the benefits of these assets are harvested only later. As a consequence, in the early years of a new GPT, its contributions to productivity growth (both labour productivity and TFP) are underestimated, while later they are overestimated. The authors posit that

> trillions of dollars of intangibles output has been produced but not counted in the national income accounts, resulting in a 15.9 percent underestimate of TFP levels 2017. There is also some evidence that the phenomenon appears to have begun again, very recently, for AI-related intangible investments.
>
> *(Brynjolfsson, Rock & Syverson, 2021: 360)*

This optimistic view contrasts with Gordon's verdict if we take both views as unconditional predictions. We may, however, reformulate it depending on what forms robotisation and AI will take.

5.2.2 What types of robots and AI?

When talking about new digital technologies, popular debates often concentrate around the robotisation of manufacturing, as suggested by catchphrases like Industry 4.0 or Second Machine Age (Brynjolfsson & McAfee, 2014). The authors paint a future in which the new technologies could ultimately make labour redundant. As increasingly less labour is needed, the share of labour in income will decline – and in the extreme case of a completely robotised production, go to zero. New ways of distributing the value added to people would then be needed, be it a universal basic income, or some form of participation from capital gains for all citizens.

To gain a clearer insight into the issues at stake, it is helpful to employ a distinction of two types of robots, recently suggested by Phelps et al. (2020), namely additive and multiplicative robots. **Additive robots** perform the same routines as human labour, thus adding to human labour and eventually substituting it. By contrast, **multiplicative robots** do not replace labour but augment it, making it more productive. Consider, for example, AI-assisted surgery. AI does not replace the surgeon, but improves the quality of her work. We may loosely associate additive robots with automation and multiplicative robots with AI, though in reality mixed forms are ubiquitous.

Automation by additive robots

Phelps et al. (2020) argue that additive robots are in effect increasing the total labour force. Thus, their likely immediate impact on wages is negative, reflecting a new abundance of labour. Unemployment may rise – at least temporarily, wages will be depressed, and a fall of the labour share is likely. But is modern automation not simply a variant of labour-saving technical progress that we are dealing with since the Industrial Revolution? And has it not – on average – gone hand-in-hand with full employment and rising wages?

Acemoglu and Restrepo (2018) argue that most robots used in manufacturing centre on **automating tasks**, thus replacing humans by machines, i.e., they are additive robots. As such they have a **replacement effect**, which reduces labour demand. Only if they also boost productivity, as was the case in the aftermath of the Industrial Revolution, this **productivity effect** would lead to lower costs and thus more production and more labour demand. The net effect depends on the relative strength of both effects. However, the authors make the point that automation technologies are often not big technological breakthroughs, but only "so-so technologies", just good enough to get adopted but not exceeding the productivity of the workers they replace by a large margin.

In sum, modern automation by additive robots is more likely to affect labour negatively than previous forms of labour-saving technical progress. By increasingly replacing labour – especially if the price of robots continues falling – without creating sufficiently new jobs, then indeed, in the extreme case, the share of labour income could move towards zero.

Artificial intelligence and multiplicative robots

Multiplicative robots make labour more productive. Higher productivity will lead to higher wages and thus to the creation of new jobs. In particular, AI has a higher potential to act as a multiplicative robot. Acemoglu and Restrepo (2020: 29) view AI as a technology platform that can be used "to restructure the production process in a way that creates many new, high-productivity tasks for labour". To be sure, AI can also be used to substitute labour, for instance, AI translation programs. Moreover, work in enabling AI, such as training and monitoring the new machines, may not be sufficient to generate enough new jobs to compensate for the losses from automation.

Rather, what Acemoglu and Restrepo (2020) have in mind are new ways in which humans can interact with AI, e.g. in education by tailoring instructions closer to the differing learning behaviour of individuals, or in the health sector by involving nurses and technicians in collecting and analysing data. In this way, their productivity could be greatly enhanced. In a similar vein, Phelps et al. (2020) are also optimistic about the long-run effects of such multiplicative robots, but they caution that in the short run, there might be factors that limit the creation of new jobs, especially a lack of a required complementary capital stock of buildings and other physical structures. Hence, their optimism is conditional on a wave of new investments.

In reality, new technologies may not fall clearly in one or the other category. But it is obvious that multiplicative robots are much more desirable from a welfare point of view. The crucial issue is, therefore, which directions the new technologies will take and whether and how these directions can be influenced.

5.2.3 Digitalisation and the future of globalisation

The advent of the computer age in the 1980s and 1990s has given rise to a slicing-up of industrial value chains and subsequently globalising them. If we follow

Acemoglu and Restrepo (2018) and think of robotisation at the level of tasks, robots have the potential to reconfigure modern global value chains.

Additive robots are not only labour replacing, but also an alternative to outsourcing, thus making de-globalisation more likely. When deciding where to locate a task within the GVC of a product, other factors will gain in importance, such as proximity to customer or suppliers, and low-labour-cost countries may lose their attractiveness as production locations. Re-shoring of activities closer to the markets may become more widespread.

This can decrease possibilities for latecomer countries to emulate the manufacturing-led catching-up growth strategies of the past. By contrast, in the service industry, digital technologies make services more tradable. However, by its very nature, services are more difficult to robotise than manufacturing tasks. This implies that increasingly the production of services will be globalised, especially since digitalised services can be delivered electronically without high trading costs. 5G and other further advances in ICT will promote this development further. As a consequence, more latecomer countries may in future be able to develop their country not by taking the traditional road of developing a manufacturing sector first, but by leapfrogging via the internationalisation of their service industry. We have seen before that India is a case in point as it has recently been able to grow by increasing the economy's productivity.

In sum, also from the point of view of technological developments it is premature to announce the end of globalisation. Rather, as argued throughout this book, and analysed in more detail in the upcoming chapters on global trade, investment, and intangibles, globalisation is changing its character.

5.3 Looking forward: the revival of industrial policies

Both climate change and digitalisation require policies that may necessitate measures to direct technical change towards a more sustainable and desirable path. The Industrial Revolution emerged against a background of a cultural change that took a different view on the material world, and finally ignited because labour-saving progress started paying off.

The world is now realising that the current growth model is not sustainable in the long-run, yet a change in incentives to move towards a different growth path can only be derived from our insights into this process, and subsequent policy that moves towards setting the right incentive to encourage both eco-innovation and labour-augmenting, rather than labour replacing technical progress to enable **inclusive growth**.

In recent years, there has been a revival of interest in industrial policies. In the times of the Washington Consensus, old-style industrial policy had a bad image. It was often associated with governments supporting unproductive industries, and picking losers instead of winners in the name of creating 'national champions'. However, the prevalence of market failures, especially regarding R&D failures and environmental external effects point to the need of public policies setting the right incentives. Moreover, the rise of China not least by means of massive industrial policy interventions, has contributed to the perception in advanced countries that own industrial strategies and policies, especially regarding new technologies, are needed.

With respect to **advanced countries** close to the technological frontier, instead of targeting individual pre-selected firms, arguments are made in favour of creating a supportive landscape for an emerging knowledge economy, e.g. supporting basic research, using incentives to redirect production and R&D to green investment and multiplicate robots, and by targeting skill-intensive industries (see, e.g. Aghion, Boulanger and Cohen, 2011). With respect to **emerging and developing countries**, there is a revival of ideas revolving around nurturing economic development by means of, amongst others, trade and industrial policies.

Recommended readings

Weil (2013) provides an accessible introduction to economic growth theory and policy. For an in-depth research-based coverage, see Acemoglu (2009). Allen (2009) provides an insightful analysis of the industrial revolution, Eichengreen (2008) is a valuable source on the history of the European economy after 1945, and Gordon (2016) offers an in-depth economic analysis of US growth.

The World Bank's website (www.worldbank.org) is a key source of analysis, such as the annual World Development Report, and data. Likewise, the website of the Organisation for Economic Co-operation and Development (www.oecd.org) is an invaluable source of timely analyses and data.

Notes

1 The British historian Robert Allen has made the point that in 18th century Britain, wages were higher than elsewhere in Europe and definitely much higher than in India and Bengal. Hence, the latter countries dominated in cotton spinning. Given that additionally energy prices were low in Britain, it paid off to invent machines to replace labour and outcompete India and Bengal in cotton spinning (see Allen, 2011).
2 To what extent the agricultural revolution caused the Industrial Revolution is still a matter of controversy. To make sense of the story, the causality should start with a productivity increase in the rural area, thus freeing people for industrial activities in the cities. An alternative narrative is that higher wages in the cities attracted people from the countryside, leading to higher wages there as well. Allen (2009) argues that high wages in London and Amsterdam were a major pull factor and thus speak in favour of the second narrative.
3 The printing press helped also in spreading the words of the Bible, especially the translation by Martin Luther.
4 See, e.g. Becker and Woessmann (2009). Kersting, Wohnsiedler and Wolf (2020) contest the literacy channel by pointing to the role of discrimination of Catholic ethnic Polish people in Prussia.
5 This summary incorporates some of the major points raised by Acemoglu (2009: 123).
6 TFP is also called multifactor productivity.

7 Equation (2.1) gives the so-called Cobb–Douglas production function. It is said to be 'well-behaved', as it assumes constant returns to scale and diminishing returns to each production factor.
8 Crafts and O'Rourke (2014: 267) argue:

> If the contribution of technological change to the growth of labor productivity is taken to be capital deepening in the modernized sectors plus total TFP growth, then this equates to 0.54 out of 0.64% per year. It remains perfectly reasonable, therefore, to regard technological innovation as responsible for the acceleration in labor productivity growth that marked the Industrial Revolution …, even though the change was less dramatic than was once thought.

9 A recent study published by the World Bank (Dieppe, 2020) provides an in-depth analysis of the productivity slowdown puzzle.
10 This is the meaning of Solow's steady state condition. It demands $s(Y/L) = d(K/L)$, where 's' is the savings rate and 'd' is the rate of depreciation of the capital stock. Hence, on the left-hand side (LHS) are the savings per working hour and on the right-hand side (RHS) are the required investments to equip each working hour with the same amount of capital. If LHS > RHS, we experience 'positive' capital deepening, otherwise 'negative' capital deepening. Hence, there is a unique equilibrium with a constant steady-state capital–labour ratio, indicated in the graph by point 'S'.
11 See http://routledgetextbooks.com/textbooks/9780321795731/resources.php. The numbers for China have been calculated by the author using the data set.
12 This can be researched in cross-country studies by testing for so-called β-convergence by regressing initial per-capita incomes of a sample of i countries (Y_i) on their growth rates g_{Yi} over a longer period of time, such as $g_{Yi} = a + \beta Y_i$. A negative and statistically significant β-value means that higher initial income implies lower growth.
13 The extensive literature on convergence differs not only by examining different conditioning factors, but also by employing different data, methodologies, and estimation methods. Reviewing the literature is beyond the scope of this book. The interested reader is directed to the survey article by Johnson and Papageorgiou (2020).
14 Asian countries in total accounted for over 52% of global production of manufactures, with Japan (7.2%), Republic of Korea (3.3%), and India (3.0%) being the largest producers after China. Germany, as the largest European supplier of manufactures, accounts for 5.8%. All data are for 2018 and are own calculations based on manufacturing (ISIC D) data for "value added by economic activity, at current prices in US Dollars" obtained from the United Nations Statistics Division National Accounts – Analysis of Main Aggregate (AMA) website: https://unstats.un.org/unsd/snaama, retrieved 31 July, 2020.
15 Chapter 5 addresses these issues in the global context in more detail.
16 Note that this figure differs from the diagram often used to illustrate ceaseless growth in the so-called endogenous growth theory where it is assumed that new knowledge is embodied in new capital. In that case, capital has constant returns to scale and allows for ceaseless capital accumulation. Hence, the capital–labour ratio would be on the horizontal axis. Such models use linear so-called AK production functions with A as a constant parameter.
17 An evidence-based approach that is often praised as the 'gold standard' are *randomized controlled trials* (RCT). The basic idea is borrowed from medical trials that test treatments on a randomly selected group of people and contrast the results to a group of non-treated people. Hence what works can be statistically tested (see, e.g., Duflo and Banerjee, 2011). However, RCTs are time-consuming, and beset with ethical issues about experimenting with people. Moreover, as argued by Deaton (2020), RCTs may not have unique advantages over other empirical methods employed.

18 The concept of the EKC is attributed to Grossman and Krueger (1991). Its name pays tribute to Simon Kuznets, who has argued an inverted-U-shaped curve for the empirical relationship between per-capita income and income inequality. The EKC works best for describing emissions of pollutants. For an early critical discussion of the EKC, see Stern, Common and Barbier (1996).
19 For example, Frankel and Rose (2005) have estimated the peak of the EKC for SO_2 at a per-capita GDP of $5,770.
20 For a discussion of the governance of global commons, see Chapter 7.
21 For a deeper discussion and a methodology to identify what holds back eco-innovations, see Sander (2016).

References

Acemoglu, D. (2009). *Introduction to modern economic growth*. Princeton University Press.

Acemoglu, D., Johnson, S., & Robinson, J. A. (2005). Institutions as a fundamental cause of long-run growth. In P. Aghion & S. N. Durlauf (Eds.), *Handbook of economic growth 1* (pp. 385–472). Elsevier.

Acemoglu, D., & Restrepo, P. (2018). Modeling automation. *AEA Papers and Proceedings*, *108*, 48–53.

Acemoglu, D., & Restrepo, P. (2020). The wrong kind of AI? Artificial intelligence and the future of labour demand. *Cambridge Journal of Regions, Economy and Society*, *13*(1), 25–35.

Acemoglu, D., & Robinson, J. A. (2012). *Why nations fail: The origins of power, prosperity, and poverty*. Crown Business.

Aghion, P., Boulanger, J., & Cohen, E. (2011). *Rethinking industrial policy*. Bruegel Policy Brief 2011/2004, June. Bruegel.

Aghion, P., & Jaravel, X. (2015). Knowledge spillovers, innovation and growth. *The Economic Journal*, *125*(583), 533–573.

Allen, R. C. (2009). *The British industrial revolution in global perspective*. Cambridge University Press.

Allen, R. C. (2011). *Global economic history. A very short introduction*. Oxford University Press.

Baldwin, R. E. (1989). *On the growth effects of 1992*. NBER Working Paper 3119. National Bureau of Economic Research.

Baldwin, R. E. (2016). *The great convergence: Information technology and the new globalisation*. Belknap Press of Harvard University Press.

Becker, S. O., & Woessmann, L. (2009). Was Weber wrong? A human capital theory of protestant economic history. *Quarterly Journal of Economics*, *124*(2), 531–596.

Bergeaud, A., Cette, G., & Lecat, R. (2016). Productivity trends in advanced countries between 1890 and 2012. *Review of Income and Wealth*, *62*(3), 420–444.

Bolt, J., Inklaar, R., De Jong, H., & Van Zanden, J. L. (2018). *Rebasing 'Maddison': New income comparisons and the shape of long-run economic development*. Maddison Project Working Paper 10, Groningen Growth and Development Centre. University of Groningen.

Boltho, A., & Eichengreen, B. (2008). *The economic impact of European integration*. CEPR Discussion Paper 6820. Centre for Economic Policy Research

Borjas, G. J. (1995). The economic benefits from immigration. *Journal of Economic Perspective*, *9*, 3–22.

Brynjolfsson, E., & McAfee, A. (2014). *The second machine age*. W.W. Norton.

Brynjolfsson, E., Rock, D., & Syverson, C. (2021). The productivity J-curve: how intangibles complement general purpose technologies. *American Economic Journal: Macroeconomics*, *13*(1), 333–372.

Campos, N. F., Coricelli, F., & Moretti, L. (2019). Institutional integration and economic growth in Europe. *Journal of Monetary Economics*, *103*, 88–104.

Cecchini, P., Catinat, M., & Jacquemin, A. (1988). *The European challenge-1992*. Wildwood House.

Cohen, W. M., & Levinthal, D. A. (1989). Innovation and learning: the two faces of R & D. *The Economic Journal*, *99*(397), 569–596.

Crafts, N., & O'Rourke, K. H. (2014). Twentieth century growth. In P. Aghion & S. N. Durlauf (Eds.), *Handbook of economic growth 2* (pp. 263–346). Elsevier.

Deaton, A. (2020). *Randomization in the tropics revisited: A theme and eleven variations*. NBER Working Paper 27600. National Bureau of Economic Research.

Dieppe, A. (Ed.) (2020). *Global productivity. Trends, drivers, and policies*. World Bank Group.

Duflo, E., & Banerjee, A. (2011). *Poor economics*. Public Affairs.

Durlauf, S. N., Johnson, P. A., & Temple, J. R. W. (2005). Growth econometrics. In P. Aghion & S. N. Durlauf (Eds.), *Handbook of economic growth 1* (pp. 555–677). Elsevier.

Eichengreen, B. (2008). *The European economy since 1945: Coordinated capitalism and beyond*. Princeton University Press.

Eichengreen, B. (2019). Trade policy and the macroeconomy. *IMF Economic Review*, *67*(1), 4–23.

Frankel, J. A. (2009). *Environmental effects of international trade*. HKS Faculty Research Working Paper Series RWP09-006. Harvard University.

Frankel, J. A., & Rose, A. K. (2005). Is trade good or bad for the environment? Sorting out the causality. *Review of Economics and Statistics*, *87*(1), 85–91.

Gordon, R. J. (2016). *The rise and fall of American growth*. Princeton University Press.

Gordon, R. J., & Sayed, H. (2020). Transatlantic technologies: the role of ICT on the evolution of U.S. and European productivity growth. *International Productivity Monitor*, *38*, 50–80.

Gorodnichenko, Y., & Roland, G. (2011). Which dimensions of culture matter for long-run growth? *American Economic Review*, *101*(3), 492–498.

Grossman, G. M., & Krueger, A. B. (1991). *Environmental impacts of a North American free trade agreement*. NBER Working Paper 3914. National Bureau of Economic Research.

Hausmann, R., Hidalgo, C. A., Bustos, S., Coscia, M., Simoes, A., & Yildirim, M. A. (2013). *The atlas of economic complexity. Mapping pathways to prosperity*. MIT Press.

Hausmann, R., Velasco, A., & Rodrik, D. (2008). Growth diagnostics. In J. Stiglitz & N. Serra (Eds.), *The Washington consensus reconsidered: Towards a new global governance* (pp. 324–354). Oxford University Press.

Hofstede, G. (2001). *Culture's consequences: Comparing values, behaviors, institutions and organizations across nations*. Sage.

Johnson, P., & Papageorgiou, C. (2020). What remains of cross-country convergence? *Journal of Economic Literature*, *58*(1), 129–175.

Kersting, F., Wohnsiedler, I., & Wolf, N. (2020). Weber revisited: the protestant ethic and the spirit of nationalism. *The Journal of Economic History*, *80*(3), 710–745.

Lakner, C., & Milanovic, B. (2013). *Global income distribution: From the fall of the Berlin wall to the great recession*. World Bank Working Paper 6719. December.

Malthus, T. R. (1798). *An essay on the principle of population*. London

Mankiw, N. G., Romer, D., & Weil, D. N. (1992). A contribution to the empirics of economic growth. *The Quarterly Journal of Economics*, *107*(2), 407–438.

Mariniello, M., Sapir, A., & Terzi, A. (2015). *The long road towards the European single market*. Bruegel Working Paper 2015/2001. Bruegel.

Mazzucato, M. (2013). *The entrepreneurial state. Debunking public vs private sector myths*. Anthem Press.

Mokyr, J. (2016). *A culture of growth*. Princeton University Press.

OECD (2011). *Fostering innovation for green growth*. Organisation for Economic Co-operation and Development.

Phelps, E., Bojilov, R., Hoon, H. T., & Zoega, G. (2020). *Dynamism: The values that drive innovation, job satisfaction, and economic growth*. Harvard University Press.

Rodrik, D. (2013). Unconditional convergence in manufacturing. *The Quarterly Journal of Economics, 128*(1), 165–204.

Romer, P. M. (1990). Endogenous technological change. *Journal of Political Economy, 98*(5), S71–S102.

Sander, H. (2016). What holds back eco-innovations? A "green growth diagnostics" approach. In V. Ramiah & G. N. Gregoriou (Eds.), *Handbook of environmental and sustainable finance* (pp. 147–163). Academic Press.

Schularick, M., & Steger, T. (2010). Financial integration, investment and economic growth: evidence from two eras of financial globalization. *Review of Economics and Statistics, 92*, 756–758.

Stern, D. I., Common, M. S., & Barbier, E. B. (1996). Economic growth and environmental degradation: the environmental Kuznets curve and sustainable development. *World Development, 24*(7), 1151–1160.

Stiglitz, J. E., & Greenwald, B. C. (2014). *Creating a learning society: A new approach to growth, development, and social progress*. Columbia University Press.

Van Ark, B., O'Mahony, M., & Timmer, M. P. (2008). The productivity gap between Europe and the United States: trends and causes. *Journal of Economic Perspectives, 22*(1), 25–44.

Voigtländer, N., & Voth, H. J. (2013). The three horsemen of riches: plague, war, and urbanization in early modern Europe. *Review of Economic Studies, 80*(2), 774–811.

Weil, D. N. (2013*). Economic growth* (3rd ed.). Pearson.

Williamson, J. (Ed.) (1994). *The political economy of policy reform*. Institute for International Economics.

World Bank (1993). *The East Asian miracle. Economic growth and public policy*. Oxford University Press.

Young, A. (1994). Lessons from the East Asian NICs: a contrarian view. *European Economic Review, 38*(3–4), 964–973.

Young, A. (1995). The tyranny of numbers: confronting the statistical realities of the East Asian growth experience. *The Quarterly Journal of Economics, 110*(3), 641–680.

Zak, P. J., & Knack, S. (2001). Trust and growth. *The Economic Journal, 111*(470), 295–321.

3

GLOBAL TRADE

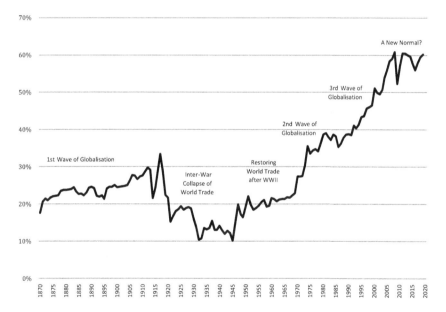

FIGURE 3.1 World Trade as a Share of World GDP (in %), 1870–2019.

Sources: 1870–1969 data are from Ourworldindata.org based on Klasing and Milionis (2014) for 1870–1949 data and Penn World Tables (8.1) for 1950–1969. The 1970–2019 data is retrieved from World Bank, World Development Indicators.
Note: Trade is measured as the sum of export and imports of goods and services.

Cross-border trade has been growing faster than global production since 1870, leading to the present record level of trade integration, as measured by the increase in the trade-to-GDP ratio (Figure 3.1). There are, however, two notable

DOI: 10.4324/9781003057611-3

interruptions: the inter-war period of de-globalisation and the cease of the trade integration process since the great financial crisis (GFC) of 2008–2009. Is the latter only a temporary standstill or are we entering the phase of a 'new normal'? This chapter explores the key features of today's trade, with a focus on global value chain trade, through the lens of modern trade theories. It highlights the implication of global trade for income (in-) equality across and within nation states, and the role of contemporary trade policies to deal with the upcoming challenges emanating from global competition, new technologies, and climate change.

1 Trade globalisation and trade costs

The key to understanding trade globalisation are trade costs in the broadest sense. Not just transportation costs, but everything that makes trading across borders more expensive or cheaper, e.g. trade barriers like tariffs, but also communication costs. Hence, technologies and trade policies are major drivers of globalisation. Interpreting the history of trade globalisation as the outcome of the interaction of technological developments and policies, allows to distinctly identify three waves of globalisation, as introduced in Chapter 1. Even more importantly, this also helps us understand the nature and possible persistence of the recent 'new normal' of stalling trade globalisation.

1.1 The first two waves of trade globalisation

From the late 19th to the early 21st centuries, the world has witnessed an unparalleled increase in economic interconnectedness. It underwent its first wave of globalisation between approximately 1870 and 1917. This process was largely influenced by the technology-driven process of industrialisation. Steamships and railways reduced transportation costs rapidly. Entrepreneurs realised the new global business opportunities and successfully lobbied for a liberal trading order. Trade barriers fell quickly, and trade started to flourish.

The aftermath of World War I (WWI) changed this. The Great Depression of 1929 caused a prolonged economic crisis and many countries became inward-looking, protectionist, and finally nationalistic. As a consequence, global trade collapsed in the inter-war period, predominantly for political reasons.

After World War II (WWII), efforts were made to restore global trade by lowering trade barriers, not least by means of a General Agreement on Tariffs and Trade (GATT), which later became the World Trade Organisation (WTO). Transportation costs declined further: shipping cost fell sharply with the introduction of container shipping, air freight costs declined, and road and rail infrastructure improved. Politically, decolonisation gave some developing countries the chance to overcome the old **complementary division of labour**. In the 1970s, we can thus identify a second wave of globalisation as some developing countries became successful exporters of manufactured products. This led to an emerging **substitutive division of labour** between advanced and newly industrialising countries (NICs). These economies, especially the Asian NICs – Taiwan, South Korea, Hong Kong, and Singapore – made inroads in a few sectors such as textiles and clothing, steel, shipbuilding, and electronics, and rapidly became super-traders, heavily competing with workers in these traditional industries in advanced countries. The NICs were the first to rapidly catch up with advanced countries in terms of productivity and per-capita income.[1]

1.2 The third wave: the rise of global value chain trade

The famous example of the pin factory described by Adam Smith (1776) in his *Inquiry into the Nature and Causes of the Wealth of Nations* can help us to understand the third wave of globalisation:

> To take an example, therefore, from a very trifling manufacture ... the trade of the pin-maker; ...the way in which this business is now carried on, not only the whole work is a peculiar trade, but it is divided into a number of branches, of which the greater part are likewise peculiar trades. One man draws out the wire, another straights it, a third cuts it, a fourth points it, a fifth grinds it at the top for receiving the head; to make the head requires two or three distinct operations; to put it on, is a peculiar business, to whiten the pins is another; it is even a trade by itself to put them into the paper; and the important business of making a pin is, in this manner, divided into about eighteen distinct operations, which, in some manufactories, are all performed by distinct hands, though in others the same man will sometimes perform two or three of them.
>
> *(Smith, 1776: 15–16)*

What Adam Smith describes here is what modern economists call the division of labour. By breaking-down the production of a good into different tasks, productivity rises, and the same number of workers can produce more pins, thus increasing the wealth of nations. Yet, what Adam Smith exhibits is the division of labour within a factory. What is distinct in the third wave of globalisation is that these tasks can, first, be **outsourced** to other companies, and second, **offshored** to foreign countries. This has created a historically unparalleled rise of what is called **global value chain (GVC) trade**, aka the **fragmentation** of global production.

1.2.1 From slicing the value chain to global fragmentation

To understand this new character of global trade, one can look back some 40 years. Back then, customers of the Swedish furniture store IKEA occasionally had experiences with table legs that did not fit when they tried to put the furniture together at home. Today this is a story of the past. Unless you are extremely unlucky, all parts of your new furniture will fit together perfectly. Similarly, veteran workers in car factories may remember the days when most car parts were produced within the factory for one simple reason: If a part did not fit on the assembly line, it could be returned to the corner of the factory where it had been produced, to be immediately adjusted accordingly.

Nowadays, computers are being used to design goods (Computer-aided Design – CAD), for computer-numerical controlled production (CNC), and computer-aided manufacturing (CAM). If parts of products can be designed and produced to fit perfectly in final assembly, the value chain can be 'sliced-up'. Production no longer has to take place in a single factory. It can be fragmented. This allows, first, outsourcing, which will occur whenever economically profitable. Second, given the huge differences in production costs and the much greater variety of specialised skills at the global level, GVCs can offer more efficient opportunities than pure domestic ones, hence boosting offshoring.

Two products perfectly illustrate this global value chain production, the Barbie doll and the iPhone. In the 1990s, the Barbie doll was the archetype example of this new way of globally fragmented production. The plastic and hair were obtained from Taiwan and Japan, the US provided the mould and decorative paintings, while China supplied the cloth. Assembling took place in low-cost locations in Indonesia, Malaysia, and China. Apple's iPhone 3G also was produced using inputs from various countries before it was finally assembled in China (see Table 3.1).

TABLE 3.1 Major Components and Cost Drivers of Apple iPhone 3G

Manufacturer	Country	Component	Cost
Toshiba	Japan	Flash memory	$24.00
		Display module	$19.25
		Touch screen	$16.00
Samsung	Korea	Application processor	$14.46
		SDRAM-mobile DDR	$8.50
Infineon	Germany	Baseband	$13.00
		Camera module	$9.55
		RF transceiver	$2.80
		GPS receiver	$2.25
		Power IC RF function	$1.25
Broadcom	USA	Bluetooth/FM/WLAN	$5.95
Numonyx	USA	Memory MCP	$3.65
Murata	Japan	FEM	$1.35
Dialog semiconductor	Germany	Power IC application processor function	$1.30
Cirrus logic	USA	Audio codec	$1.15
Rest of bill of materials			$48.00
Total bill of materials			**$172.46**
Manufacturing costs			**$6.50**
Grand total			**$178.96**

Source: Xing (2011).

The third wave of globalisation is therefore distinct from the second wave because of the **new technological possibilities for slicing up the value chain**. The globalisation of the created tasks has been enabled by two major factors:

- Drastically falling information and communication costs since the 1990s, which facilitated the creation and management of complex value chain production across borders.
- Trade liberalisation in the 1990s has reduced barriers to trade and FDI and facilitated GVC trade. Especially regional trade liberalisation efforts of emerging economies have often been driven by the intention to enable participation in global and regional values chains.

1.2.2 Adding value in GVCs: the smile curve

Globalised value chains take advantage of global differences in labour costs. Going back to our example of Barbie, the doll was sold for $10 in the US. The export value of a Barbie was just $2 when it left Hong Kong, the remaining $8 covered transportation, marketing, wholesaling, and retailing in the US, and a $1 profit for Mattel. Even more remarkable, of the $2 for the export value, only about 35 cents cover the labour cost for assembling in China, while the rest is for the cost of materials, regional transportation, overhead, and profits.[2] Likewise, and as shown in Table 3.1, the iPhone also features a cost structure, where assembling costs are $6.50, representing just 3.6% of total costs, and a meagre 1.3% of the $500 sales price.

This very feature of GVC production can be visualised by the so-called smile curves (Figure 3.2). Typically, pre-production activities, such as developing and branding new products, as well as post-production activities, such as distribution and marketing, often create the highest value added. These activities are often

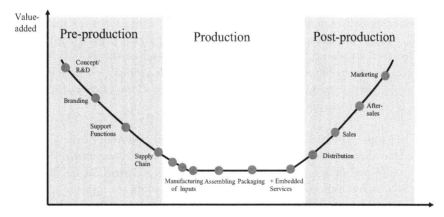

FIGURE 3.2 The Value Chain and the Smile Curve.
Source: Own graph based on Figure IV.9 in UNCTAD (2020: 143).

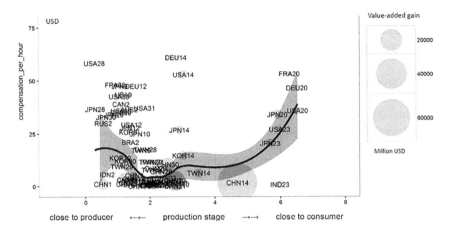

FIGURE 3.3   Estimated Smile Curve for China's Exports of Electrical and Optical Equipment, 2009.

Source: Figure 2.18 in World Bank (2017: 55), based on Meng, Ye and Wei (2017).

knowledge-intensive and located in advanced economies. In contrast, the actual production of the goods, from manufacturing of inputs to assembling and packaging them, often creates a lower value added, especially when no specialised knowledge is required and the production can easily be offshored to emerging economies.

Reality, of course, is more complex. To illustrate this, first take a look at the estimated smile curve for China's export of electrical and optical equipment in 2009 (Figure 3.3). The curve shows the predicted low level of value added, here measured by labour compensation per hour, around the production stage. The low level of compensation in China (indicated CHN in the graph) in the production stage, demonstrates that in industries like electronics, assembling especially has often been relocated to low wage countries. Yet, the fit of the curve is far from perfect. Especially, suppliers of manufactured inputs, such as Germany (indicated DEU) and the US, can realise a high value added by providing specialised inputs.

However, whether the GVC actually 'smiles', depends on the industry. Counterexamples can be found for the German automobile industry, where the curve 'frowns' (Figure 3.4). The World Bank's *Global Value Chain Development Report 2017* gives the following explanation:

> To some extent, this may reflect the successful transition of the German auto industry from traditional mass producer to mass customizer and to individual design based on digital technology and artificial intelligence. The mass customized and individual design manufacturing stage accounts for a relatively large portion of the total value gain, while the traditional high-end design and sales functions account for only a small portion of total value gain and mostly in foreign countries.
>
> *(World Bank, 2017: 56)*

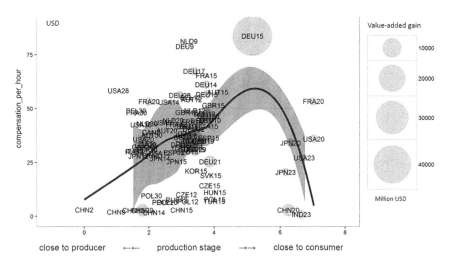

FIGURE 3.4   Estimated Smile Curve for Germany's Automobile Exports Production, 2009.

Source: Figure 2.20 in World Bank (2017: 57), based on Meng, Ye and Wei (2017).

1.2.3 The emergence of regional production networks

More often than not, GVCs show a high degree of regional concentration. For example, in the electronics industry many of the inputs originate from the same region, namely South-East Asia and China, suggesting the importance of **regional production networks**.

If we take a closer look at the degree of trade integration for selected regions and countries (Figure 3.5), we can first observe that it increased fastest in China, peaking around 2007. This is mainly due to China's participation in GVCs, in particular in the electronics industry. Consider again the iPhone example. As an assembler, China has to import many intermediate inputs, of which many came from other countries in Asia. Hence, the dramatic increase in trade has largely been driven by this GVC trade, which however, is at the same time regionally concentrated.

Another salient feature is the outstandingly high degree of trade integration in Europe. Europe's openness is specific in three ways. First, European countries are relatively small and need to trade more as not all goods can be produced economically at home. Second, the European Union (EU) single market, created in 1992, has helped a surge in intra-European trade. Third, the integration of the Central and Eastern European countries (CEECs), especially with the eastern enlargement of the EU from 2004 onward, facilitated the creation of regional production networks such as those in the automobile industry, which generated a massive intra-regional trade in intermediate goods (see European Perspective 3.1).

While regional production networks have also been created and facilitated within North America by the North American Free Trade Area (NAFTA), which came into force in 1994, the impact on overall openness is much smaller as the two advanced countries involved are large, and Mexico is the only low-labour-cost producer in the regional value chain.

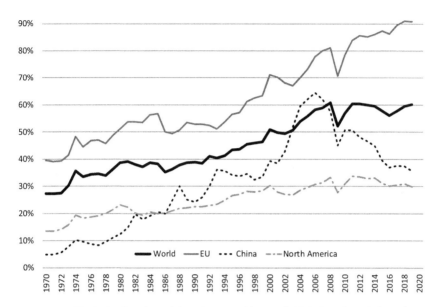

FIGURE 3.5 Trade in Goods and Services as a Share of GDP (in %) in Selected Regions, 1960–2019.

Data Source: World Bank, World Development Indicators, http://data.worldbank.org.

EUROPEAN PERSPECTIVE 3.1

The European automotive production network

Technical advancements have made it possible to unbundle the value chain in automotive production. As stated in WTO (2019: 85) "A car is an extremely complex system containing over 15,000 different components, including key components that are often design-specific and difficult to substitute. During the assembly stage, the parts must be carefully aligned with one another in harmony, and the risk of interference between parts is not uncommon." ... "However, developments in design schemes have spurred changes that have increased modularity in the auto industry." ... "Volkswagen devised the 'modular transverse matrix platform' to develop a wide range of different products including its standard models, such as the Golf, as well as luxury cars, such as Audi."

These developments have supported both the offshoring of tasks and its regional clustering in the European automotive industry. In a study of the European automobile supplier industry, Klier and McMillan (2013) argue that high level of agglomeration of the industry is driven by three main factors: (1) highway access for connecting the value chain, (2) the desire to locate near assembly plants, and (3) the desire to locate near other parts producing plants. The industry has therefore been shaped by strong centripetal forces that favoured the regional agglomeration, with a strong involvement of the CEECs neighbouring Germany.

1.3 The world is not flat

Our look at the GVCs for the Barbie doll, the iPhone, and in European automotive industry has revealed strong regional concentration. While sometimes popular books on globalisation make the point that "the world is flat", this view has been criticised in academic literature.[3]

Centrifugal forces

In a borderless world without physical and political obstacles, full arbitrage would ultimately create flatness by equating prices, wages, and returns on everything. The major 'world-flattening' centrifugal forces are:

- falling transportation costs,
- falling information and communication costs, and
- falling political barriers to cross-border activities.

These forces have been strong in the past decades in pushing globalisation. Container ships, air freight, and more and better highways have helped to bring down transportation time and costs. The advances in information and communication technologies (ICT) have made it easier to shop around globally, and – even more importantly – to co-ordinate globalised production processes. All this has been politically backed by falling barriers to trade and reduced obstacles to investing abroad. Yet, a flat world has not emerged yet. Hence, obstacles to full globalisation must be present.

Distance still matters

In a flat world with shrinking transportation and communication costs, one would expect the role of distance between two trading partners to become less important over time. However, the 'distance effect' is quite sizeable: empirical studies find distance coefficients close to one, which means that bilateral trade is about 10% lower for a country pair with a 10% higher distance relative to an otherwise comparable country pair. In other words, trade shrinks rapidly with distance. Even more interestingly, many studies also find that despite falling trading costs, the distance effect has increased since the 1990s. While there is an extensive discussion on what causes this result, including questioning the methodologies, a plausible and widely held view is that this **distance paradox** is caused by regionally concentrated production networks in many industries.[4]

Centripetal forces

Why do industries concentrate regionally? The most crucial, so-called **centripetal forces** are:

- **Market size**. Market size matter for industries in which economies of scale are important.[5] Hence firms tend to locate their production close to agglomerations where the demand for their products is high. This is more so when the trade costs are higher. Hence, automobile production is often located close to large markets, while light-weight electronic products are often produced in one region for the whole globe.
- **Clusters**. It is often useful to locate a company within an industrial cluster where specialised supplier, customers, experts, and other relevant resources are located.[6] Silicon Valley is a classic example. Moreover, modern so-called flexible production systems, employ methods such 'just-in-time' or 'continuous innovation', which increase the importance of physical closeness of suppliers and customers.
- **Regional trade and investment policies**, like free trade areas or special economic zones, promote regional production network by bringing down regional trade barriers. If countries open up only towards a region, thus reducing tariffs and other obstacles to cross-border activities faster regionally than globally, this tends to promote regionally concentrated production.

In sum, a regionally concentrated globalisation can thus be viewed as the outcome of the interaction of globalising centrifugal and localising or regionalising centripetal forces (Sander, 1996). In many industries, most prominently in automobiles and electronics, regional clusters make economic sense, either producing for a large regional market (automobile), or for a global market (electronics in Asia). As a consequence, in many industries, regional production networks have emerged since the early 1990s, creating regionally or even locally concentrated, but globally connected hubs, introduced in Chapter 1 as **glocalisation**, rather than a flat world.

1.4 Towards a new normal?

Since 2009 trade globalisation has levelled-off. Is it just a temporary flattening after the shockwaves created by the GFC of 2008–2009? The enduring slowdown of trade growth speaks against this interpretation.

Could increasing anti-globalisation sentiments and trade policy conflicts explain the slowdown? Basically yes, but increasing protectionism can hardly be blamed for the slowdown of trade integration in the first decade after the GFC.

In fact, policy makers around the globe were aware that they wanted to avoid the mistakes of the inter-war period and protectionism has been rising only recently.

Thus, we have to explore other structural, potentially enduring, factors for understanding the 'new normal'. Three factors come to mind:

- First, it can be argued that especially GVC trade is levelling as everything that can be sliced-up has already been sliced-up.
- Second, robotisation is making labour costs less important for the decision where to locate production. Hence, it might lead to nearshoring and thus reduce trade.
- Third, China has de-globalised drastically since the mid-2000s as can be seen from Figure 3.2. China has made rapid economic and technological progress, which has enabled the country to produce previously imported intermediate products, like displays and microchips for smartphones, at home. For comparison, in 2018 China produced so many electronic inputs for the iPhone X, that its share in the bill of materials is now $104, or 25.4% of the bill of materials (Xing, 2019). When China only assembled the iPhone 3G, the corresponding numbers were $6.40 or 3.6% of the bill of materials. In a way, China increasingly resembles a large country like the US with a relatively low trade share, as many things can and will be produced at home. Not surprisingly, the phrase 'the new normal' originated in China.

To explore more closely the future of trade globalisation, we discuss, first, the underlying causes of trade integration (Section 2), its (distributional) consequences (Section 3), and the impact of trade policies (Section 4), before returning to the future of trade globalisation in Section 5.

2 Understanding global trade

2.1 Trading across borders

Why do countries trade with other countries and why does it matter that trade takes place across borders rather than within the same jurisdiction?

2.1.1 Trade motives

The answer to the first question seems simple if you refer to the normal experience of a traveller: First we can discover things unknown to us, such as exotic spices. Trade economists speak of 'trade based on availabilities'. There is little to theorise about this form of trade. The main question is how much of our goods we have to pay for these spices, the so-called terms-of-trade. Second, some products are (relatively) cheaper abroad, and in turn some of our goods are (relatively) cheaper for foreigners. In this case, **inter-industry trade**, e.g. exchanging wine

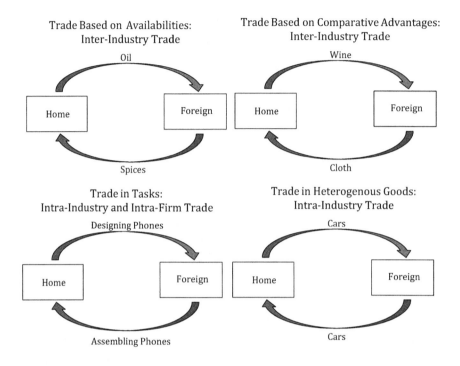

FIGURE 3.6 The Major Trade Motives.

for cloth makes sense. This is trade based on comparative advantages, as argued by David Ricardo already in 1817.

Third, with the rise of GVC trade we increasingly have to explain why nations engage in **trade in tasks**. e.g. designing for assembling mobile phones, rather than wine-for-cloth. Finally, we may want to buy goods because they come in a different appearance. For example, Germans may buy French cars for their style and the French buy German cars for their reputation. Variety – or heterogenous goods as economists would say – is another main reason for trading. In this case, **intra-industry trade** takes place.

Whatever the reasons for trading are, the consumer benefits. This is precisely why we bring goods home from our travels and engage in international trade: because we cannot produce the goods at home, because they are produced cheaper abroad – in whole or in parts, or because they are different from our goods and we value this variety. Figure 3.6 illustrates these major trade motives.

2.1.2 The importance of borders

Is there anything special that distinguishes cross-border trade from trade within a country? After all, our trade motives also apply to trade within a country. A key difference is that borders matter, and **international** trade is often much lower than **intranational** trade.

An influential study has shown that significant border effects exist. Subsequent research confirms the border effects, and reports that on average intranational trade is 13.3 times higher than international trade.[7] However, advances in methodology helped to shrink the effects on average. Best practice studies report on average a border effect of 5.8, which is much lower than the initial estimate, but still substantial. The results differ by region and size of the country. Borders are more important for small countries than for big countries. For example, they have been found to be 8.9 for Canada and 1.9 for the USA in a study on US–Canada trade. For Europe, the average border effect is 4.3, while it is very substantial for emerging economies (22.2).[8]

The reasons are manifold. They are not only the obvious ones like tariffs and border controls. Different regulations on both sides of the border, language differences, and other cultural barriers, or even political animosities can hold back trade. However, even if we would be able to get rid of all the obvious obstacles to cross-border trade, we may still have border effects, as the experience of the EU's single market project shows (see European Perspective 3.2).

EUROPEAN PERSPECTIVE 3.2

The home bias in the EU's single market

In the 1980s, the EU was considered to suffer from 'Eurosclerosis', a lack of international competitiveness of its major industries, particularly vis-à-vis Japan, whose automobile and electronics companies made inroads into the European market. In response, the EU Commission, under its president Jacques Delors, launched the 'Europe 1992' initiative to create the European Single Market, and abolish all tariffs and other trade obstacles on cross-border trade. Additionally, free movement of services, labour, and capital were envisaged. In the words of the EU Commission*:

> The single market refers to the EU as one territory without any internal borders or other regulatory obstacles to the free movement of goods and services. A functioning single market stimulates competition and trade, improves efficiency, raises quality, and helps cut prices.

However, researchers still find a **home bias** in the single market, i.e., consumers continue to prefer domestic products to a larger extent than distance and other explanatory variables predict. A recent European Central Bank (ECB) study by Mika (2017) confirms border effects for the EU. However, the author also finds that these border effects are decreasing with the time of a country's EU membership. Hence, CEECs which joined only from 2004 onward, typically show a stronger home bias. Moreover, the home bias is much stronger in services than in goods trade.

* See: https://ec.europa.eu/growth/single-market_en.

2.2 The origins of trade theory: making the case for free trade

Making the case for free trade is deeply ingrained in an economist's DNA. The advocacy of free trade and the birth of the science of economics go hand in hand. But why do economists insist on the advantageousness of free trade? On the one hand, it is based on a deep insight that economists have developed, in particular David Ricardo's **principle of comparative advantage**. In fact, the principle still goes a long way in explaining modern trade, especially when adapted to the new realities. On the other hand, the insight has been instrumental in disclosing the anti-business stance of European monarchies.

Until the 18th century, Europe was largely ruled by monarchies, sometimes in fragmented and small states, not least in Germany, where the aristocrats earned income by collecting border taxes. Kingdoms like France based policies on the ideology of **mercantilism** that advocates restricting imports and promoting exports. The idea is to 'earn' and accumulate gold for the monarchy. Consequently, in the mercantilist view imports are 'bad', exports are 'good', and the higher the export surplus, the better it was for the country. In contrast, in England, where industrialisation started, businessmen increasingly opposed this wrong-headed logic. They were aware that importing raw materials without tariffs is beneficial for them in two important ways: first, it allows the consumption of foreign goods, such as spices and tea, at low costs; and second, imported goods often are the base for producing manufactures that could be sold with higher profit margins, both nationally and internationally, if no tariffs are applied.

Adam Smith's writings lend scientific support for free trade. The argument that all countries gain from trade when each country specialises in the production of the goods they are better in, i.e., to specialise according to **absolute advantages** was already an intellectual challenge for the mercantilists. However, it took the wit of David Ricardo to demonstrate that specialisation across borders, and subsequent trading, is beneficial to both trading partners even if one country is superior in producing everything. The theory of **comparative advantage** was born and became a powerful argument for promoting free trade. Late industrialisers in continental Europe, though, took the idea only reluctantly on board, arguing that an adjustment period is needed to develop their relatively backward industries behind 'infant-industry' tariff walls. But finally, after some catching up, the idea of mutually beneficial free trade became widely accepted in the advanced countries of the 19th century.

Nevertheless, the theory of comparative advantage is a difficult idea, often challenged for false (mercantilist) reasons, but at times overused by free-trade enthusiasts, and – carefully formulated – even compatible with (temporary) infant-industry protection. In other words, it deserves a closer look.

2.3 Comparative advantages and the globalisation of trade

2.3.1 Comparative advantages: an old, difficult, and still relevant idea

The insights from the principle of comparative advantage are indeed very powerful ones. David Ricardo (1817) developed the idea at the level of goods. If Portugal is relatively better in producing wine and England relatively better in producing cloth, then both are better off by specialising according to their comparative advantage, and then trading wine for cloth. The surprising insight of Ricardo is that specialisation and subsequent trade is also mutually beneficial if one country is absolutely better in producing both goods. This is something businesspeople find hard to believe. Hence, we need to dig deeper to understand Ricardo's difficult idea.

2.3.1.1 An old idea: the 200 years-old principle of comparative advantage

The two key assumptions of Ricardo's idea are:

- Countries are constrained in their production possibilities.
- Countries are different in terms of their productivity in producing the goods.

Hence, they must choose what to produce. If both countries concentrate on what they can do relatively best, both countries can jointly produce more than in autarky. In other words, they are obtaining efficiency gains – a bigger global cake, so to speak.

A simple numerical example can illustrate this (Table 3.2). Assume that Portugal is more productive in producing both, wine and cloth: For producing a bottle of wine Portugal needs one day, England 6. In the clothing industry Portugal's unit labour requirements for producing a piece of cloth are, with two days, also lower than in England, which needs three days. Hence, Portugal is six times

TABLE 3.2 Illustrating the Principle of Comparative Advantage

Country	*Labour*			*Allocation of Labour*			
	Wine	*Cloth*	*Availability*	*Autarky*		*Specialisation*	
	Unit Labour Requirements	*Unit Labour Requirements*	*Number of Working Days*	*50% of Working Days on Wine*	*50% of Working Days on Cloth*	*Portugal Producing Only Wine*	*England Producing Only Cloth*
Portugal	1	2	100	50 wine	25 cloth	100 wine	0 cloth
England	6	3	300	25 wine	50 cloth	0 wine	100 cloth
"World"				**75 wine**	**75 cloth**	**100 wine**	**100 cloth**

better in wine (6/1), and 1.5 times (3/2) more productive in producing cloth. England is then said to have a **comparative** advantage in producing cloth, as its absolute disadvantage vis-à-vis Portugal is lower in the clothing industry. Conversely, Portugal has a comparative advantage in producing wine.

Invoke now the constraints on production possibilities, and the Ricardo proposition follows immediately. In our example, we equip Portugal with 100 working days and England with 300 working days. If then each country (while still in autarky), for example, uses 50% of its labour days on producing each good, respectively, Portugal can produce 50 bottles of wine and 25 pieces of cloth, while England produce 25 wine and 50 pieces of cloth. This results in a 'world' production of 75 units for each good. Now assume complete specialisation according to comparative advantages. This would allow producing 100 units of each good. We obtain efficiency gains of 25 bottles of wine and 25 pieces of cloth. It should be noted that efficiency gains can always be obtained regardless which numbers are chosen for labour endowment or consumption pattern.[9] In other words, the principle is 'always true' as a matter of the model's logic. Yet, as once quipped by Nobel laureate Paul Samuelson, it is not trivial.

The efficiency gains accrue because limited resources are now used in both countries on what they can do relatively better by considering **opportunity costs**: For each piece of cloth additionally produced in Portugal the country would forgo two bottles of wine. England, by contrast, would only lose half a bottle of wine.

How much of the enlarged cake will go to whom depends on the actual prices, i.e., how much wine Portugal has to pay for a piece of cloth after starting to trade, and vice versa. These so-called **terms-of-trade** depend on supply and demand factors. The less wine Portugal has to pay for cloth, the more of the efficiency gains will go to Portugal, and the less to England. If Portugal would have to pay two bottles of wine for a piece of cloth, as they had to in autarky, all efficiency gains would go to England. Conversely, if the price would be only half a bottle (the autarky price in England) all gains would go to Portugal. Anything between these two extremes distributes the efficiency gains between both countries. However, as the terms-of-trade determine who gets how much of the additional cake they are **zero-sum gains** – the more Portugal gets, the less England gets, and vice versa. Efficiency gains are, however, clearly **positive-sum gains**.

As simple as the argument looks, comparative advantage is often misunderstood as it seems to be at odds with the normal business experience: If a company is better in everything than its competitors it will expand and eventually even take over the competing firm. Conversely, if a company is worse in everything it will go bankrupt and eventually disappear. This is, of course, not what happens to countries. If a country is superior in producing everything, it is still limited by its resources. Hence, if the whole world wants all your products, you cannot deliver fully and thus your prices (and ultimately your wages) will increase and maybe also the value of your currency. As a consequence, you will lose your least productive industry, namely the one with the comparative disadvantage.

By contrast, a country that is less productive in producing everything will see its prices and wages decreasing, and the value of its currency deteriorating until it is absolutely cheaper in the good with the comparative advantage. In other words, wage, price, and exchange rate movements turn comparative advantages into *competitive* price advantages.

Consequently, the more productive countries are, the higher are their wages relative to the wages of the less productive countries. In fact, in reality we can observe that productivity and income levels of countries are strongly correlated. Relatively low levels of productivity are a major cause of relatively low income and wage levels of countries (for details see Chapter 2).

Another way of positing Ricardo's idea is that countries should specialise in goods where their productivity is somewhat above their average productivity. Because the latter determines – at least partly – the relative wage, industries with comparative advantages will be price-competitive. To illustrate this point, assume your average productivity and, hence, your wage is only 20% of the corresponding number of your competitor, but the productivity in your best industry is 50% of the productivity of the foreign industry, e.g. when they need one day for a bottle of wine and you need two days. If wage abroad is $10 per day and, thus, in your country only $2, you can offer the wine for $4 and they for $10. Hence, you are price-competitive despite being less productive in everything.

2.3.1.2 A difficult idea: a Ricardian model with many goods

If you want to formalise all conditions that turn the old idea of David Ricardo into a theoretically coherent model, one in which you can clearly identify all hidden assumptions and evaluate what happens if these assumptions are violated, then it indeed gets very difficult. For example, you can relax the assumption of only two countries or only two goods. A model with many goods (in fact, with a 'continuum of goods') has been developed by Dornbusch, Fischer and Samuelson (1977) and become an important 'workhorse' for trade economists. It can help us to understand both the logic of comparative advantage as well as many features of global trade much better.[10] We do not go into the technical details here, but present a simple graphical version to capture some of the most important insights.

For simplicity, one can think of five industries in which both countries work with different labour requirements and hence productivities. In our example below, the home country's car industry is ten times more productive, the machinery industry eight times, the textile industry four times, and so forth. In Figure 3.7 we arrange the sectors according to the home country's decreasing productivity advantages.[11] The actual distribution of comparative advantages depends on the relative wage between both countries. For example, if the home wage is three times the foreign wage, all industries with a productivity advantage of less than a factor 3 will become import sectors, here clothing and agriculture, while the others will become export sectors. If the relative wage increases, and our wage becomes five times foreign wages, we will also 'lose' the textile industry.

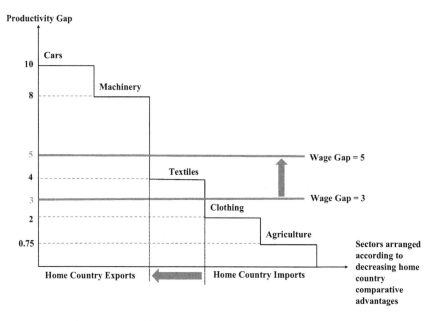

FIGURE 3.7 The Structure of Trade in a Ricardian Model with Many Goods.

2.3.1.3 A relevant idea: insights from a comparative advantage perspective

Even this extremely simplified presentation of a difficult model allows us to draw a number of important insights for today's trade issues.

- First, whether an industry is competitive is partly beyond the companies' control. It depends on the productivities in other sectors and countries, even if they seem to be unrelated to 'our industry'. Two examples can illustrate this interdependence:
  - If population abroad grows faster than at home, this will result in relatively lower wages abroad and may lead to a loss of home industries with the smallest productivity advantage. As a consequence, the home country will produce a smaller range of goods. For home workers this implies a welfare gain as their relative higher wages allow buying more foreign goods. Conversely, foreign workers suffer welfare losses because they can now buy less foreign goods.
  - Technology advancements have similar, though not identical effects as demographic developments. If technology improvements happen abroad, this will again lead to a loss of our industries with the smallest advantages. Likewise, home workers will benefit from higher productivity abroad as it allows for relative cheaper imports. This time, however, these positive spillover effects are not coming at the net expense of the foreign workers as their effective wage is also increased by a higher availability of goods after the technology boost. To illustrate, just think of general

productivity increases in China. The West's relative wage will increase and a loss of some marginal industries may result, but Western workers are also able to buy more Chinese goods at lower prices. China, despite some term-of-trade losses, will be better off, too.

- Second, wage and exchange rate development caused by relative demand shifts, e.g. a higher demand for the goods produced by our best industries, can lead to a loss of our least-best industry. A case in point is the Chinese shoe industry. With a booming electronics industry, Chinese wages increased relative to neighbours' wages. This can lead to a migration of the shoe industry even though the neighbours are less productive in making shoes.

- Third, capital movements and exchange rate developments can have direct consequences on the specialisation of a country. Consider the following cases:
  - Many observers have indicated that until recently, China has been keeping its currency value artificially low over several years. While popular arguments often highlight the subsequently occurring trade surplus, the more interesting insight is that an under-evaluation of a currency can help to turn a not fully competitive industry into an export sector. It can therefore be considered as a type of industrial policy (see also Section 4), sometimes dubbed as 'exchange rate protectionism'.
  - In the 1980s, market-oriented reforms by then British Prime Minister Margaret Thatcher, coupled with high interest rates, led to a huge inflow of capital into the UK and the British Pound appreciated dramatically. Our model predicts then a loss of export industries. In fact, the UK lost a lot of its industrial export industries in that period in favour of the most productive British industry: finance. In a scholarly article, sub-titled 'The competitive consequences of Mrs. Thatcher', Paul Krugman (1987) employed the Ricardian model with many goods to analyse the case. However, he extended it by 'learning effects', suggesting that once an industry with a high learning potential is lost, the competitors may catch up and it might not be possible to win this industry back, even if the exchange rate returns to its previous level.
  - In the Eurozone, the group of countries that have adopted the Euro as a single currency, an exchange rate does not exist anymore. Hence, all adjustments fall on wages and prices. Prior to the Eurozone crisis, which started in 2010, several southern member countries experienced an economic boom with prices and wages rising relative to the northern member countries. The loss of marginally competitive industries is the predicted consequence in our model. However, regaining competitive advantages, especially when the Eurozone crisis hit southern members, is difficult without exchange rate adjustments. To regain competitiveness either wages and prices have to fall in the south, or to increase in the north. However, wages and price are often downward-rigid in the short run, while the northern countries opposed the idea of inflating their prices. Finally, increases in productivity could help, but this takes time.

In sum, when taking Ricardo seriously, the model can offer plenty of insight into the modern trade environment. It is clear, however, that the basic version has its limitations. Notably, it focuses only on labour as a production factor, only on goods and not on tasks and GVCs, and it gives no role for companies and corporate strategies.[12] Further, it ignores economies of scale, an important feature of production in manufacturing. In the following, we will discuss these issues in more detail.

2.3.2 Comparative advantages and the second wave of globalisation

Trading on the basis of comparative advantages relies on the existence of cost differences between the trading countries. Being different, not only in terms of productivity as in the original Ricardo model, but also in terms of production factor availabilities is another cause for producing things relatively cheaper in another country.

2.3.2.1 The role of factor endowments

In the early 20th century Eli Heckscher (1919) and Bertil Ohlin (1933) shifted the focus of comparative advantage theory away from productivity to factor endowments and, consequently, factor prices. Under the condition that productivities are similar across industries and countries, their **factor proportion theory** predicts:

- relatively labour-rich countries have relatively lower wages, and thus a comparative advantage in producing labour-intensive goods;
- relatively capital-rich countries have relatively higher wages, and thus a comparative advantage in producing capital-intensive goods.

For a correct interpretation one should however note (as always when dealing with comparative advantages) the word 'relative'. Hence, it is not the absolute amount of labour and capital that matters, but the factor proportions of capital to labour and the relation of wages to capital income.

The basic assumption of an at least relative equality of productivity is indeed not too farfetched at least for some manufacturing industries like clothing or simple electronics, where the production process is rather standardised. Such goods are therefore often labelled as 'Heckscher–Ohlin Goods'. It is then predicted that, e.g. relatively labour-rich developing economies have a comparative advantage in producing labour-intensive goods like clothing because of the relative wage advantage, while capital-rich advanced countries specialise in producing goods that require a high proportion of capital inputs. As such, the theory seems to offer a good explanation for the second wave of globalisation, and the rise of emerging economies as a producer and exporter of standardised, labour-intensive manufactures.

2.3.2.2 Unpleasant consequences

Unfortunately, the theory predicts some unpleasant consequences of trade in Heckscher–Ohlin goods. Starting trading along Heckscher–Ohlin lines with a labour-rich country leads to a shrinking of the labour-intensive manufacturing industry in capital-rich countries. While capital-intensive industries will expand, this comes at the expense of workers: The shrinking labour-intensive industry will displace more workers than the expanding capital-intensive industries will hire at given factor prices. Conversely, many new jobs are created in labour-rich economies, and only few lost. Hence, relative wages in advanced countries tend to fall and in emerging economies they tend to rise. This is the unpleasant conclusion of the **factor price equalisation theorem**. While commentators and critics of 'globalisation' often refer to it, it is helpful to summarise some insights from standard trade textbooks before blaming all ills of advanced countries on trading with developing countries.

- First, technology and, hence, productivity differences prevail in the real world. Most empirical studies show that technology matters most in explaining wage and per-capita income differentials.
- Second, the theorem is about equalisation of the wage-profit relation. Consequently, it is not about absolute factor-price equalisation, or – to put it more colloquially – about working for Chinese wages in advanced countries.
- Third, relative factor price equalisation requires total goods price equalisation. But as there are still transportation and other trade costs as well as tariffs and non-tariff barriers to trade, the equalisation is incomplete.
- Fourth, not all advanced countries are affected alike. The prediction of the factor price equalisation theorem assumes that labour-intensive goods are still produced in a country when trade with the labour-rich country starts. China's return to the global marketplace in the 1990s, is a case in point, notably for Europe. Instead of affecting all European countries alike, it mostly affected those who were still specialised in labour-intensive goods where China had comparative advantages, namely southern European countries which, e.g. still had a large textile and clothing sector, and which, by contrast, the northern EU countries had already offshored long before.
- Fifth, the Heckscher–Ohlin theory has not performed well when confronted with reality. Wassily Leontief already found in 1953 that the supposedly capital-rich USA exchanged labour-intensive exports for capital-intensive imports. This **Leontief paradox** has led to a re-formulation of the original Heckscher–Ohlin model into a **neo factor proportion theory**, which differentiates labour according to different skill levels and hypothesises that human capital-rich countries have a comparative advantage in human capital-intensive goods while low-skilled labour-rich countries will specialise in industries using less qualified labour more intensively.

However, we can take away two major insights from these theories:

- First, the relative endowment with production factors matters for the specialisation pattern (see European Perspective 3.3).
- Second, trade may hurt low-skilled workers and benefit high-skilled workers in rich countries. Conversely, trade may have the potential to lift low-skilled workers out of poverty in poor labour-rich countries.[13]

EUROPEAN PERSPECTIVE 3.3

Factor proportions and European enlargement effects in Austria

The Heckscher–Ohlin model, like all comparative advantage models, reminds us that international trade is influenced by relative country conditions. In other words, the development of your trading partner matters as well. If they invest more in human capital development than your country, the pattern of comparative advantage may take an unexpected turn. A case in point is Austria, as argued by Dalia Marin (2016):

> At first, Austria benefited from the European Union's eastern enlargement. International trade soared, Austrian firms invested heavily in the region, and Austrian banks opened subsidiaries there, financing these countries' modernization. All of this was good for business, and the Austrian economy grew rapidly. But a hidden dynamic ultimately turned the tables on this success. Central and Eastern European countries had low per capita income, but were rich in skills. Austria, far wealthier, was not. In 1998, 16% of Central and Eastern Europeans (including Russia and Ukraine) had academic degrees, compared to just 7% of Austrians. So, when Austrian firms invested in Eastern Europe, they did not just relocate low-skilled manufacturing jobs; they also offshored the parts of the value chain that required specialised skills and produced valuable research.

2.3.2.3 Dynamics of comparative advantages

While the neo factor proportion theorem helps us to understand the 'global shifts' in international trade during the second wave of globalisation, it misses out on some points, which played an important role with the **passage of time** as both, the factor requirements by products as well as the factor endowments in countries, can change over time.

The first point has been highlighted by the 'Product Cycle Theory of International Trade and Investment', advanced by Raymond Vernon (1966) as a theory of 'dynamic comparative advantage'. Products typically go through a so-called product-cycle from an innovation phase to a maturing phase, and finally to a standardisation phase. Over this cycle, the factor requirements of a product change. Take the example of electronic calculators: when developed in the 1970s, they required a lot of engineering and thus human capital. Hence, from the point-of-view of factor proportion theory the comparative advantage is then in countries, which are considered to be human capital-rich, i.e., with a relatively high proportion of engineers in the workforce, like the USA. However, over time the product matures. Mass production requires large factories and thus a lot of physical capital. The comparative advantage is now in capital-rich countries, mainly in Europe and Japan, where the demand for these goods was rising rapidly. Production shifted accordingly. Today, electronic calculators are relatively standardised products, using standardised integrated circuits, simple displays, and a lot of plastic. This makes the products now a largely labour-intensive goods, which are best suited for production in low-skilled labour-rich countries, conditional on complementary investments in assembling factories from international companies (Table 3.3). For industries this implies relocation of production of the product cycle. For countries this implies that their comparative advantage in certain products is indeed temporary.

In a way, the resources needed to produce goods, which are at a time in high demand and booming, and the factor endowment of countries can make a good 'fit' in certain times, and thus facilitate rapid economic development. Cases in point are capital-rich Western Europe, catching up rapidly with the USA, and China's fast economic growth in the last two decades, based on its focus on labour-intensive manufacturing. However, as the experience of Western Europe shows, there is no guarantee that the old 'fit' is appropriate in new times.

This leads to the second source of dynamics: changing factor proportions in a development and industrialisation process. South-East Asian countries, especially, have been going through a fast process of changing factor proportions over time – from being classified as labour-rich to capital-rich, and finally human-capital rich ones. As countries become more capital-rich relative wages for unskilled

TABLE 3.3 The Product Cycle Theory of International Trade and Investment

Product Cycle Phase	Innovation Phase	Maturing Phase	Standardisation Phase
Major factor requirements of the product	Human capital	Physical capital	Labour and physical capital
Relative factor endowment of countries	Human-capital-rich economies	Capital-rich economies	Labour-rich economies, foreign investment in physical capital often needed
Examples	Calculators & PC in the 1980s USA	Calculators & PC in the 1990s Europe	Calculators & PC in the 2000s South-East Asia

workers also increase and low-skilled labour-intensive industries are then relocating production. In Asia, this process has become known as the 'flying geese' effect. Like geese, Japanese electronics industries, often relocated production to neighbouring countries with a 'better' factor-proportion fit, whenever the host countries developed above a certain benchmark. At the same time, the rapid developer became an attractive location for capital-intensive or even human-capital intensive industries as can be seen from the first NICs.[14]

2.3.2.4 Comparative advantage and the role of institutions

So far, we have focused on hard economic facts: measurable productivities, factor proportions and intensities, as well as factor prices. Of course, all these things do not fall from heaven but are man-made – or at least man-influenced. Acemoglu and Robinson (2012) argue that man-made (good) political and economic institutions often underlie economic success.

In a similar vein, a new strand of literature on institutions and comparative advantages is emerging that suggests that institutional quality matters for comparative advantages too.[15] In particular, it is hypothesised that institutions become the more important for creating comparative advantages, the more the product requires good institutions to be produced. To give an example, compare the production of potatoes to the development and marketing of a new pharmaceutical product. The former requires some food safety regulations and a few rules for self-marketing potatoes at the local market. The latter, however, needs a much more complex drug-safety regulation, rules for patent rights, possibilities to enforce contracts within and across borders, and much more. Hence, a country with a low institutional quality is less expected to produce 'good-institution-intensive goods'.

The argument is relevant for advanced countries (see European Perspective 3.4) and emerging economies alike. For example, if China wants to move up the ladder towards more knowledge-intensive production, it will ultimately have to provide the right fit of institutions to make new industries flourish.

EUROPEAN PERSPECTIVE 3.4

Institutional factors in European trade performance

The EU is not simply a trading bloc, it effectively 'exports' good institutions to its member countries. If such institutions are important in helping comparative advantages to emerge, and recent research supports this, then EU membership may have had an important impact on these developments as all EU-member countries have to adopt the whole body of laws and regulations of the Union, the so-called *Acquis Communautaire.*

However, institutions may not only need to be 'good', but – as discussed before – should provide the right 'fit' at a time. As argued by Eichengreen, an important reason why Western Europe was able to catch up rapidly after 1945 relates to

> ...the fact that Europe possessed a set of institutions singularly well suited to the task at hand. Catch-up was facilitated by solidaristic trade unions, cohesive employers' associations, and growth-minded governments working together to mobilise savings, finance investments, and stabilise wages at levels consistent with full employment. ... In a nutshell, then, opportunities for catch–up and convergence were realised of the conformance, or more colloquially, the 'fit' between the structure of the Western European economy and the economic and technological imperatives of the day.
>
> (Eichengreen, 2007: 3–4)

From this point of view, it is also evident that Europe today needs different institutions than during the catch-up growth phase.

2.3.2.5 Summing up: the second wave of globalisation visualised

The ascent of emerging economies as exporters of low-labour-cost manufactures can be largely attributed to the fall in trade costs, especially transportation costs, driven by the containerisation of the shipping industry, lower-cost air transportation, and road-infrastructure improvements. Moreover, the trend towards trade liberalisation was extremely supportive. Figure 3.8 illustrates this process. It is based on the Ricardian model with many goods as shown in Figure 3.7. Instead of 'steps' it features a continuously falling line for the underlying technological gap. Left from where it cuts the wage gap line, would thus our export sectors, right of it the import sectors. However, we need to make adjustments for trading costs because just a one-cent cost advantage is not sufficient to start exporting. The outer lines show that after adjusting for trading costs, fewer goods will be imported and exported than in a frictionless world. In between are non-traded goods. Thus, in a very simple sense, a reduction of trading costs allows for competition from abroad, especially in areas where the differences in comparative advantages are the lowest. This is where exports and imports are expected to be boosted most: formerly non-trading industries start exporting or face competition from imports. Both led to a massive increase in trade. But is the world like this in the 21st century as well?

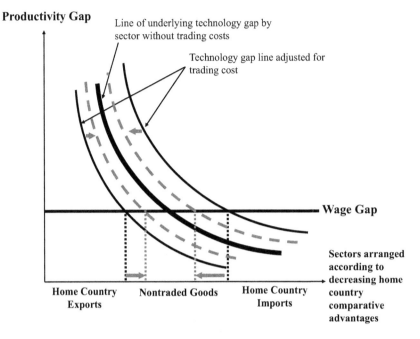

Productivity Gap

Line of underlying technology gap by sector without trading costs

Technology gap line adjusted for trading cost

Wage Gap

Sectors arranged according to decreasing home country comparative advantages

Home Country Exports   Nontraded Goods   Home Country Imports

FIGURE 3.8 Falling Trading Costs and the Second Wave of Globalisation.
Source: Based on Figure 3 in Baldwin (2006: 17).

2.3.3 The third wave of globalisation: trade in tasks

Tasks, like those in Adam Smith's pin factory, are not anymore allocated within one factory but distributed across borders in countries where they can be performed most efficiently. As such, the principle of comparative advantage goes some way in explaining modern value chain trade between countries with differing productivities and factor proportions, as discussed before. As Timmer et al. (2014: 116) note: "In essence, international fragmentation expands the opportunities of countries to specialise according to comparative advantage and hence to gain from trade. As such, it is on average welfare improving, but not necessarily for all workers and owners of capital." While this sounds familiar after our review of 19th and 20th century trade theories, is there something fundamentally different with trade in tasks?

Fragmentation means 'unbundling' (Baldwin, 2006), Adam Smith's pin factory writ globally. Fragmentation can be viewed as specialisation along comparative advantages at the task level, which has the potential to produce high efficiency gains. It can therefore be expected to increase labour productivity. However, there are two major differences between trade in tasks and wine-for-cloth trade:

• Global competition is not between home and foreign factories as institutions that bundle capital and labour anymore, but between national workforces competing for different tasks. Hence, the individual worker is much more exposed to global competition and left on his/her own.

• Advances in technology, especially in communication technologies and technological abilities to slice-up the value chain, allow for fragmentation of the production process of a wide range of products. Such disruptions are less predictable in both occurrence and direction than the impact of trade cost reductions in the 20th century.

Figure 3.9 illustrates the issue: a fall in trading costs can result in changes in the international division of labour that are very difficult to predict. The home country may gain a comparative advantage (1), lose it (2), or may not be affected at all (3).

According to Baldwin (2006), the consequences are much more severe than previously seen, in particular because of

• an increased unpredictability of changes at sector and skill-group level, and
• the suddenness as a major characteristic of changes.

While on the positive side wage increase for the remaining workforce in sectors that engage in outsourcing is possible if productivity increase overcompensates the effect of job losses, the dark side is particularly severe. It requires much more flexibility and adjustment at individual worker level than the previous waves of globalisation. As we will discuss in Section 3, this has important effects on income distribution and equality both within and between countries.

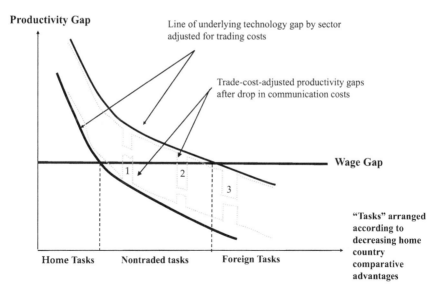

FIGURE 3.9 Falling Trading Costs and the Third Wave of Globalisation.
Source: Based on Figure 7 in Baldwin (2006: 26).

2.3.4 Creating comparative advantages

Up until now we have taken the distribution of comparative advantages for granted. However, in Chapter 2 we have discussed how industrial latecomers, the USA or Germany in the 19th century, were concerned about the lead of England in many industries. The idea of **infant-industry protection** was born and promoted by the German economist Friedrich List. In the 20th century, the idea became prominent among development economists, and has led to a wide adoption of 'import substitution (IS) strategies' in developing countries. In the 1980s, the strategy came under attack for producing an 'IS-Syndrome' of protecting uncompetitive industries, which impose a high toll on customers, on other producers who needed the protected, now costly items (quite often steel) for producing goods, and ultimately whole economies. While Latin American economies were typically identified as those suffering from the syndrome, East Asian countries had meanwhile experienced an economic miracle. The famous World Bank (1993) 'East Asia Miracle Study', attributed most of the success to market-oriented reform in the spirit of the Washington Consensus of market-oriented economic policies.[16] However, this interpretation has been hotly debated. Today many observers, not least the World Bank, concede that the visible hand of 'developmental states' played an important role in devising a successful East Asian 'import substitute first, then export' strategy.[17] Therefore, two questions stand out:

- What are the intellectual underpinnings of an infant-industry protection strategy?
- Why have these strategies worked in some cases and failed in others?

The modern arguments for infant-industry protection relate to learning effects and so-called externalities. Consider learning first. In Figure 3.10, the upper-right curve depicts the average costs of the USA in producing a good – say microchips – depending on their experience in producing the chips, measured by the cumulated previous output. The learning curve is falling, suggesting that with more experience average costs are lower. If historically the USA was first in producing microchips, its production costs will be as low as AC_{USA}. Now consider that China has an underlying comparative advantage, meaning that at any level of experience, China will have lower average costs. However, as a latecomer it has no or little experience and hence higher costs. At AC_{China} the USA is relatively cheaper and will outcompete China. The infant-industry argument then holds that history should not govern the future. If China manages to learn through experience, it will be able to produce cheaper than the USA. Some kind of industrial policy would then bring China's underlying comparative advantage to the fore, which otherwise would stay with the USA.

A similar argument also applies to so-called **external economies** through industrial clusters: Firms may experience lower costs when located in an industry

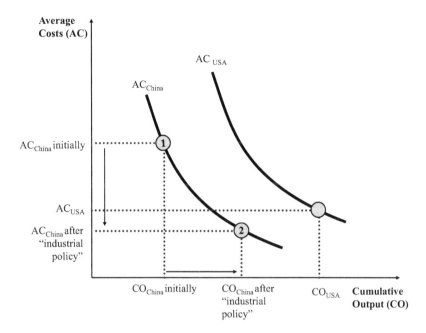

FIGURE 3.10 The Learning Curve and the Infant Industry Argument.

cluster. Take the example of Silicon Valley which provides a much easier access to specialised suppliers, human capital, and nearby customers. The larger the size of the industry (cluster), the lower the average costs will be. If then a country is a latecomer in developing a certain cluster, it may never be able to compete with the incumbent. Again, some form of support may help to overcome this issue and shift the comparative advantages from the incumbent to the newcomer.

An earlier version of this argument related to economies of scale within the company, i.e., the ability to spread fixed costs over a larger scale of production, thus lowering the average costs. Infant-industry protection would, in this case aim at making domestic companies large enough to realise an underlying comparative advantage. Today, however, the argument is somewhat discredited and has largely vanished from textbooks. The main reason is that in an open trade environment, it is possible to target the global market directly. Hence, a too small local market to obtain economies of scale is not anymore seen as a major limiting factor.

This brings us to the second question: Why have these strategies often worked in Asian countries but not in others? The answer is twofold: first, for the strategy to work, the countries must indeed have an underlying comparative advantage, i.e., the AC curve must be below the one of the incumbents, only then one promotes a potential 'winner'. Second, the policy design of picking and supporting targeted industries is crucial for success.

Picking winners, however, is not easy and more often than not governments pick losers – industries in which the countries will not be able to obtain a cost advantage within a reasonable time. This is, however, not a major argument against the strategy for two reasons: first, it can serve a reminder that the selection of targeted industries needs to be done very carefully. Second, and even more importantly, if a mistake is made one should be ready to correct mistakes early on. The negative experiences with targeting industries show that often unsuccessful industries have been supported open-endedly. In contrast, clear performance criteria conditioned on becoming successful exporters, as well as sunset clauses for terminating support, were essential to the success of many East Asian NICs in the 1990s (Amsden, 1989; Rodrik 1996, 2006).

How, then, to support emerging industries? After WWII until the mid-1990s often simple trade policies like quotas and tariffs were used for infant-industry protection. With the creation of the WTO in 1995, and the implementation of the new world trade rules, developing countries are more constrained in using tariffs and quotas. Hence, other forms of industrial policy support, like government subsidies, became more prominent. Nevertheless, nowadays the scope for infant-industry protection is much more limited than it was in earlier days. We will return to these issues in Section 4 when discussing trade policies.

2.3.5 Comparative advantages today: taking stock

Comparative advantage is a still powerful concept to understand the trade between countries that are different in many aspects: technology, productivity, factor endowment, skills, institutions etc. Given the relevance of comparative advantage theory today, it should not be discredited for 'carving comparative advantages in stone'. In fact, the theory can well serve as a base for a constructive dialogue on how to bring underlying but hidden comparative advantage in industrial latecomer countries to the fore.

In recent years, the Ricardian model has seen a revival, not least because better data is now available at the level of the firm for in-depth scrutiny of the causes of comparative advantage. The main message from this new and ongoing research program is that firms are the main drivers of comparative advantages. The classical Ricardo model has highlighted productivity differences across countries at the industry level. However, companies within an industry also operate with different levels of productivity. The argument, then, is that only the most productive firms will be able to compete in global markets.[18] We discuss this approach more deeply in Chapter 4 with respect to multinational enterprises.

Trade based on comparative advantages can lead to significant efficiency and productivity gains, but it also creates winners and losers. While this problem can, in principle, be addressed by compensating the losers from the gains of trade, this is often not common practice. However, not addressing these issues carefully will ultimately undermine the case for open trade. Before we return to these issues in the Section 3, we turn to a much less controversial way of trading.

2.4 Intra-industry trade: a less controversial globalisation?

Not all trade is based on comparative advantage. What if countries are rather similar in all aspects that contribute to comparative advantages? After all, many European countries are very much alike in terms of per-capita income, productivity levels, wages, education, human capital endowment etc. Yet, intra-European trade dominates the trade of most European countries. The majority of this trade is often not based on comparative advantages, but largely features **intra-industry trade**. For example, Germany exports cars to French consumers who like German cars, while some German aficionados buy French cars. Intra-industry trade allows offering more variety to both countries, while the car producers can take advantage of a larger scale of production. This is the key message of the 'new trade theory', which only emerged in the 1980s to explain the hitherto unexplained phenomenon of intra-industry trade, which then constituted about 60% of world trade.

The argument is fairly simple in principle but difficult to implement consistently into economic theory. For convenience, a simplified graphical version of Paul Krugman's (1980) seminal model is presented in Figure 3.11. Consider a certain domestic industry, say cars, in which a given number of firms produce and sell cars. These cars are all of one class, e.g. economy size, but heterogenous in detail. Such a market can be analysed as a market form known as **monopolistic competition**: There are enough suppliers to guarantee price competition, but each firm has some room to set prices based on the special features of the product.

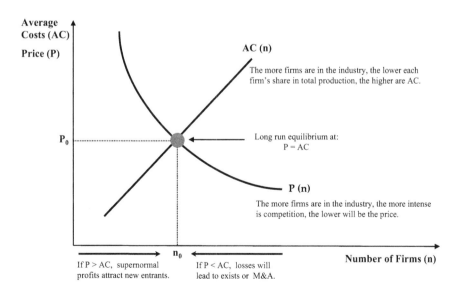

FIGURE 3.11   The Model of Monopolistic Competition in the Krugman Version.
Source: Own graph based on Krugman, Obstfeld and Melitz (2018: 205).

It is therefore assumed that the price will be lower with more firms are in the industry. Hence, the price curve in Figure 3.11 is downward sloping. On the cost side, the model assumes that manufacturing is characterised by economies of scale because of high fixed costs. With only one supplier, the cost per car would be lowest. The more firms that are present in the market, the lower their market share, and thus the scale of production and the cost per car. Hence, the average cost curve is upward sloping. In a purely domestic market, the price would settle at P_0 and the number of firms in the industry would be n_0. If there were fewer firms, the price would exceed the costs. Monopoly profits would then attract new entrants, which would drive the price down until P_0 is reached. Conversely, if there were more firms than n_0, they would make losses. Some may exit the market; others may rather opt for mergers and acquisitions (M&A) to cut costs and restrict the competition, until the long run equilibrium is reached where average costs equal the price.

What does this have to do with trade? Take the example of the European car industry again. Consider that the above analysis has been made for Germany with n car producers. Assume now that France also has a car industry in which n⋆ firms compete (the asterisk indicates 'foreign' firms). For simplicity assume that France is identical to Germany, i.e., having the same market size, the same number of firms, and the same prices and costs. What happens when we integrate these two hitherto completely separated markets? Figure 3.12 illustrates this. After integration, the number of firms (from n_0 to n_{01}) that can supply at the same cost as before doubles. Hence, the AC curve shifts to the right. However, with double the number of firms, rivalry will increase and put pressure on the price.

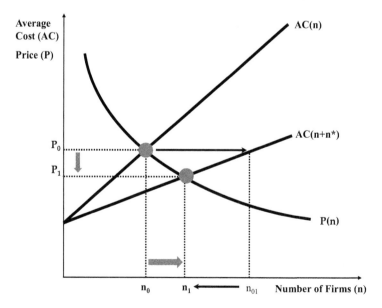

FIGURE 3.12 Integrating Two Markets in the Krugman model.
Source: Based on Krugman, Obstfeld and Melitz (2018: 208).

As firms would then make losses, they will either exit or engage in M&As until they can recover their costs at P_1 with n_1 companies surviving.

The overall result from integrating the two markets, therefore, brings several benefits:

- Lower prices for consumers as P_1 is lower than P_0.
- More variety as both German and French consumers can now choose from n_1 firms.
- Lower costs and prices allow for an increased joint market.
- Lower costs and prices increase the competitiveness vis-à-vis third countries.
- Both countries can keep a competitive car industry.

From this list it is immediately visible that intra-industry trade among similar countries is much less controversial than trade along comparative advantage, yet also brings high benefits. Not surprisingly, it has become an important inspiration for the creation of the European Single Market in 1992 (see European Perspective 3.5).

EUROPEAN PERSPECTIVE 3.5

The EU single market and the new trade theory

The idea of the EU's Single Market project (see European Perspective 3.2) took advantage of the insights of the new trade theory to deal with increasing international competition in the 1980s, especially from Japan, whose automobile and electronics industry made inroads into the European Market. In preparation for the single market decision, the EU commissioned a report on the 'Cost of Non-Europe'. The report was based on a large number of industry studies. Many of these sector studies directly or indirectly related to the insights of the new trade theory as a quote from the report* shows:

> A study of potential economies of scale in European industry shows that, in more than half of all branches of industry, 20 firms of efficient size can co-exist in the Community market whereas the largest national markets could only have four each. It is evident, therefore, that only the European internal market could combine the advantages of technical and economic efficiency, 20 firms being more likely to assure effective competition than 4 firms. Comparing the present industrial structure with a more rationalized but still less than optimal one, it is estimated that about one third of European industry could profit from varying cost reductions of between 1 to 7%, yielding an aggregate cost-saving of the order of 60 billion ECU.

*Source: Commission of the European Communities (1988: 18). Available at: www.ec.europa.eu/economy_finance/publications/pages/ publication7412_en.pdf.

2.5 A summary on trade theory with a view

Modern trade theories help us understand the causes and effects of trade globalisation. Broadly speaking, we can distinguish between theories that are based on comparative advantage, highlighting trade-relevant country differences, and theories highlighting trade in variety between fairly similar countries.

Specialising according to comparative advantage can be in goods, services, and at the level of tasks. Country differences, especially in productivity, factor availabilities, and institutions influence the pattern of specialisation. While trade according to comparative advantage is considered to boost efficiency, these gains often come with pains as adjustment requirements are high.

In contrast, trade among more similar countries is much less controversial but also expected to lead to huge efficiency gains. The EU's Single Market project has shown that market integration can be mutually beneficial and less painful than trading along comparative advantage lines.

That said, it is also clear that especially with the EU's eastern enlargement, the present day EU Single Market combines both worlds, intra-industry trade and comparative advantage trade, in particular with respect to GVC trade in regional production networks. In this sense, the now more heterogeneous EU of 27 members offers both, opportunities for increasing efficiency and competitiveness of European industries, and more adjustment needs at the individual worker level. Dealing with the challenges of the distributional consequence is therefore a key issue in both global and European trade.

3 The distributional consequences of global trade

Most economists agree that trade is beneficial. However, our review of trade theory has also revealed the pains that can be associated with opening up – in particular those arising from structural change and affecting particularly vulnerable groups. Moreover, recent research has shown that economic inequality is rising, especially within countries. Is too much openness responsible for this? This section reviews the recent evidence on the link between trade and the associated gains and pains.

3.1 Gains

In public debates the gains from trade as advocated by trade theory are often not well understood. In fact, they are not about obtaining revenues from exporting – as wrongly assumed by the mercantilists. Rather, gains from trade emanate from access to goods, which are supplied at a lower cost from a foreign source, or come in different varieties, or both. In any case, it is the consumer who benefits. In a comparative advantage world, trade expands the consumption possibilities, in a world of economies of scale, it means access to more variety at lower prices. But how large are these gains?

The size of the gains depends on the degree and type of trade liberalisation: lowering tariffs, removing import quotas, and many other measures. Empirical research attempts to quantify the impact of free trade agreements. Hence, the results of such studies differ depending on the scope of the agreement (global, regional, bilateral), and the liberalisation efforts made. In most cases, they find non-negligible though not dramatically high positive effects somewhere around 1% of GDP (see European Perspective 3.6).

EUROPEAN PERSPECTIVE 3.6

The potential welfare gains of T-TIP

A study of the potential benefits of the proposed and later abandoned Trans-atlantic Trade and Investment Partnership (T-TIP) (Felbermayr, Heid & Lehwald, 2013) between Europe and the USA estimates an average increase of real per-capita income in Europe of 0.27%, resulting from tariff reductions. The authors explain that these low numbers are due to the already very low level of tariffs between the USA and the EU.

In an extended scenario they calculate income gains close to 5%, but these include a number of additional and indirect effects from a 'deep liberalisation', such as more investment induced by a more stable economic environment. However, these effects are much more uncertain.

Larger gains are possible but also less certain as they depend on whether and how opening up leads to economies of scale, increases investment, and labour productivity. For example, according to Global Trade Watch (2016), a 10% increase in global value chain participation increases average labour productivity by 1.7%.[19]

A more ambitious attempt to measure the gains from trade is to compare – like in the simple Ricardo model – the autarky case with the open trade case. Helpman (2011: 52–56) reviews studies of two cases: for the case of the US trade embargo of 1807–1809, a lower bound of a loss of 4.9% of GDP is found plausible. The second case relates to Japan's policy of near autarky between 1639 and 1859. According to some research, Japan's terms-of-trade increased after opening up 3.5-fold, leading to a 65% increase of real income. This study has been criticised, and alternative estimates suggest gains in the range of 5.4%–9.1%.

We therefore conclude that welfare gains from reallocating resources are non-negligible but not excessive when opening up further from an already very low level of trade barriers. However, opening up an isolated country or shutting up economies almost completely, like in the inter-war period, can have huge effects.

3.2 Pains

Even the basic version of comparative advantage model reveals the pains that come with opening up to trade:

- Opening up leads to structural change with some industries expanding and others declining or disappearing, thus creating winners and losers.
- Adjustment to structural changes is often slow as it takes time for displaced workers to find jobs in expanding industries. In the meantime, structural unemployment can emerge and impose high costs.
- Often certain groups of workers are more seriously affected than others – in rich countries, especially, low-skilled workers may be hit hard.

Regarding the first point, how big are the costs of a required structural change relative to the benefits of liberalising trade? Harvard economist Dani Rodrik argues, based on a simplifying numerical example, that the redistribution following a tariff reduction can easily dwarf the net gains:

> For example, in an economy like the United States, where average tariffs are below 5 percent, a move to complete free trade would reshuffle more than $50 of income among different groups for each dollar of efficiency or 'net gain' created!... It's as if we give $51 to Adam, only to leave David $50 poorer.
>
> *(Rodrik, 2011: 57)*

Rodrik's argument critically depends on the assumed low level of initial tariffs. With higher initial average tariffs of, say, 40%, the ratio of redistribution to net gains would not be 50 but 'only' 6. Nevertheless, trade liberalisation requires substantial structural changes. This leads to the question whether this change can simply be left to market forces or whether the consequences of trade liberalisation should be managed (see Chapter 7).

This point is reinforced by looking at the underlying reasons for the sluggishness of the structural change. Many people have specialised skills in certain industries, which they cannot easily take to another industry without experiencing income losses. For these people, the income losses are not transitory (as often claimed by economists) but permanent. This is a key point of a recent empirical study of the impact of the 'China shock' on regions in the US (Autor, Dorn & Hanson, 2016).

Regarding vulnerable groups, the factor-proportion theory has pointed early to low-skilled workers in advanced countries as potential losers from global trade. But the previously made point on people with specialised skills already indicates an eventually wider group of losers. In fact, it could even be that specialised medium-skilled people may suffer less than low-skilled as we will see in the next section.

3.3 The distributional implications of global value chains

With the third wave of globalisation, the described structural changes and their consequences can be even more severe as they hit at the level of tasks and introduce a global competition between skill groups. In many GVCs, the share of value-added accruing to physical production is often less than 20% of the total value added, and much less for assembling, as we have seen in the case of the iPhone. Developing countries are thus worried about concentrating on low value-added activities, while in high-wage countries semi-skilled workers are concerned because of directly competing with the workforces in developing countries.

Generally speaking, one would expect that in advanced countries low-skilled workers would lose relative to higher-skilled workers, while in emerging economies the opposite effects should be observed. However, global value chain trade can have other redistribution effects than predicted by the factor-proportion theory. A recent study on factor-share developments in GVCs found that the share of value-added going to capital has increased between 1995 and 2008 from 40.9% to 47.4%. Labour lost accordingly, but the loss was concentrated on low-skilled labour, a fall from 16.6% to 12.8%, and – most surprisingly – on medium-skilled workers, a decrease from 28.7% to 24.4%. Only high-skilled labour gained moderately, increasing its share from 13.8% to 15.4% in GVCs (see Timmer et al., 2014). Similar developments have also been found not only at the economy-wide level but also for some industries (see European Perspective 3.7).

These results are surprising because they also report losses of income shares for medium-skilled and low-skilled workers in emerging economies. According to the factor proportion theory one would expect rising wages for these skill groups, and, hence, a larger income share for these groups. However, in two major aspects the third wave of globalisation seems to differ markedly from the second wave:

*   Companies may hire for their GVCs predominantly relatively high-skilled workers in emerging economies to ensure high production standards.
*   New manufacturing technologies can be biased against low-skilled labour. Digitalisation may have already taken its toll on the demand for low-skilled and medium-skilled labour in emerging economies, too.

EUROPEAN PERSPECTIVE 3.7

Distributional effects of globalising the German car industry

According to a study by Timmer et al. (2014), the globalisation of the German car industry has led to a reduction of the German share of value-added from 79% to 66% from 1995 to 2008. German medium- and low-skilled workers have lost the most as their share in total value-added declined the most. Regarding foreign value-added, the clear winner is foreign capital (see Table EP 3.7).

TABLE EP 3.7 Shares in Value Added of the Global Value Chain of German Cars (in % of Final Output Value), 1995 and 2008

German Value Added	79 (%)	66 (%)
High-skilled labour	16	17
Medium-skilled labour	34	25
Low-skilled labour	7	4
Capital	21	20
Foreign value added	**21**	**34**
High-skilled labour	3	6
Medium-skilled labour	6	9
Low-skilled labour	4	4
Capital	8	15

Source: Timmer et al. (2014).

In sum, GVCs show complex effects on value-added creation and, hence, the distribution of income, both across and within countries. These effects are not carved in stone but change over time, differ widely across industries, and are often difficult to predict. Hence, they require the attention of policy makers.

4 A brief introduction to trade policies

4.1 The rationale for trade policies

Trade policy is motivated by two major intentions: nurturing new infant industries, and a defensive intention to restrict or slow down emerging competition to an incumbent industry.

Starting with nurturing infant industries, the use of trade policies goes back to the times of the Industrial Revolution. Latecomers in Europe engaged in infant-industry protection, and the US followed this example particularly between the Civil War and the outbreak of WWI (see also, Chapter 2). After WWII, tariff reductions remained limited in Europe, as the countries aimed at shielding their industries from US competitors in the reconstruction phase. Japan protected its industry with many non-tariff bureaucratic measures until the 1970s. Many developing countries also embarked on infant-industry protection policies. However, while the original four Asian NICs were largely successful in nurturing an industrialisation that ultimately led to export accomplishments, governments elsewhere often failed to pick winners, notably in Latin America and Africa. Nevertheless, second and third generations of Asian NICs, such as Thailand, Malaysia, Vietnam etc. have become successful emerging economies. Finally, the rise of China is largely attributed to trade and industrial policies, which many see in contradiction to the principles of the world trading system. As we have discussed in Section 2.2.4, the interpretation of the 'Asian Miracles' has been controversial. Yet, we have also seen that much depends on how governments attempt to nurture industries. Broadly speaking, four major concepts are being debated with respect to latecomer catching-up:

- **Attracting FDI** and participation in GVCs, is the modern alternative to infant-industry protection, and has played a major role in successful catching-up in the last two decades. FDI is a major channel of technology transfer and learning. However, the devil is in the details. Investors care about protecting their core technology, while host countries have an interest to learn as much as possible. This is a controversial issue as can be seen from the debate about the Chinese requirement to enter into joint ventures when investing in China.[20]
- **Infant Economy Protection**, proposed by Stiglitz and Greenwald (2014), argues the case for supporting the development of the manufacturing sector as a whole, as it is viewed as the sector with easiest and fastest potential for igniting learning processes.[21] The advantage of such a broad approach would be that the argument that governments are not good at picking winners, would not apply. Of course, the concept has been discussed critically.[22]
- The **New Industrial Policy**, as advocated by Rodrik (2004), highlights identifying country-specific constraints that hold back crucial investments. The policy should then support **new** activities, including new **tasks in GVCs**, rather than whole sectors. In Rodrik's view it is important that this support is temporary and conditional on success, a major lesson learned from the debate on Asian miracles.
- The **New Structural Economics,** developed by former World Bank Director Justin Yifu Lin (2012), highlights the interaction of the upgrading of a country's resources over time, especially the quality of human capital, and the gradual extension of its product space. This process should be based on an effectively working market mechanisms, but supported by government policies to facilitate industrial upgrading. In a way, the concept rationalises China's industrial policy approach, at times also revealing its contradictions and counter-productive results, yet also recommending it as a role model for other latecomer countries.

By contrast, **defensive trade policies** aim at prohibiting or at least slowing down the market entry of foreign competitors. The main arguments for protection are:

- Adjustment costs in terms of unemployment, falling wages, or other social costs, e.g. decline of weak economic regions;
- Pressure from interest groups to protect certain industries from competition;
- Securing domestic supply of goods considered to be of special importance, e.g. for national security reasons.

Many economists argue that adjustment costs caused by international competition are not very different from those emanating from new technologies. Whether your job is taken by a foreign worker or a robot, does not make much of a difference. In both cases economists recommend active labour market policies. This is especially of relevance with respect to trade in tasks, which has made jobs even more prone to sudden changes and exposes workers to high uncertainties. Baldwin (2006) has therefore argued that **protecting people** rather than protecting industries should have priority.

4.2 Understanding trade policy instruments

Tariffs and quotas are the standard instruments of protectionism. Tariffs can be levied on imported goods as a **specific tariff** per unit of the imported good, or as an **ad valorem tariff**, in percent of the import value. An alternative is the use of import quotas. However, quotas have largely been phased out after WWII, and the WTO neither allows to introduce new quotas nor to raise tariffs once they have been agreed upon in a global trade agreement.

This situation gave rise to a grey-area protectionism in the 1980s. The US and European countries were suddenly confronted with fast increasing imports from Japan and other Asian NICs, especially automobiles and electronics, as well clothing from many other developing economies. As resorting to the classic instruments was no option, **voluntary export restraint** (VER) agreements with the governments of the new successful exporter were arranged, because no trade law at that time ruled out that exporters could voluntarily restrict their exports. For example, at their peak between 1986 and 1988, VERs covered 12% of US imports. Most prominent were VERs with Japan (6.4%) and the so-called 'Multifibre Agreement', an export quota system for the garment industry, covering 3.1% of US imports (Bown & Keynes, 2020).

Why should countries agree to a VER? One answer is that in case of no agreement, the protectionist countries could resort to two other instruments, anti-dumping allegations and safeguards. The latter allow a country to protect an industry against a sudden surge in imports. While only a temporary measure, it still may hurt the exporter, especially when the restriction is faced all of a sudden. Anti-dumping tariffs must be justified. While the allegation may not be substantiated in the end, the trade 'remedies' can still harm the exporter. We will soon see that there is also a carrot for the exporter, but for this we have to take a short look at the simple economics of protectionism.

4.2.1 The simple economics of tariffs and non-tariff barriers

What are the effects of tariffs and on the protectionist economy? In the simplest (textbook) case a 'small country case' is analysed.[23] The assumption of a small country means that the barriers-imposing country has no influence on the world market prices, even if it would stop importing altogether. The case of a tariff can then be analysed in a standard supply-demand diagram (Figure 3.13).

Without foreign trade, a country would produce a product, say solar panels, at an autarky price where domestic supply and demand curves intersect. If the world market price is, however, below this price – as indicated in the figure – the domestic market would be flooded with imports from abroad. At this price, only a few domestic suppliers would be able to stay in the market, namely those on the supply curve that are willing and able to supply at or below the world price, thus limiting the domestic supply to S_0. At this low price, domestic demand is D_0, thus the difference between S_0 and D_0 are imports. A tariff on imports, here for simplicity as a specific tariff per unit would push the domestic price upward. This allows more domestic companies to stay in the market. Domestic supply increases from S_0 to S_1, which is the intended protection effect (PE) of the tariff. The consumers now have to pay a higher price and cut back demand from D_0 to D_1, which is the consumption effect (CE) of the tariff. Jointly PE and CE make the trade effect of a tariff, namely the reduction of imports.

What are the effects on the welfare of the protecting country and the involved actors? To start with, the consumers pay a higher price and lose what is

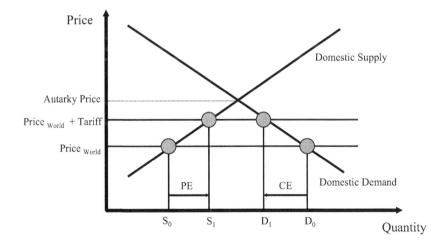

FIGURE 3.13 Analysis of Tariff (Small Country Case).

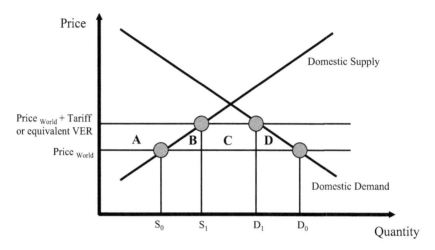

FIGURE 3.14 Welfare Analysis of a Tariff and a VER (Small Country Case).

graphically indicated by the area ABCD, as indicated in Figure 3.14. This is a loss of a so-called **consumer surplus** because the consumers now pay not only a higher price (area ABC) but also lose from reducing demand (area D). The domestic producers gain directly from higher prices. Thus, they receive the equivalent of area A, which increases their so-called **producer surplus**. Finally, the state receives **tariff revenues**, which equals the area C (C measures the product of tariff rate and imports). Hence, there is a redistribution from consumers to producers and the state. However, the two triangles B and D cannot be recovered. They represent **deadweight losses** of welfare because the protectionist economy now buys the product, in our example the solar panels, from a less efficient domestic source, thus forgoing gains from trade.

It is insightful to contrast the welfare effects of a tariff with those of a quota. We consider here the case of a VER, which for comparability, should limit imports by the same amount as a tariff, hence constitute an equivalent VER. Under a typical VER arrangement, the restriction of imports increase the domestic price to the same level as it would be in the case with the tariff. The major difference is that the area C is not going to the state but to the foreign producers, who can now enjoy a higher selling price. Hence, a VER subsidises the foreign producer. This is the aforementioned carrot for the exporter.[24]

Empirical studies have shown that the welfare losses from efficiency losses (the triangles B and D) are typically small and dwarfed by the transfers to the foreign producers, which can be substantial. It is widely acknowledged that in the case of Japanese car producers, these transfers have helped them to upgrade their products by investing into new technologies.

Under the new WTO rules, many VERs negotiated with foreign governments were banned and phased out. In the conflict between the EU and China over solar panels, a way was found to circumvent this rule by threatening Chinese manufacturers with the possibility of imposing an anti-dumping duty. As these duties would likely have been in line with WTO rules because of high government subsidies to the solar industry in China, Chinese exporters accepted the 'carrot' of charging higher minimum prices, thus 'earning' the area C. The main losers were the consumers in Europe.

The economics of protectionism is of course more complex than sketched here. In particular, the following modifications could be of importance:

- If the country is large enough, a tariff could impact the price of the imported good. Lower demand from the large country could lead to lower prices. In consequence, the welfare losses from inefficiencies could be overcompensated by terms-of-trade gains. While large countries might be tempted to apply such an optimum tariff, it is more a theoretical possibility, which, in practice is largely not applied, as it might provoke retaliation from other large countries.
- If the protected industry is imperfectly competitive, for example, characterised by a monopoly, protectionist policies allow the domestic producers to exercise monopoly power. Hence, quotas do much more harm than tariffs as they provide more protection to the monopolist.
- If the industry is characterised by economies of scale, trade restrictions limit the potential of realising cost reductions by accessing foreign markets. Hence, trade liberalisation can be more beneficial, and protectionism more costly, than indicated by the standard analysis of tariffs and quotas.

4.2.2 Non-standard measures: labour and environmental standards

More recently, the use of labour and environmental standards in international trade relations is increasingly winning support among policymakers and civil society. Do standards reflect justified concerns and preferences of a country, or do they constitute a new type of protectionism? The key word here is 'justified'.

Starting with **labour standards**, it must first be noted that if a country has lower labour costs because it has a lower average productivity, this surely does not justify banning imports from the country. In fact, not allowing countries to capitalise on their comparative advantages would strip them of export opportunities, and chances to develop their economies.

However, if labour costs are pushed down by using forced labour, slavery, or suppressing basic labour rights, it is justified not to import from such a country. In such cases, Rodrik (2017) argues in favour of 'social dumping' actions because then

> ...trade may undercut the social bargains struck within a nation and embedded in its laws and regulations. ... After all, this is no different from keeping out imports that violate, say, domestic health and safety regulations, which most countries already do.

However, for the time being, the WTO does not recognise 'social dumping' as a case for using trade remedies. An increasingly popular alternative is to ask companies to take more responsibility for their GVCs. While some favour voluntary actions, a recent study prepared for the EU Commission has argued that they have "not brought about the necessary behavioural change".[25] As a consequence, there is an ongoing debate on introducing value chain laws, which would make companies legally more responsible if violations of basic labour rights occur within their value chains.

Next to typical **environmental standards**, such as rules regarding pollution or preserving nature, climate policies raise new questions that touch on international trade. Despite the Paris Climate Agreement, climate policies differ by countries and regions. Consider carbon taxes: if one country introduces a carbon tax on carbon dioxide (CO_2) emissions and another does not, exporters from the latter gain a competitive edge. A border carbon adjustment tax can then re-establish a level playing field by putting an equivalent levy on imported goods that have not been subjected to a similar carbon tax in the production country.

In sum, non-standard measures raise a number of open questions. Using them unilaterally is not always in line with global trading rules. Countries therefore often resort to including clauses on labour rights and environmental standards in regional or bilateral trade agreements. The disadvantage here is that countries are not always treated alike, as some might be able to negotiate softer conditions than others. We discuss this issue in more detail in Chapter 7.

5 The future of global trade

Three major driving factors influence the future of trade globalisation: technology, economic behaviour, and policy. Starting with **technology**, the most relevant current technological developments are in the areas of robotisation and digitalisation.

- **Robotisation** makes labour costs less important for the decision of where to locate production. It can be understood as a process where tasks in the production process are automated (Acemoglu & Restrepo, 2018). Hence, robotisation is an alternative to offshoring labour-intensive tasks. Moreover, if robots continue getting less and less expensive, this trend is likely to be reinforced. However, the argument comes with two caveats:
  - Instead of reshoring, nearshoring to a close-by country is also possible. Hence, trade would not be reduced but become more regionally concentrated.
  - Rapidly developing countries like China may increasingly offshore low value-added tasks to lower income countries rather than automating them.
- **Digitalisation** can give rise to new possibilities for slicing up the value chain, especially with respect to services. As labour costs are still important

in the service industry, and the cost of cross-border digital delivery is low or even close to zero, the next trade globalisation may be in the area of services.

- The impact of new technologies on **transportation cost** is important. Paul Krugman (2020: 4) argues that "trends in globalisation should be seen as the result of a race between the technology of transportation and the technology of production". If transportation technologies win the race, trade globalisation intensifies. Arguably, this could be the story behind the three waves of globalisation, where first steamships and railways, then containerisation, and finally ICTs outpaced progress in production. By contrast, only in the late 1970s did trade globalisation reach the level attained before WWI. This 'failure' to globalise fast, may not be caused by too small improvements in transportation technologies but by an even faster growth of technological progress in industrial mass production.[26] If correct, the hypothesis lends support to the two propositions above: If future technical progress is mainly in the production of goods but not services, while the advancements in cross-border delivery are more pronounced in the service industry, globalisation of merchandise trade could slow down while service globalisation could be boosted.

With respect to **economic behaviour**, two arguments are of relevance especially with regard to corporate strategies:

- The **diminishing returns to GVCs** argument, namely that everything that could be sliced-up, has already been sliced-up, may be relevant to manufacturing but not yet in services.
- GVC trade in manufacturing, even when not expanding, may not shrink but just stagnate. Antràs (2020) points out that firms have made high investments in their global sourcing strategies. These **sunk costs** make it unlikely that global firms will reconfigure their value chains if changes are considered to be temporary, e.g. such as changes emanating from shocks like the GFC or the Covid-19 pandemic. Or to put it differently, value chains will de-globalise only when changes are considered to be permanent.

Regarding **policies**, there are several trends and feedback loops that can either reinforce or undermine trade globalisation trends:

- As trade globalisation produces winners and losers, this could lead to a **backlash against globalisation**. Three, not mutually exclusive scenarios are:
  - Outright trade wars and increasing old-style protectionism that aim at protecting industries.
  - Cushioning the negative side effects of globalisation by means of social and active labour market policies. The focus here would be on protecting people not industries, as Baldwin (2006) has argued with respect to dealing with trade in tasks.

- Managing globalisation, for example by means of protecting labour standards from social dumping.
- If, and when **climate policies** will become part of a global policy, e.g. by pricing CO_2 emissions, this will increase trading costs and thus promote regional trade at the expense of long-distance trade. Similarly, if border carbon adjustments are to come in the future, as currently discussed in the EU and in the US, this will have similar centripetal, de-globalising effects.
- If countries like China increasingly perform **higher value-added activity within the country** rather than importing these goods, this also leads to less global trade. While this can partly be the effect of deliberate policies,[27] it is also, if not predominantly, the consequence of economic development within China.
- The rise of a **multipolar world** poses the question whether these 'poles' will ultimately choose to remain open to the global economy, or whether they become more inward looking and protectionist to the outside.

What then is the future of trade globalisation? From both the technological, and the subsequent economic behaviour side it is not fully clear what the implications for trade in goods are. But since centripetal and centrifugal forces are at work at the same time, it is likely that **glocalisation** will continue to shape the global trading landscape. This depends, on the one hand, on the internationalisation strategies of corporations (Chapter 4). However, trade in intangibles, such a digitally-enabled trade in services, data, and knowledge, will surely become more important, both in absolute terms as well as relative to merchandise trade (see Chapter 5).

Finally, the rise or demise of trade globalisation as the outcome of technological or market developments is neither good nor bad per se. If it makes more sense to locate production close-by, thus leading to de-globalisation or slowbalisation, there is nothing wrong with it. What would, however, be worrying is a backlash against globalisation that would ignite devastating trade wars.

Recommended readings

For a more detailed coverage of trade theories, the reader may consult standard textbooks of international economics such as Daniels and Hoose (2017), Feenstra and Allen (2017), and Krugman, Obstfeld and Melitz (2018).

Helpman (2011) provides an accessible non-technical review of recent theoretical advances in international trade theory. For an in-depth presentation of theoretical and empirical research, see Feenstra (2016).

For up-to-date information and analyses the reader may consult the WTO website (wto.org). Especially the annual World Trade Reports and the occasional Global Value Chain Development Reports (World Bank, 2017; WTO, 2019) are invaluable sources of information.

Notes

1 Chapter 2 provides an in-depth discussion of income divergence and convergence.
2 For data and an in-depth discussion, see the seminal paper by Feenstra (1998).
3 This is the title of a popular book by Friedman (2005). Leamer (2007) provides an extensive review and critique of the book.
4 The gold standard for quantifying the role of distance in trade, is estimating a so-called gravity equation. The gravity model conjectures that trade between two countries is proportional to the product of the economic size of the countries – typically measured by the GDP – and inversely related to the geographical distance that separates them. Other explanatory variables are often added to capture effects of common borders, a common language, cultural differences, trade agreements, a common currency, etc. For a review of gravity model estimates for the distance coefficient see the meta study by Disdier and Head (2008). On the distance paradox, see also Carrere, De Melo and Wilson (2013).
5 This market-size argument comes with the crucial qualification that production cost must be subject to economies of scale. If production costs do not depend on the size of production, what only matters are whether differences in production costs are not overcompensated by trade costs. If production costs at home plus trade costs sum up to less than production costs abroad, it makes sense to export to that market, irrespective of the market size. Conversely, a company may enter the market, again irrespective of the market size. Strictly speaking, in the latter case, the costs to enter a new market must also be considered. If these costs are fixed regardless of the market size, then market size matters again. But in this case, we have economies of scale, namely decrease entry costs per unit.
6 This is what economists call 'external economies of scale': Average production costs are lower when a (small) company is located close to other (small) companies that belong to the same industry. For a theoretical analysis see Section 2.3.4.
7 The classic reference is McCallum (1995).
8 The data reported for best practice studies are from Havranek and Irsova (2017). This meta study reviews 61 different studies published between 1995 and January 2014 and provides averages of all estimates.
9 For a general exposition of the validity of the principle of comparative advantage allowing for incomplete specialisation, the reader may consult a textbook on international trade.
10 For a recent non-technical presentation, see Helpman (2011).
11 The size of these sectors may differ, and thus also their potential for exporting. It is then the relative demand and supply in all industries and in both countries, which will finally determine the wages at home and abroad, as well as the exchange rate. In other words, the model invokes a balance of payments constraint that requires exports to be equal to imports, in order to determine the relative wage. For our purposes, we skip this difficult step and simply ask what happens at different relative wage levels.
12 It is also possible to extend the Ricardian model to a multi-country model. For a non-technical discussion, see Helpman (2011).
13 We look more closely at the distributional consequences of global trade in Section 3.
14 For a more detailed discussion of catching-up growth the reader is again referred to Chapter 2.
15 For an overview of the role of institutions in creating comparative advantages, see Nunn and Trefler (2014).
16 The term "Washington Consensus" is attributed to Williamson (1990). Next to sound monetary and fiscal policies it includes a set of market-oriented reforms such as price liberalisations, opening up to trade, and privatisation of state-owned enterprises.
17 For the critical reception of the Miracle study, see, e.g. Amsden (1994) and Singh (1994).

18 Among the first important contributions to this "new, new trade theory" are Eaton and Kortum (2002) and Melitz (2003).
19 For an in-depth discussion of the determinants of (productivity) growth, see Chapter 2.
20 We discuss these issues in more detail in Chapter 4.
21 For a discussion of the role of manufacturing in promoting growth and convergence, see Chapter 2.
22 The reader may consult the Stiglitz and Greenwald (2014) book, which also contains commentaries on their arguments by leading economists.
23 This is a so-called partial equilibrium analysis, which focusses on a single market. A general equilibrium analysis, which is beyond the scope of this introduction, takes into account the impact of tariffs on other sectors of the economy.
24 A classic quota imposed by a country would typically allocate an import license to an importer. The difference between the world market price and the domestic price would then accrue to the importer. If the state prices the license, e.g. by auctioning them, the area C would, depending on the price, not go (fully) to the importer.
25 See the speech by EU Commissioner Reynders, available at: https://responsiblebusinessconduct.eu/wp/2020/04/30/speech-by-commissioner-reynders-in-rbc-webinar-on-due-diligence.
26 See Chapter 2 for a discussion of high technical progress in manufacturing in that 'golden age' period.
27 This is the core of the 'Made in China 2025' strategy of the Chinese government. See the website of the Chinese government: http://english.www.gov.cn/2016special/madeinchina2025/.

References

Acemoglu, D., & Restrepo, P. (2018). Modeling automation. *AEA Papers and Proceedings*, *108*, 48–53.

Acemoglu, D., & Robinson, J. A. (2012). *Why nations fail. The origins of power, prosperity, and poverty.* Crown Business.

Amsden, A. (1989). *Asia's next giant: South Korea and late industrialization.* Oxford University Press.

Amsden, A. (1994). Why isn't the whole world experimenting with the East Asian model to develop? Review of the East Asian miracle. *World Development*, *22*(4), 627–633.

Antràs, P. (2020). *De-globalisation? Global values chains in the post-COVID-19 age.* NBER Working Paper 28115. National Bureau of Economic Research.

Autor, D. H., Dorn, D., & Hanson, G. H. (2016). The China shock: learning from labor-market adjustment to large changes in trade. *Annual Review of Economics, 8*, 205–240.

Baldwin, R. (2006). *Globalisation: The great unbundling(s).* September. Prime Minister's Office, Economic Council of Finland.

Bown, C. P., & Keynes, S. (2020). Why Trump shot the sheriffs: the end of WTO dispute settlement 1.0. *Journal of Policy Modeling, 42*(4), 799–819.

Carrere, C., De Melo, J., & Wilson, J. (2013). The distance puzzle and low-income countries: an update. *Journal of Economic Surveys, 27*(4), 717–742.

Commission of the European Communities (1988). European Economy. The Economics of 1992. No. 35 (March).

Daniels, J. P., & Hoose, D. D. (2017). *Global economic issues and policies* (4th ed.). Routledge.

Disdier, A.-C., & Head, K. (2008). The puzzling persistence of the distance effect on bilateral trade. *The Review of Economics and Statistics, 90*(1), 37–48.

Dornbusch, R., Fischer, S., & Samuelson, P. (1977). Comparative advantage, trade, and payments in a Ricardian model with a continuum of goods. *American Economic Review, 67*(5), 823–839.

Eaton, J., & Kortum, S. (2002). Technology, geography, and trade. *Econometrica, 70,* 1741–1779.

Eichengreen, B. (2007). *The European economy since 1945. Coordinated capitalism and beyond.* Princeton University Press.

Feenstra, R. C. (1998). Integration of trade and disintegration of production in the global economy. *Journal of Economic Perspectives, 12*(4), 31–50.

Feenstra, R. C. (2016). *Advanced international trade: Theory and evidence.* Princeton University Press.

Feenstra, R. C., & Allen, A. M. (2017). *International economics* (4th ed.). Worth Publishers.

Felbermayr, G., Heid, B., & Lehwald, S. (2013). *Transatlantic trade and investment partnership (TTIP). Who Benefits from a Free Trade Deal?* Bertelsmann Stiftung.

Friedman, T. L. (2005). *The world is flat. A brief history of the twenty-first century.* Farrar, Straus and Giroux.

Global Trade Watch (2017). *Trade developments in 2016: Policy uncertainty weighs on world trade.* World Bank Group.

Havranek, T., & Irsova, Z. (2017). Do borders really slash trade? A meta-analysis. *IMF Economic Review, 65*(2), 365–396.

Heckscher, E. (1919). The effect of foreign trade on the distribution of income. *Ekonomisk Tidskrift, 21,* 497–512.

Helpman, E. (2011). *Understanding global trade.* MIT Press.

Klasing, M. J., & Milionis, P. (2014). Quantifying the evolution of world trade, 1870–1949. *Journal of International Economics, 92*(1), 185–197.

Klier, T., & D. McMillen (2013). Agglomeration in the European Automobile Supplier Industry. Federal Reserve Bank of Chicago, WP 2013–15, November.

Krugman, P. (1980). Scale economies, product differentiation and the pattern of trade. *American Economic Review, 70*(5), 950–959.

Krugman, P. (1987). The narrow moving band, the Dutch disease, and the competitive consequences of Mrs. Thatcher: notes on trade in the presence of dynamic scale economies. *Journal of Development Economics, 27*(1–2), 41–55.

Krugman, P. R. (2020). Notes on Globalisation and Slowbalization, November. www.gc.cuny.edu/CUNY_GC/media/LISCenter/pkrugman/Notes-on-globalisation-and-slowbalization.pdf.

Krugman, P. R., Obstfeld, M., & Melitz, M. (2018). *International economics. Theory and policy* (11th ed.). Prentice Hall.

Leamer, E. A. (2007). A flat world, a level playing field, a small world after all, or none of the above? *Journal of Economic Literature, 45*(March), 83–126.

Lin, J. Y. (2012). *New structural economics: A framework for rethinking development and policy.* The World Bank.

Marin, D. (2016). What's the matter with Austria? Project Syndicate.org. June 15.

McCallum, J. (1995). National borders matter: Canada-U.S. regional trade patterns. *American Economic Review, 85*(39), 615–623.

Meng, B., Ye, M., & Wei, S.-J. (2017). Value-Added Gains and Job Opportunities in Global Value Chains. IDE Discussion Paper 668, IDE-JETRO, Chiba City, Japan.

Melitz, M. J. (2003). The impact of trade on intra-industry reallocations and aggregate industry productivity. *Econometrica, 71,* 1695–1725.

Mika, A. (2017). Home Sweet Home: The Home Bias in Trade in the European Union. European Central Bank Working Paper No. 2046. April.

Nunn, N., & Trefler, D. (2014). Domestic institutions as a source of comparative advantage. In G. Gopinath, E. Helpman, & K. Rogoff (Eds.), *Handbook of international economics 4* (pp. 263–315). Elsevier.

Ohlin, B. (1933). *Interregional and international trade.* Harvard University Press.

Ricardo, D. (1817). *On the principles of political economy and taxation.* London.

Rodrik, D. (1996). Understanding economic policy reform. *Journal of Economic Literature, 34*(1), 9–41.

Rodrik, D. (2004). Industrial Policy for the Twenty-First Century. Working Paper Series RWP 04–047. John F. Kennedy School of Government, Harvard University.

Rodrik, D. (2006). Goodbye Washington consensus, hello Washington confusion? A review of the World Bank's "economic growth in the 1990s: learning from a decade of reform". *Journal of Economic Literature, 44*(4), 973–987.

Rodrik, D. (2011). *The globalisation paradox. Democracy and the future of the world economy.* W.W. Norton.

Rodrik, D. (2017). It's time to think for yourself on free trade. *Foreign Policy,* 27 January.

Sander, H. (1996). Multilateralism, regionalism and globalisation: the challenges to the world trading system. In H. Sander & A. Inotai (Eds.), *World trade after the Uruguay round. Prospects and policy options for the twenty-first century* (pp. 17–36). Routledge.

Singh, A. (1994). Openness and the market friendly approach to development: Learning the right lessons from development experience. *World Development, 22*(12), 1811–1823.

Smith, A. (1776). *An inquiry into the nature and causes of the wealth of nations.* London. The Glasgow edition of the works and correspondence of Adam Smith, vol. II, edited by R. H. Campbell and A. S. Skinner. Oxford University Press, 1976.

Stiglitz, J. E., & Greenwald, B. C. (2014). *Creating a learning society. A new approach to growth, development and social progress.* New York.

Timmer, M. P., Azeez Erumban, A., Los, B., Stehrer, R., & de Vries, G. J. (2014). Slicing up global value chains. *Journal of Economic Perspectives, 28*(2), 99–118.

UNCTAD (2020). *World investment report 2020.* United Nations Conference on Trade and Development.

Vernon, R. (1966). International investment and international trade in the product cycle. *Quarterly Journal of Economics, 80,* 121–125.

Williamson, J. (1990). What Washington means by policy reform. In Williamson, J. (Ed.), *Latin American adjustment: How much has happened?* Institute of International Economics.

World Bank (1993). *The East Asian miracle. Economic growth and public policy.* Oxford University Press.

World Bank (2017). *Global value chain development report 2017.* International Bank of Reconstruction and Development/World Bank.

WTO (2019). *Global value chain development report 2019.* World Trade Organisation.

Xing, Y. (2011). How the iPhones Widens the US Trade Deficit with China, VoxEU.org, 10 April. www.voxeu.org/article/how-iphone-widens-us-trade-deficit-china.

Xing, Y. (2019). How the iPhone widens the US trade deficit with China: The case of the iPhone X. VoxEU.org, 11 Novemberr www.voxeu.org/article/how-iphone-widens-us-trade-deficit-china-0.

4

GLOBAL INVESTMENT

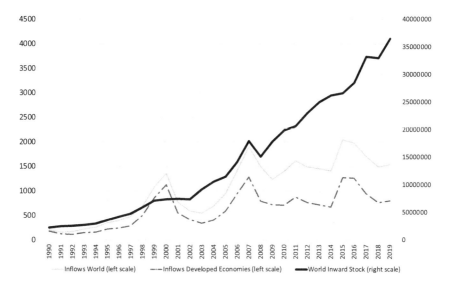

FIGURE 4.1   Foreign Direct Investment Inflows and Inward Stocks, 1990–2019 (in million $).

Data source: UNCTAD (2020), Annex 1 and 3.

Foreign direct investment (FDI) has been a major driving force behind the third wave of globalisation. It has been key in establishing global value chains (GVCs), with about half of the inflows going to developing countries and countries in transition in the 2010s. However, recently FDI inflows are more or less stagnating, yet the global stock of FDI remains at a high and even increasing level (see Figure 4.1). This chapter explores the main reasons why firms involve themselves

DOI: 10.4324/9781003057611-4

by means of FDI in global production, and discusses the future of FDI under the conditions of the emerging new global economy (NGE).

1 What is FDI?

A foreign investment is considered a foreign **direct** investment if a firm creates a subsidiary abroad, e.g. a production plant, or acquires more than 10% of the capital of a foreign company. For the concept of FDI, full or partial **control** over the business operations is key. In the case of creating a fully-owned subsidiary, or so-called greenfield investments, this is obvious. In the case of brownfield investments, usually mergers or acquisitions (M&As), the 10% cut-off benchmark classifies a foreign investment either as a portfolio or a direct investment.

Of course, this benchmark is arbitrary, but short of asking the investor whether or not she exercises control over the business operations, it has been adopted as standard procedure in international statistics that, hence, needs to be interpreted with care. For example, big sovereign wealth funds may only be interested in dividends even when their share in companies is occasionally above 10%. Conversely, two or more hedge funds, which individually hold lower shares, may liaise to exercise influence. Likewise, foreign investors may choose to acquire less than 10% to circumvent national restrictions to foreign participation.

FDI inflows (measured as inward inflows from the point of view of all receiving economies) reached a peak before the great financial crisis (GFC) in 2008, amounting to 4% of the world's gross domestic product (GDP). Since then, new inflows lost importance relative to global production, but the accumulated stock of FDI, the sum of all past inflows minus depreciations, continued to increase.[1] M&As became a major part of inflows in the early 2000s, even amounting to over 70% of all inward FDI in 2000 (see Table 4.1).

With direct investments abroad, a national firm becomes a multinational corporation (MNC), aka multinational enterprise (MNE). An MNE is thus an enterprise that owns or controls value-adding activities across boundaries in more than one country (Dunning, 1992). As such, it is distinct from companies that just serve foreign markets via exports or source intermediate inputs from abroad via imports.

An MNE headquarters its management typically in the home country, but operates (also) in the host country. Hence, for the classification of investments

TABLE 4.1 FDI Inwards Flows and Stocks in Percent of World GDP

	1990	2000	2007	2010	2019
FDI inward inflows	0.9	4.0	4.0	2.1	1.8
Of which: M&As	0.4	2.8	2.2	0.5	0.6
FDI inward stocks	9.3	21.8	39.2	29.9	42.2

Source: Own calculation based on Table IV.1 in UNCTAD (2020: 124).

TABLE 4.2 Activities and Size of Foreign Affiliates of MNEs in Percent of World GDP

	1990	2000	2007	2010	2019
Sales	30.1	35.0	55.5	35.4	35.9
Value added	5.6	9.0	12.9	9.9	9.2
Total assets	26.1	67.3	156.6	125.0	128.7

Source: Own calculations based on Table IV.1 in UNCTAD (2020: 124).

as FDI, it is important to identify the home and host countries. Differing classifications across countries can therefore lead to statistical discrepancies between inward and outward FDI, which theoretically should match. While identifying the home country of an MNE is occasionally not easy, it is even more difficult to identify the true nationality in terms of ownership, especially for MNEs that are listed on various stock exchanges across different jurisdictions. Moreover, the increasing complexity of corporate structures – often created for tax avoidance reasons by setting up affiliations in financial offshore centres or domiciling headquarters in low tax countries –blurs the nationality of an MNE further.

MNEs have become important players in the global economy. While their activities also peaked before the GFC, the sales of their affiliates abroad still amounts to almost 36% of GDP, while the contribution of the affiliations to world GDP is close to 10%. Note that these numbers do not include the activities of the MNEs in their often large home countries. Moreover, the total assets of all foreign affiliates still exceed world GDP (Table 4.2).

2 FDI motives

Why do corporations choose to operate foreign affiliations? There are three main answers: they seek resources, they seek new markets, or they seek both.

Resource seekers invest abroad to have access to specific resources. The main reasons for such a **vertical FDI** are lower costs and/or to secure access, as can be discerned from looking at three key types of resource-seeking:

- MNEs seek **physical resources**, such as raw materials or agricultural products, but also attractions for tourism. By investing in these sectors, it is often possible to circumvent market imperfections, e.g. when supply of a mineral is highly concentrated in companies that charge monopoly prices. Moreover, sole suppliers can also use their position to discriminate among customers, e.g. for political reasons.
- MNEs seek **cheaper labour** in the sense that unit labour costs are sufficiently below those at home to make offshoring of production meaningful. It is not sufficient that labour costs are below those at home. Rather, a labour-cost

advantage should not be overcompensated by a productivity disadvantage, thus resulting in a unit-labour-cost advantage that is high enough to make foreign production profitable after taking into account the trade costs of delivering the product to the home market.[2]

- MNEs seek **specialised skills**, like technological capabilities, management and marketing expertise, or other organisational skills. Here again, both cost and access matter. In some cases, professionals in foreign countries may have an edge in certain capabilities, e.g. like IT competencies in Silicon Valley. In other cases, such capabilities may be available in the required abundance only abroad, e.g. IT programming capabilities in India.

Market seekers typically set up a replication of their home country production facilities to serve the foreign market. Such **horizontal FDI** takes place because for a variety of reasons it is cheaper to produce in the target market rather than at home, and access the market by export. There are three main groups of reasons:

- Trade costs, understood as both physical trade costs, like transportation costs, and political trade costs, such as tariffs and other trade restrictions as well as investment incentives, make production in the target market more attractive. Hence, the latter are often used by host countries to attract market-seeking FDI.
- Going abroad facilitates adaption to tastes as well as to specific regulations in the target market, which may best be done within the country, often using local staff. Examples range from adjusting movies to local regulations to creating vegetarian hamburgers for countries where a large part of the population does not eat beef.
- Companies are often following a main supplier or customer who moved to a foreign market. This is particularly relevant, when closeness between suppliers and customers is important. For example, suppliers of batteries for electric cars may follow a car producer moving to a large foreign market, in order to develop new battery technologies in close cooperation with its customer.

It is important to recognise, however, that contrary to common beliefs, it is not simply the market size as such that makes a country attractive for market-oriented FDI. Rather, it is the market size in conjunction with trade costs. To understand this qualification, imagine a world with no trade costs at all. This is not a very farfetched assumption. Just think of digital markets, such as streaming portals. If the stream is not subject to digital taxes or national firewalls, the delivery does not require to set up (often expensive) subsidiaries abroad. In fact, if the production is characterised by economies of scale, it makes full sense to produce at home and deliver as (service) exports.

Finally, especially the third wave of globalisation has led to a sharp proliferation of GVCs, and thus boosted a new type of **efficiency-seeking FDI** that aims at taking advantage of both, differences in costs and availability of production factors world-wide, and locating close to different markets. This often leads to **complex integration** in GVCs, which requires to decide and coordinate where to perform which task in a globally fragmented production process, taking into account both sourcing and market consideration at the same time. Such decisions will be taken at every stage of the value chain, starting from pre-production over the actual production to post-production distribution activities.

Finally, and for completeness, there are a number of **other FDI motives** (see Dunning, 1992; Dunning & Lundan, 2008), such as:

- **Strategic asset-seeking investment**: Examples are access to specific expertise and knowledge, or access to production capacity to increase production in a very short time, e.g. to produce new vaccines in a pandemic.
- **Escape investment**, e.g. as a response to a weak legal framework, bad governance, or instable macroeconomic environment at home.
- **Support investment**, e.g. to establish a distribution network abroad for products exported to or produced in the foreign market.
- **Passive investment**, e.g. real estate investment as alternative to portfolio investment.
- **Tax-avoidance induced investment**, which is solely or predominantly undertaken for this reason.

All these motives are present today, yet historically some forms have been dominating certain historic periods since the Industrial Revolution. In a somewhat simplifying way, one can allocate the listed FDI motives to our three waves of globalisation:

- In the first wave of globalisation (1870–WWI), vertical FDI played an important role, not least in colonies, to exploit primary goods and to obtain agricultural products.
- In the second wave of globalisation (after WWII–approximately 1990), mass markets in advanced countries developed fast and created a boom of horizontal market-seeking FDI, especially among developed countries. However, in the late 1970s and 1980s, labour-seeking vertical FDI increased fast, often concentrating on newly industrialising countries (NICs) in Asia.
- In the third wave of globalisation, efficiency-seeking FDI became the major driver of FDI. By 2012, for the first time more than 50% of global FDI flowed to developing economies and transition economies. In particular within the European Union (EU), efficiency-seeking FDI into new member states soared (see European Perspective 4.1).

EUROPEAN PERSPECTIVE 4.1

FDI in the EU

A major objective of the EU Single Market is to stimulate intra-EU FDI. In fact, for most EU countries, investments from other EU countries contribute more than half of its FDI stocks, as Figure EP 4.1 shows. It is striking that in many new member countries, such as Slovakia (SK), Poland (PL), Romania (RO), Czech Republic (CZ), Croatia (HE), Slovenia (SI), Estonia (EE), and Lithuania (LT) more than 80% of all FDI inward stocks are originating from other EU member states. This clearly reflects how much these countries have become part of the European value chain production. Another striking feature is that countries like the Netherlands (NL) Luxembourg (LU), Ireland (IE), and Cyprus (CY), which are known as tax havens, are obviously not only attractive for intra-EU investments but also for FDI from outside the EU.

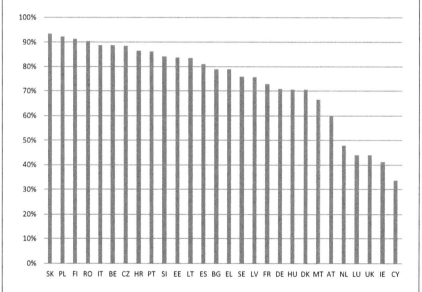

FIGURE EP 4.1   Share of Intra-EU Inward FDI Stocks in Percent of Total Inward FDI Stock of EU-Countries, Averages 2016–2018.

Source: Own calculations based on EU Single Market Scoreboard data, available at: https://ec.europa.eu/internal_market/scoreboard/integration_market_openness/fdi/index_en.htm.

---

3 Understanding global production

The key character of FDI is to exercise control over the operations of a foreign affiliation. Hence, for FDI to take place, it should pay off for a company to engage in often costly control procedures, e.g. by having a management team at the production site rather than having a different foreign company organising the production. Doing things inside a company, rather than outsourcing it to other companies is called **internalisation**.

3.1 FDI and the entry-mode decision

Internalisation plays a key role in one of the most celebrated theoretical models of FDI, the OLI-model of John Dunning (1992). Dunning's model posits that a company only undertakes a foreign investment when three specific advantages are present simultaneously:

- Ownership-specific advantages (O)
- Locational advantages (L)
- Internalisation advantages (I)

As an example, consider a pharmaceutical company that holds a patent on a vaccine, which is in high demand. The patent constitutes the company's O-advantage. If this vaccine is best produced in the home country of the company (after correcting for trade costs), it can simply be exported, and there is no need to invest abroad. However, if it is more efficient to locate production abroad, be it for serving the target market or the home market, the L-advantages suggest relocating production. This, however, does not mean that the company must engage in market-seeking or resource-seeking FDI. Instead, it could give a production license to a foreign company. At this point, I-advantages come in: The firm has to decide whether it a good idea to outsource the production to a subcontractor, or to keep control over the production process, e.g. to secure the quality of the vaccine, or to protect the know-how. If, and only if, the firm decides to exercise control, it will consider a direct investment. Table 4.3 summarises this logic of what is also known as the **entry-mode decision**.

O-advantages are often based on property rights, such as a patent or a brand name. In the emerging knowledge economy, they are, however, increasingly based on intangible assets, such as innovative capacity, unique production management skills, experience, and specialised know-how, or a particular experience in orchestrating and governing complex GVCs.

L-advantages can be identified on the basis of all the trade determinants that trade theory enumerates (see Chapter 3): availability of raw materials; climate and natural productivity advantages in the production of agricultural goods;

TABLE 4.3 The Entry Mode Decision in the OLI-Model

Entry Mode	Ownership Advantage	Locational Advantage	Internalisation Advantage
Export	Yes	No	No
Licensing	Yes	Yes	No
FDI	Yes	Yes	Yes

input prices, such as wages, energy prices, and costs of intermediate products; productivity, quality, and motivation of the labour force; transportation and trading costs, including trade barriers; and last but not least economies of scale and network externalities, which favour concentrated large production units or production within industrial clusters, respectively.

Once it has become clear that an activity of a firm is best located abroad, it has to be decided whether or not to do it outside or inside the firm by means of FDI. A general **I-advantage** that favours FDI is that using subcontractors causes transaction costs. It starts with search and negotiation costs to finalise a contract with the 'right partner', and ends with litigation costs in case the 'wrong partner' has been chosen. Other I-advantages differ depending on the type of investment. For **vertical FDI**, the major reasons for exercising direct control are:

- to circumvent price distortions, especially when external suppliers or buyers have a monopoly, or other forms of imperfect competition are prevalent;
- to avoid or reduce uncertainties in the supply chain of intermediary inputs; and
- to control the quality of inputs and distribution channels.

With regard to **horizontal FDI**, key issues are:

- to control and guarantee quality, e.g. to protect the brand name; and
- to take advantage of host government's incentives to attract FDI, such as tariffs or tax holidays (see Section 4).

Since **efficiency-seeking FDI** often combines aspects of vertical and horizontal investment, everything mentioned above is relevant here as well. However, given the complexities of modern GVCs, which often use new technologies, protecting core technologies is a major motive for FDI. Licensing or joint ventures, in contrast would make it easier for host country companies to acquire the technology or the key technological skills. For this very reason, China has for a long time insisted that foreign investment must take place as a joint venture with a Chinese company (see Section 4).

3.2 The multinational enterprise in global production

How do companies involve themselves in global production? From the OLI-model, we have seen that two elements are crucial: **outsourcing** and **offshoring**.

Outsourcing, especially regarding intermediate inputs, is fairly common. Just think of cotton for the local production of cloth. Most of the time cotton or cotton fabrics are bought from the market. Only in rare cases, fashion companies involve themselves in producing cotton. Outsourcing can occur at all stages of the value chain, from product development over manufacturing to post-production activities, such as marketing and retailing. The alternative is **integrated production**, which, in an extreme case, would control the production over the whole value chain from the development of the product concept to market delivery.

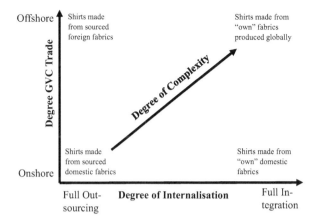

FIGURE 4.2   Integration and Offshoring in Global Production.

The more the company controls the value chain by means of integration, the more complex the process of managing production becomes. Likewise, this complexity also increases, the more inputs are sourced globally rather than domestically. Figure 4.2 illustrates this. The least complex form of production is to buy domestic inputs in the local market and produce at home. Sourcing offshore is more complex. Likewise, even controlling and governing a purely domestic value chain can be a formidable challenge, especially when the value chain is rather long, whereas governing a fully integrated global value chain is surely the most complex management challenge.

The examples of offshoring and outsourcing given in Figure 4.2 suffice to explain the basic principles, but the reality of advanced GVCs production is more complex.

- First, most inputs are not simply sourced in an anonymous (global) market, but are customised inputs, manufactured according to specifications provided and controlled by the lead company. Whenever a company uses external suppliers, is has to invest in finding the best supplier and make relationship-specific investments with this supplier. Likewise, the suppliers also invest into this (contractional) relationship. Moreover, these relationships may not last forever, thus entailing insecurities for both sides. For example, Apple can decide to use another supplier (e.g. for assembling iPhones in India) or to produce inputs within the company (e.g. Apple's decision to develop its own chips). Likewise, suppliers can contract with other customers (see Antràs, 2020a).
- Second, the complexity of the value chain increases also with the sheer length of the value chain. Complex products like the iPhone or Boeing's 787 clearly have a much longer value chain, than shirts made of cotton.

From all this, it is clear that firms are not equally equipped to internationalise, participate in, or ultimately govern complex GVCs. Trade economists are increasingly focusing on the role of firms as the key drivers of comparative advantages of

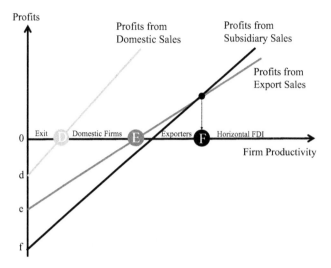

FIGURE 4.3 Productivity Level and Internationalisation of Firms.
Source: The figure is based on Figure 6.2 in Helpman (2011: 139).

nations.[3] The classical Ricardo model highlights productivity differences across countries at the industry level. However, companies within an industry also operate with different levels of productivity. The argument is, thus, that only the most productive firms are able to compete successfully on global markets. Moreover, this approach advocates a pecking order in the sense that the more productive the firm is, the more complex its involvement in global production.

Figure 4.3 illustrates this argument for the case of market-oriented FDI. On the horizontal axis, companies are ordered according to their level of productivity. The vertical axis measures profits or losses emanating from domestic sales, exports, and sales from subsidiaries abroad created by FDI, respectively.

Consider 'profits from domestic sales' first. With zero productivity, the company would produce and sell nothing and make a loss (d) equal to its cost. The more productive the firm, the lower the loss. At point D, the productivity is sufficient to break even, while higher productivity allows making profits. Compare this with profit from exports. Selling abroad requires upfront investments, like market research, setting up distribution channels, preparing staff for dealing with foreign operations etc. With higher fixed cost, the loss of a potential exporting company at zero productivity (e) would exceed the losses of a purely domestic company. Moreover, as exporting causes trade costs, e.g. from transportation, insurance, etc., the profit curve for the exporting company is flatter than the one for the purely domestic company. Consequently, only companies with a productivity level of E or higher will engage in exports. Setting up subsidiaries abroad via FDI involves even higher fixed costs (f) than selling to foreign markets. Variable costs, however, are lower because of lower trade costs due to proximity to the market. Horizontal FDI is thus more profitable than exports when the companies' productivity level exceeds point F. This gives a clear pecking order: only the most productive firms will become MNEs.

While the general message is that, the deeper the companies' involvement is in international business the more productive it should be, the devil is in the detail, especially when it comes to GVCs. Nevertheless, some predictions and insights are possible. For example, Antràs and Helpman (2004) have developed a model that predicts that the least productive firms produce at home, sourcing most inputs from the domestic market, while only the most productive ones pursue a complex global integration strategy, thus creating a lot of intra-firm trade.

Kohler and Smolka (2009) find in an empirical study of Spanish companies that 91% of the firms outsourced at home, while only 28% pursued complex global strategies. While this result confirms the prediction, it appears, however, that integration strategies are much less common (34%) than outsourcing-cum-offshoring (66%), hinting that integration is a strategy which is reserved only for the most productive firms in an industry. The latter results contradict the Antràs and Helpman model, which assumes that manufacturing costs are lower abroad, and fixed costs of a complex integration strategy are higher than simple outsourcing. This suggests that the predictions vary depending on the applicability of the assumptions. For example, if the fixed costs of integration are lower than those of outsourcing, the pecking order will reverse, making intra-firm production more attractive for less productive firms. An illustration could be a firm that has difficulties finding a reliable and cheap supplier of key inputs, e.g. because the suppliers have high market power.

Allowing for heterogeneity of firms help us to understand the process of globalisation, and especially the role of MNEs for the rise (and potential demise) of GVCs. That said, the new approach also points to the need of detailed studies at the national and company level (see European Perspective 4.2).

EUROPEAN PERSPECTIVE 4.2

The internationalisation of European firms

In a study on European firms, Mayer and Ottaviano (2007) apply the heterogeneous-firm approach to the international performance of European companies. They confirm that in line with the theory "the relative export performance of countries at the macro level is positively correlated with the relative productivity of their firms measured at the micro level" (2007: 49). In other words, European export champions tend to be those with the highest productivity.

The detailed findings show that aggregate European exports are driven by a few top exporters, which export a large fraction of their turnover to many locations. As predicted by the theory, the authors also confirm that truly multinational firms have been found to perform better than exporters, and exporters perform better than non-exporters. Moreover, "the happy few" are different from other firms: "They are bigger, generate higher value added, pay higher wages, employ more capital per worker and more skilled workers and have higher productivity" (2007: 1).

4 FDI policies

FDI policies are inspired by the positive or negative effects foreign investments have – or are assumed to have – on the host and home country, respectively. Historically, especially vertical FDI in colonies and – later – developing countries, have often met fierce critique for being exploitive. Especially in the 1960s and 1970s, a wave of expropriation threatened foreign investors. Since the 1980s, and with the rise of GVCs, many developing countries increasingly view FDI as a means of helping industrialisation and getting access to technology, thus promoting productivity and economic growth. Advanced countries – especially when their economies are operating below capacity with a high level of unemployment – often hope that inward FDI will create new jobs.

On the side of the FDI home countries, concern have been growing that host country policies are against the interests of the home countries and/or the home country companies. In consequence, this has resulted in a number of new regulations on FDI.

The United Nations Conference on Trade and Development's (UNCTAD) Investment Policy Monitor differentiates three major categories of investments measures[4]:

- **Entry and establishment**. The major measures here are regarding ownership and control, access to land, and approval and admission.
- **Treatment and operation**. Major categories here are non-discrimination, nationalisation and expropriations, capital transfers and foreign exchange, dispute settlement, and operational conditions.
- **Promotion and facilitation**. The major categories here are investment facilitation, investment incentives, and Special Economic Zones (SEZs).

While it is beyond the scope of this book to go into the details of all these measures, two policy areas of special interest, restrictions of ownership and investment incentives shall be highlighted.

Restrictions on ownership are particularly controversial. For one, there is the infamous 'joint-venture requirement' for investors in China, which restricts the ownership of foreign investors to 50% of the capital of the venture in key industries. A major objective of the old Chinese Joint Venture law was to get access to foreign technologies – or at least familiarise Chinese companies with them. Whether this is already an unfair practice is a matter of debate. The counterargument is that investors still can and will weigh the costs of sharing their knowledge with the benefits of producing in China and/or for the Chinese market.

Another key issue with the treatment of FDI in China is reciprocity. Advanced countries became increasingly dissatisfied with the joint venture requirement, while Chinese investors have been able to buy themselves into Western companies without restrictions. Hence, Chinese outward investments have come under scrutiny as well. Short of a new global trade and investment agreement at the global level, many countries have embarked on negotiating regional or bilateral investment agreements.[5]

However, on January 1, 2020, China has liberalised and unified its foreign investment regulations in a new Foreign Investment Law (FIL), which is much less restrictive on ownership, and guarantees more protection of intellectual property rights. Hence, one may interpret this change as the outcome of a changing constellation of demand for FDI in China and the supply of investments from abroad.

Turning to **investment incentives**, host countries often use a plethora of instruments to attract foreign investments. Low(er) taxation (than at home), or even tax breaks are amongst the most prominent and controversial ones. Differences in taxation are nothing unusual. It is a key element of nation states' sovereignty to decide about taxes and their use, and the preferences regarding taxation may vary considerably across countries. What matters therefore is not low taxation per se, but a more favourable treatment of foreign investors relative to local investors. To do so, many countries use **Special Economic Zones** (SEZs). While in 1975, 29 countries had established 79 SEZs, their number increased to 845 in 1997 and 3,000 in 2002. In 2018, approximately 5,400 SEZs were operated by 147 countries (UNCTAD, 2019: 129).

Tax incentives to attract foreign firms to produce within the host country should, however, be distinguished from **pure tax havens**. The latter are only interested in obtaining tax revenues from foreign companies that re-domicile their headquarters to the tax haven to minimise taxation. This is typically being done by 'profit shifting', i.e., booking costs in the high tax home country and shifting the revenues to a tax haven. A classic example of **transfer pricing** is to book the research and development (R&D) expenditure for developing a new technology at home, then selling the technology for a low price to a subsidiary in a tax haven, and finally paying high fees for the use of the technology. Hence, profits are shifted to tax havens (see European Perspective 4.3).

EUROPEAN PERSPECTIVE 4.3

Intra-EU profit and tax shifting

Tax avoidance through profit shifting is a worldwide phenomenon. Yet, while it may be difficult to reach a global agreement on tax havens (see Chapter 7), it is striking that profit shifting within the EU is remarkably high. According to recent research by Tørsløv, Wier and Zucman (2020), four EU countries, namely Ireland, the Netherlands, Luxembourg, and Belgium, are the major EU profit shifting destinations. The four largest EU countries, namely, Germany, France, Italy, and Spain, lost between 14% and 26% of their corporate tax revenues to tax havens in 2017, predominantly to these four EU havens. For the tax havens, tax revenues from shifted profits are a substantial, occasionally even a major part, of their corporate tax revenues (Table EP 4.1).

TABLE EP 4.1 Profit Shifting and Corporate Tax Shifting in Selected EU Countries, 2017

Shifted Profits From	Profits (In Billion $) Lost To							Tax Revenue Lost		
	EU					Non-EU Tax Haven	Total Lost Profits	In billion $	In % of Corporate Tax Revenue	
	Ireland	Netherlands	Luxembourg	Belgium	Other				To All havens	To EU Havens
Germany	10.0	16.9	20.8	4.4	1.4	12.5	**65.9**	19.6	26%	21%
France	5.7	7.4	12.5	7.3	0.4	6.8	**40.0**	13.3	22%	18%
Italy	6.2	3.5	11.2	2.1	0.2	3.3	**26.5**	6.4	15%	14%
Spain	3.3	5.7	4.2	1.0	0.1	2.5	**17.0**	4.2	14%	12%
Sum	**25.2**	**33.5**	**48.7**	**14.9**	**2.1**	**25.0**	**149.4**	**43.6**		
Other countries	101.0	45.8	17.3	5.6						
Total	**126.2**	**79.3**	**66.0**	**20.5**						
Tax revenue from shifted profits (in billion $)	6.2	10.5	1.9	4.0						
Tax revenue from shifted profits in % of total revenue	67%	39%	58%	19%						
Tax rate on shifted profits	5%	13%	3%	19%						

Source: Own table based on data by Torslov, Wier and Zucman (2020), available on https://missingprofits.world.

Next to the well-known small tax havens, such as the Cayman Islands, several advanced economies can be classified as financial centres, as argued by Lane and Milesi-Ferretti (2018). These centres distinguish themselves by an extraordinarily high ratio of external assets and liabilities to GDP, such as Belgium, Hong Kong, Ireland, Luxemburg, the Netherlands, Singapore, Switzerland, and the United Kingdom. What is behind these high ratios? Two reasons are given:

- Parent enterprises create 'special purpose entities', whose purpose is not to perform production activities, but to raise capital or hold assets (and/or liabilities). For example, according to the authors more than 75% of all FDI claims and liabilities in the Netherlands are related to such entities.
- MNEs move their domicile to a financial centre. Even if only the headquarters is moved but not the production facilities, it will add to the FDI stocks of the financial centre. For example, re-domiciling helped Ireland to bring FDI claims in 2014 to a level that exceeds the Irish GDP by more than a factor of 5.

Figure 4.4 reveals that the most successful hosts of FDI within the EU are some of those mentioned above, which are attractive for both investors from EU and from third countries.

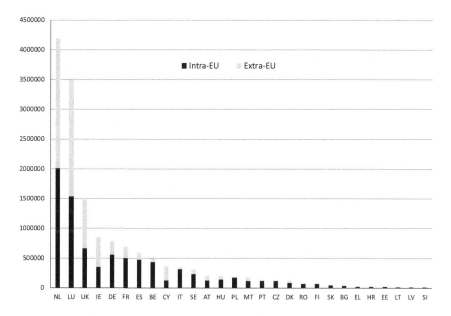

FIGURE 4.4   Intra- and Extra-EU Inward FDI Stock in EU Countries, Average 2016–2018 (in million €).

Source: Own calculations based on EU Single Market Scoreboard data, available at: https:// ec.europa.eu/internal_market/scoreboard/integration_market_openness/fdi/index_en.htm.

Measures on investments are not fully within the discretion of a country. Rather, several measures are prohibited for the World Trade Organisation (WTO) members by the trade-related investments measures (TRIMs) agreement, such as some forms of local-content requirements. These rules are, at the same time, often intensified by bilateral and regional trade agreements. Moreover, the treatment of tax havens is currently under scrutiny at both regional levels, such as within the EU, and the global level where - at the time of writing - a global minimum corporate tax rate is being debated. These governance issues are discussed in Chapter 7 in more detail.

5 The future of global investment

The future of global investment is closely intertwined with the future of GVCs. In this sense, many arguments discussed in Chapter 3 are valid for FDI, too. In fact, most data reveal that growth in GVC trade and FDI have both been stagnating in the second half of the 2010s. However, while the share of foreign value added in trade is stagnating, it is nevertheless still high. The same applies to the stock of FDI. This suggests that firms do not reconfigure their global supply chains in reaction to shocks that are considered of temporary nature because of the high sunk cost of their prior investment in their value chains (Antràs, 2020b). Rather, only structural changes considered to persist, will have a long-term impact on FDI.

What can then be expected from longer-term persistent technological changes is:

- **Robotisation** and new technologies such as additive manufacturing (3D-printing) will favour production closer to the market. Hence, more reshoring and/or nearshoring becomes likely. In the former case, we expect less FDI.
- **Digitalisation** offers continuing opportunities for globalising service tasks (Baldwin, 2019). In fact, FDI in services has remained high and may even increase.

With respect to **policies**, in recent years trade conflicts have been increasing, and more generally, national and regional industrial policies tend to focus more and more on promoting domestic activities. To what extent nationalistically motivated trade conflicts continue to prevail remains to be seen. However, trade wars between two countries may not lead to de-globalisation but to a relocation of production from one location to another. For example, a trade war between the US and China may lead to a reshoring from China to India or Vietnam. Moreover, regional policies could also stimulate FDI, but within a region at the expense of extra-regional FDI.

In a more extreme case of nationalistic industrial policies, there is a risk of a divergence of technological developments, especially if two or more different (industrial) standards emerge, like, e.g. two internets. Increasingly, governments and regional clubs are aiming at setting standards, e.g. in data exchange. Whether this will lead to a bifurcation, which restricts the exchange between two standards, or whether this results in a competition in which the 'best standard' will be adopted globally, remains to be seen.

With respect to **environmental threats**, especially climate change, a response with policies aiming at curbing carbon dioxide (CO_2) emissions, like emission taxes, will clearly add to transportation costs and promote production closer to the market, yet not necessarily a reshoring to the domestic economy, if nearby jurisdictions offer locational advantages.

Health and security threats, like pandemics or dependencies on foreign supply, can promote tendencies towards reshoring sensitive production activities. However, as it is well-known from portfolio investment strategy, multi-country sourcing could be superior to putting all eggs in one basket.

In sum, FDI may thus not simply be stalling but slowly reconfiguring global value chains. However, as argued with respect to GVC trade in Chapter 3, a slowdown in global investment is nothing to worry about per se. If it reflects what is best in terms of economic efficiency given the key features of new technologies, it must not be a bad thing. Nevertheless, robotisation especially can imply that poor countries may not be able to follow the successful development paths of the NICs by finding their place in GVCs in manufacturing. Nonetheless, as discussed in the upcoming Chapter 5, the globalisation of intangibles may offer new alternatives.

Recommended readings

Classic texts on FDI are Dunning and Lundan (2008) and Caves (2007). For a non-technical review of recent theoretical advances see Helpman (2011), while Antràs (2016) provides an in-depth coverage.

For up-to-date information and analyses, the annual *World Investment Report* published by the United Nations Conference on Trade and Development (unctad.org) is an invaluable source of information data and topical analyses.

Notes

1 The high value of FDI stocks in 2019 is partly due to rising evaluations in global capital markets in 2019 (UNCTAD, 2020: 11).
2 For a detailed discussion, see Chapter 3.
3 See, e.g. Eaton and Kortum (2002) and Melitz (2003) for the seminal contributions to the so-called "new new trade theory". Helpman (2011) provides an accessible introduction to the approach.
4 UNCTAD's website www.investmentpolicy.unctad.org provides information on all investment measures by countries, regions, and sectors.
5 See Chapter 7 for a discussion on such deep trade agreements, including the new EU-China Investment Agreement (CIA).

References

Antràs, P. (2016). *Global production*. Princeton University Press.
Antràs, P. (2020a). Conceptual Aspects of Global Value Chains. Background Paper to the World Development Report 2020. World Bank Policy Research Working Paper 9114.

Antràs, P. (2020b). *De-globalisation? Global values chains in the post-COVID-19 age.* NBER Working Paper 28115. National Bureau of Economic Research.

Antràs, P., & Helpman, E. (2004). Global sourcing. *Journal of Political Economy, 112*(3), 552–580.

Baldwin, R. (2019). *The globotics upheaval. Globalization, robotics, and the future of work.* Oxford University Press.

Caves, R. S. (2007). *Multinational enterprises and economic analysis.* Cambridge University Press.

Dunning, J. H. (1992). *Multinational enterprises and the global economy.* Addison-Wesley.

Dunning, J. H., & Lundan, S. M. (2008). *Multinational enterprises and the global economy.* Edgar Elgar.

Eaton, J., & Kortum, S. (2002). Technology, geography, and trade. *Econometrica, 70,* 1741–1779.

Helpman, E. (2011). *Understanding global trade.* MIT Press.

Kohler, W. K., & Smolka, M. (2009). Global Sourcing Decisions and Firm Productivity: Evidence from Spain. CESifo Working Paper Series 2903.

Lane, P. R., & Milesi-Ferretti, G. M. (2018). The external wealth of nations revisited: international financial integration in the aftermath of the global financial crisis. *IMF Economic Review, 66,* 189–222.

Mayer, T., & Ottaviano, G. I. P. (2007). *The happy few: The internationalisation of European firms.* Bruegel Blueprint Series, III.

Melitz, M. J. (2003). The impact of trade on intra-industry reallocations and aggregate industry productivity. *Econometrica, 71,* 1695–1725.

Tørsløv, T., Wier, L., & Zucman, G. (2020). The Missing Profits of Nations. April 22. Available on: www.missingprofits.world.

UNCTAD (2020). *World investment report 2020.* United Nations Conference on Trade and Development.

5
GLOBAL INTANGIBLES

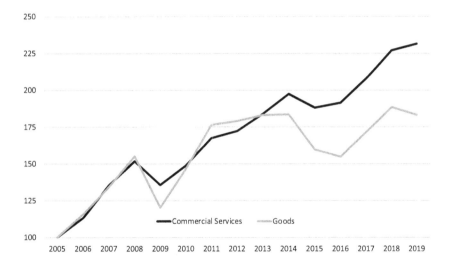

FIGURE 5.1 World Trade in Commercial Services Versus Trade in Goods, 2005–2019; (2005 = 100).

Source: Own calculations based on WTO Database data (https://data.wto.org) on "World Commercial Service Exports and World Goods and Services Exports in Million US Dollar".

Unlike trade in goods, trade in commercial services has been continuously rising in the past years, and most recently outpaced the stalling trade in goods (Figure 5.1). Moreover, many advanced countries, while often experiencing deficits in merchandise trade, are exhibiting trade surpluses in intangibles. Services have long been viewed as non-tradable, or at least costly to trade. Digitalisation is changing this rapidly. The very combination of a high share of labour in

DOI: 10.4324/9781003057611-5

producing services and drastically falling trading costs in digital delivery across borders, makes services a potential key driver of a fourth wave of globalisation. This chapter explores the increasing tradability of services, with a special emphasis on two intangibles of particular importance in the new global economy (NGE), data and knowledge.

1 Trade in services

Devoting a whole chapter to trade in services is not straightforward. After all, do trade theories as discussed in Chapter 3 not explain most of the trade patterns observed? A first answer is: in principle yes, and increasingly so. Comparative advantages, e.g. based on productivity, factor abundance or technological gaps, often play a role. Learning effects are important, too, and many offered services are heterogenous enough to offer consumers choices between differentiated services products. With the advent of digital technologies, services have become much more like manufactures. The Indian service industry is a case in point. The country is a well-established exporter of information technology (IT) services, including programming services for major soft- and hardware producers. The 'products' can be delivered via internet connections. Likewise, outsourced call centres and other so-called business process outsourcing activities, such as billing and ticketing services for airlines, are already well-established service export sectors in India.[1] Like manufactures, these services are tradable, scalable, and innovation and learning effects are important in the industry (Baldwin & Forslid, 2019).

There are, however, major differences to manufacturing, which makes it worthwhile to give intangibles additional attention. Many services still have to be performed by human beings and cannot easily be substituted by robots. At the same time, trade costs, especially of digital cross-border delivery, have fallen drastically over the last decades. Under these conditions, arbitrage in labour-intensive services is becoming increasingly attractive. In a way, services showcase the argument by Paul Krugman (2020) that globalisation sprints occur whenever the productivity increases in transportation costs exceed those in the industry itself.

Having said that, it should be noted that trade in services is still at a low level, commanding only about 25% of total world trade in goods and services. Yet, we should take the argument by Baldwin (2019) seriously that service production can be expanded much faster than industrial production, which requires a lot of physical investments. Thus, the ongoing process of globalisation of services could be even faster and more disruptive than the third wave of globalisation.

1.1 What is trade in services?

Trade in services is difficult to conceptualise and, subsequently, quantify in all its aspects. Some cross-border activities are easy to identify, for example, buying

(=importing) an insurance from a foreign insurance company, or hiring a foreign tax consultant. Other services are more difficult to classify correctly. Consider that you would like to watch a new movie. In case you download or stream it from a foreign media portal it will be classified and counted as a service import. However, if you import it as a DVD, it is counted as a goods import. Given, that printing a DVD and packaging accounts for only a fraction of the DVD's price tag, this seems not very logical. Moreover, when people shift from buying DVDs to streaming, trade in services grows at the expense of goods trade.

Nevertheless, it may make sense to treat both 'modes of delivery' differently. The DVD import can be checked at the border, and eventually a tariff is levied on it, while the distribution of DVDs via retailers within a country has to be in line with the importing country's regulations. Another example are professional services, such as tax advice. If the advice is delivered by a tax consultant who flies in, it is counted as a service import. It the tax consultant sets up a commercial presence in the country where she delivers the advice, it is not counted as a service import but rather as the domestic activity of a foreign investor. Yet, the logic of service trade would clearly classify it as a service import.

With the establishment of the World Trade Organisation (WTO) in 1995, the General Agreement on Trade in Services (GATS) went into force, which brought service trade under the umbrella of the world trading system. In doing so, GATS defines four modes of delivery of cross-border services, namely:

- **Mode 1**: Cross-border supply of services, e.g. digitally via the internet.
- **Mode 2**: Cross-border consumption. This occurs when a foreign customer consumes services within the territory of the supplier, e.g. as a tourist.
- **Mode 3**: Establishment of a commercial presence in the host country, which delivers services in the host country, but is an affiliate of a foreign company.
- **Mode 4**: Presence of natural foreign persons to deliver a service, such as a foreign tax consultants.

All but mode 3, the commercial presence, are counted in the balance of payments statistics, which constitute the official data for trade in services, like the ones used in Figure 5.1. Hence, our graph misses an important part of trade in services and, thus, underestimates the importance of global service trade. In fact, commercial presence is responsible for more than half of all trade in services (see Figure 5.2).

1.2 The globalisation of intangibles in the global value chain

The new digital technologies can do to services what information and communication technology (ICT) did to manufacturing value chains in the third wave of globalisation: slicing services into tasks and making them tradable. As soon as services can be delivered digitally, they can be globalised, too. This increasingly allows to separate and globalise services along the manufacturing value chain.

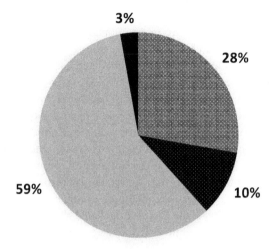

Cross-border transactions (Mode 1) ▨ Consumption abroad (Mode 2)
Commercial Presence (Mode 3)   ■ Presence of Indidivduals (Mode 4)

FIGURE 5.2   World Trade in Services by Mode of Supply, 2017.
Source: Own graph based on Figure B1 in WTO (2019: 24). Data are WTO estimates from the "experimental" TISMOS (Trade in Services by Mode of Supply) dataset.

Figure 5.3 synthesises graphs and elaborations in the 2020 World Investment Report (UNCTAD, 2020). Using a standard, though quite granular 'smile curve', which posits higher value added towards the beginning and the end of the value chain,[2] the report identifies three major areas where services impact on the value chain:

- **Service commodification**: In both, the pre- and post-production phases of the value chain, services are becoming increasingly like commodities, e.g. hiring marketing experts for developing products based on consumer preferences, or developing marketing and distribution strategies. As commodities these services can be standardised, become scalable, and, hence, be fragmented and offshored, similar to trade in production tasks as discussed in Chapter 3.
- **Servicification**: Manufacturing, be it manufacturing of inputs, assembling, or packaging, is increasingly offered as a service.
- **Servitisation**: Embedding services in products is also become more widespread, implying that the dividing line between products and services is being blurred further.

Finally, Figure 5.3 also incorporates the plausible argument that (big) data is playing a more important role in creating higher value added in research and development (R&D), and from the use of customer data.

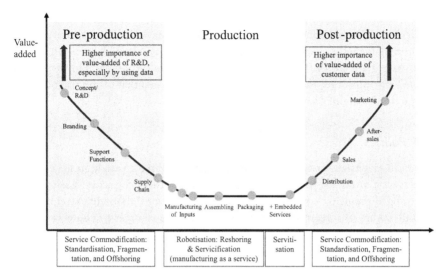

FIGURE 5.3   The Globalisation of Intangibles in Production.
Source: Own compilation based on Figures IV.9–IV.11 in UNCTAD (2020: 143-145).

1.3 The emergence of new digital global services

Will there be a new wave of globalisation via novel forms of delivery of digital services? Baldwin (2019) argues that digital technologies could bring down the face-to-face costs of communication, not least through virtual reality (VR) and augmented reality (AR) applications. Tele-presence, tele-conferencing, VR, and AR are an alternative to costly and time-consuming business travel. While this can also help to promote traditional manufacturing-based global value chains (GVCs), Baldwin sees the major potential in globalising digital services. This might allow countries that previously have not benefitted from the GVC-driven third wave of globalisation, to develop new competitive advantages based on labour cost differentials, which finally have the potential to connect even remote countries, like Argentina, and many landlocked countries in Africa and Asia, which have not been part of the 'partial convergence' process, discussed in Chapter 2.

On a more visionary note, Baldwin (2019) argues the case of an emerging world of tele-robotics and tele-migration. In the words of Baldwin and Forslid (2019: 8):

> As various forms of virtual-presence technology are combined with human-controlled robots, an expanding range of manual services could be provided at a distance. At the high end, technicians could conduct inspections or undertake repairs from remote locations, and nurses in the Philippines could care for elderly people in Japan. At the low end, hotel rooms in Oslo could be cleaned by robots controlled by cleaners in Kenya. Lawns in Texas could be maintained by robots steered by Mexican gardeners sitting in Mexico.

As with tele-presence, the widespread use of telerobots is still constrained by high costs. Whether such tele-migration will become a dominant activity in the NGE remains to be seen and depends – as the authors acknowledge – on a rapid and sharp reduction of the current high costs of tele-robotics. However, if it comes, the impact on the global economy could exceed that of the rise of GVCs in the third wave of globalisation.

1.4 Policies

Trade in services is creating other challenges compared to trade in goods. The effects often make deeper inroads into the social fabric of countries, posing complex and difficult to communicate technical questions about their regulation, and their very character makes rapid and disruptive changes in competitiveness possible.

The World Trade Report 2019 summarises its findings on the welfare effects of trade in service as follows:

> Trade in services creates welfare gains for society through a more efficient allocation of resources, greater economies of scale, and an increase in the variety of services on offer. In addition, some service sectors, such as infrastructural services, play a critical role in the functioning of the entire economy while others affect the productivity of the economy's factors of production. An important avenue through which services trade benefits societies is the improvement in firms' competitiveness, both in the services and manufacturing sectors.
>
> *(WTO, 2019: 6)*

However, opening up to trade requires adjustments on the side of the exporter and on the side of the importer, alike. Thus, like trade in goods, it creates winners and losers. Moreover, as the 'presence' of foreign services is much more directly felt, trade is services is often more controversial than trade in goods. Hence, countries frequently regulate the service sector more tightly than goods trade (see European Perspective 5.1).

The choice of policy instruments depends on the specific character of services. In goods trade, tariffs are the most common form of trade restrictions, while quantitative restrictions, like quotas are (in principle) not in line with WTO rules. The situation is reversed for services. For dealing with cross-border delivery, establishment of commercial presence or movement of natural persons, tariffs are clearly not suitable. Hence, the WTO rules allow quantitative restrictions. Most importantly, while the rules for trade in goods require non-discrimination, i.e. foreign and domestic companies within a country must be treated alike, in the service sector specific national treatment is allowed, making a differential treatment, e.g. via taxes, of foreign suppliers possible.

EUROPEAN PERSPECTIVE 5.1

The EU single market for services

The European Single Market is explicitly a single market for cross-border services. However, cross-border service delivery is still relatively low in the EU, with the main mode of service trade being FDI. While this is partly so because of the limitations in tradability, the dominance of small 'micro' firms in the service sector in Europe as well as remaining regulatory barriers play a role. This has prompted the EU to launch a *Service Directive* in 2006 to:

- remove red tape and simplify the establishment of service providers in their home country and abroad;
- simplify the cross-border provision of services into other EU countries;
- strengthen the rights of service recipients, in particular consumers;
- ensure easier access to a wider range of services.*

A recent International Monetary Fund (IMF) study (Ebeke, Frie & Rabier, 2019) argues that political factors play an important role in holding back service sector reforms, in particular vested interests of home country suppliers, a general fear of social dumping, and the widespread belief that cross-border liberalisation would reduce service quality.

* Quoted from https://ec.europa.eu/growth/single-market/services_en.

---

2 Global data

Data traffic has increased drastically over the past two decades and outpaced all other economic cross-border activities by far. However, globalisation of cross-border data traffic is not evolving evenly. Rather, some countries are standing out by the sheer size of data traffic, while some emerging Asian countries have been catching up fast.

As can be seen from Table 5.1, in 2019 China (including Hong Kong) has recorded the highest level of cross-border data traffic measured in megabits per minute, even outpacing the USA. India already ranks fourth, while Germany and France fell in the ranking if compared to 2001. Of course, part of this ranking is due to the sheer population size. However, scaling the data per-capita shows that China's per-capita cross-border data traffic (like Vietnam's) is close to that of Germany and France. Singapore and the UK stand out in per-capita terms, and the US has a per-capita traffic twice as high as the listed European Union (EU) countries. If past trends give any indication, and it might well be so especially considering the previously discussed digitalisation of the service sector, it appears likely that countries such as India, Brazil, and Vietnam will further

TABLE 5.1 Cross-Border Data Traffic by Countries in Megabits per Minute (Mbpm), 2019

Rank by Mbpm	Ranking 2001	Ranking 2019	Mbpm	Mbpm per Capita
1	USA	China/HK	6,660	4.76
2	UK	USA	3,600	10.97
3	Germany	UK	3,073	45.99
4	France	India	1,978	1.45
5	Japan	Singapore	487	85.37
6	China/HK	Brazil	482	2.28
7	Brazil	Vietnam	479	4.97
8	Russia	Russia	454	3.15
9	Singapore	Germany	436	5.25
10	India	France	332	4.95

Source: Own calculations based on data from **NIKKEI** Asia at https://vdata.nikkei.com/en/newsgraphics/splinternet/. Population data are from World Bank at https:/.data.worldbank.org.

catch up with the leaders in terms of per-capita data traffic. Regarding China, the future development may crucially depend on China's policy stance regarding cross-border data traffic.

2.1 Why data markets are different

Digital data markets are characterised by strong **network externalities**. With this term, economists describe that a company's digital network is more valuable for the user when it has more users. Just think of social media platforms, like Facebook or Twitter. Monopoly positions emerge almost naturally in such a **winner-takes-it-all** environment. These markets are characterised by a lack of effective competition, thus generating high monopoly profits. In consequence, digital markets are often dominated by global **digital superstar firms**, especially the so-called 'big five': Alphabet, Apple, Amazon, Facebook, and Microsoft, but also increasingly by corporations active in the so-called platform economy, such as Uber or Airbnb.

Given the high rate of concentration in digital markets, it is not surprising that the higher profit margins of superstar firms can lead to a lower share of the value added distributed to labour. Autor et al. (2020) blame the rise of superstar firms for the secular fall of the share in national income going to labour because a rising share of superstar firms in the national value added, reshuffles income shares from labour to capital.

2.2 How digital multinationals are different

Delivering data services to the customer often requires less internationalisation of capital than in traditional manufacturing. According to the United Nations

TABLE 5.2 The International Footprint of Top 100 Multinational Enterprises, 2015

	Tech MNEs	Telecom MNEs		Other MNEs
Share of foreign assets	41%	66%		65%
Share of foreign sales	73%	57%		64%
Ratio share of foreign sales to foreign assets	**1.8**	**0.9**		**1.0**
Of which: *Internet platforms*	*2.6*			
Digital payments and other digital solutions	*1.9*		*Of which: automotive and aircraft*	*1.3*
IT	*1.8*			
E-commerce	*1.1*			
Digital content	*1.1*			

Source: Based on UNCTAD (2017: 170–171).

Conference on Trade and Development (UNCTAD, 2017), in 2015, 73% of the sales of tech multinationals were from abroad, while only 41% of their assets were located abroad. Hence, one dollar of assets abroad, generated 1.8 dollars of sales. By contrast, for non-tech multinationals the ratio is about 1. Internet platform and other digital IT solutions, including digital payments, particularly exhibit an 'asset-light' form of internationalisation (Table 5.2). As a consequence, such digital multinationals are more closely linked to their home countries than non-tech multinationals. Moreover, the foreign presences of digital companies has often been driven by tax (avoidance) considerations, in a way that exceeds the extent observed for other multinational enterprises (MNEs) (UNCTAD, 2017).

2.3 Data policies and the future of data

Unlike traditional companies, digital superstar firms often do not even charge for their services. Rather, customers pay with their data for free-of-charge services. This raises two questions:

- Without having a price for data, how can we know how much data shall be produced?
- Who owns the data, or to frame it as a normative question: Who should own the data?

Regarding the first question, the value attached to data is often the price at which it can be sold to advertisers. But does this price really reflect the value customer attach to using the service, say, an internet search? The demand for a physical good, say a car, determines in conjunction with supply the price of a car. Hence, the willingness to pay for a car provides important information for the allocation of resources to produce cars. This link is cut in the case of data. We have therefore little, if any, indication whether we produce enough, too little, or too much data.

Therefore, some experts have raised the question, 'Who owns the data?' Arrieta-Ibarra et al. (2018) argue that the current barter deal "free digital services for free data", treats **data as capital** that is owned, just like a machine, by a corporation. As such, the main criterion for utilising data is delivering a return on investment. However, what happens if this leads to investing into artificial intelligence (AI) technologies that replace human work with machines? A world without work could emerge, in which people will have to live on universal and unconditioned incomes and receive their self-esteem from activities beyond work. Against such a vision, the authors propose to treat **data as labour**, which is owned by individuals who sell their data as work on a (to be designed) data labour market as the source of both, income and self-esteem.

The authors, however, note that if AI does not deliver on its promise to replace human work, it would not matter much how we treat data. However, it may well be that the way data is owned has an impact on the direction in which AI-technology will develop. Acemoglu and Restreppo (2020) argue against incentives that stimulate the "wrong type of AI", which focuses on replacing labour rather than on enhancing labour-productivity.[3] If in fact, treating data as capital would encourage the wrong type of AI, a transition period to treat data (at least partially) as labour could be beneficial. This would, however, require strengthening "countervailing power" to digital superstar monopolists, by means of competition policies, a data labour movement, and regulation (Arrieta-Ibarra et al., 2018).

The quest for regulating data markets requires an answer to who should regulate the market. Data is a global business, yet the industry is largely regulated at the national level as multilateral regulations are missing. National regulation may, however, not be adequate, given the characteristics of this industry, discussed earlier. Even if we accept that national regulation is the only way, the crucial question is who then should regulate: the countries where the firms domicile, or the countries of their customers?

For the time being, the US, China, and the EU are the main actors. Occasionally, this can help to influence global standards in dealing with data (see European Perspective 5.2), but it can also lead to a bifurcation of technological

EUROPEAN PERSPECTIVE 5.2

The EU's general data protection regulation

The EU already has a long history of competition cases against digital MNEs. Moreover, the EU's *General Data Protection Regulation* (GDPR) has an important impact on the global data market. *The Economist* (September 22, 2018: 13) argues that "the principles of the GDPR are now being used as a benchmark for good data practice in markets well beyond Europe".

development, e.g. an emergence of two internets. Chapter 7 scrutinises the issue of supranational versus national governance more deeply.

3 Globalisation of knowledge

Knowledge is increasingly created globally, and not anymore dominated by advanced high-income countries. In particular, the rise of China and Korea has changed the landscape of global innovation. Figure 5.4 illustrates this, using patent applications as an indicator of knowledge production.[4]

Moreover, knowledge is increasingly crossing borders, as documented in a recent study, which utilises cross-patent citations (IMF, 2018). While in the 1990s, the spillovers were mainly between the US, the EU, and Japan, this analysis shows an increasing importance of South-North trade and South-South trade in knowledge, with Korea and China as major actors.

3.1 How knowledge spreads

Patents and their use, be it in applications in production, or by building upon them for developing new patents (as measured by cross-citations) is only one way how knowledge spreads. In principle, knowledge can cross borders in three major ways[5]:

- **Codified knowledge**. From early hand-writings over printed books to today's internet, codified knowledge is the classic way to spread knowledge. In the ancient times before the printing press, hand-written books were rare and precious. Only few books travelled, often key religious works like the

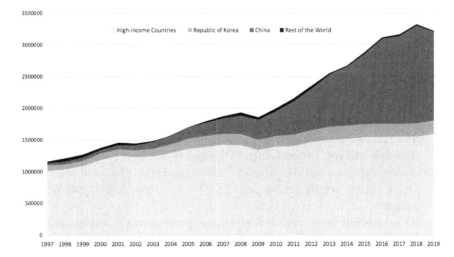

FIGURE 5.4 Total Patent Applications, 1985–2019.
Source: Own graph based on data from WIPO Statistics Database. www3.wipo.int/ipstats.

Koran, the Bible, or the Talmud. Libraries played a major role, and travelling was a major means to get access to knowledge. The printing press made books more widely accessible and affordable. Its impact on the Industrial Revolution by means of knowledge diffusion, including spreading the ideas of the Enlightenment can hardly be underestimated (see Chapter 2). The advent of the internet has increased the speed of knowledge diffusion further, but has not necessarily decreased the cost of accessing the knowledge. This very much depends on the use of paywalls by copyright owners, and the ability of different countries to pay for access to codified knowledge.

- **Embodied knowledge**. Products can reveal the knowledge needed to produce them. Thus, knowledge travels with goods. A now classic case is the 'reverse engineering' of the first IBM personal computers (PCs) in the 1980s. Hence, trade is key for knowledge spillovers. Conversely, trade boycotts are often directed at cutting a country off from new knowledge, as was the case in the 1980s when Western countries blocked technology exports to the Soviet Union.

- **Tacit knowledge**. Tacit knowledge, aka 'know-how', is often too complex to describe fully. Take as an example the knowledge of how to walk. Walking is typically learned by a combination of imitation and repetition, and requires both a role model and time. It is therefore slow to be transmitted across borders. Yet, it is often the most important source of productivity advances and overcoming technological backwardness and inefficiencies (see Chapter 2). Hence, cross-border movements play a key role as a vehicle of knowledge globalisation. Especially movements of natural persons, e.g. migration or studying and working abroad are very effective means of knowledge transfer. Likewise, cross-border knowledge and R&D networks are extremely useful in creating new knowledge, as the fast development of a Covid-19 vaccine has demonstrated.

From a more practical point of view, Fu and Ghauri (2021) provide a useful differentiation of five different modes of trade in intellectual property:

- **Licensing and franchising**. This can be related to a patented technology and business model but also to a brand, and specialised know-how.
- **Intellectual services**. In this category fall the provision of knowledge to individuals and organisations, including consultancy and training.
- **Foreign direct investment**. FDI exposes foreigners directly to new technologies and business practices which can create massive learning-by-doing effects. Yet, ownership can be used to control and restrict knowledge transfer.
- **Outsourcing**. Involving other companies participating in a value chain can lead to important know-how spillovers, especially regarding the increasing outsourcing of intangibles.

- **Globalisation of R&D**. International research collaboration and the establishment of cross-border research networks are, in fact, creating knowledge spillovers prima facie.

3.2 Knowledge transfer and intellectual property rights

From the perspective of an innovating company the transfer of knowledge is a double-edged sword. On the one hand, selling know-how has increasingly become a major source of income, hence generating direct benefits. There can also be indirect beneficial effects. More widely-spread knowledge can boost productivity and income in the receiving economy, and may thus contribute to a higher demand for the innovating companies' products. On the other hand, the company's monopoly position could be eroded.

This raises two questions: first, how strongly should intellectual property rights (IPR) be protected and, second, how should a global IPR system be designed?

3.2.1 How strongly should IPRs be protected?

To be frank, there is no consensus about the right degree of IPR protection. To start with, IPR protection has to strike a delicate balance. On the one hand, it should provide sufficient protection from competition to stimulate innovation. On the other hand, this protection should at some point cease, to allow enough competition to make the innovation available to customers at affordable prices (technology diffusion), and second, to incentivise new innovations. Hence, the key task is to design an IPR system that is favourable to productivity by stimulating both innovation and technology diffusion.

However, the evidence for a link between IPR protection, on the one hand, and innovation and productivity, on the other hand, is weak. Boldrin and Levine (2013: 3) point to the case of the US and its "patent puzzle":

> in spite of the enormous increase in the number of patents and in the strength of their legal protection, the US economy has seen neither a dramatic acceleration in the rate of technological progress nor a major increase in the levels of research and development expenditure.

Instead, the authors point to historical and international evidence that weak patent systems may be more supportive to innovation that stronger ones, and suggest that a competitive environment may be more stimulative than government-granted temporary technology monopolies.

The major conclusion that can be drawn from this evidence is a **need to review the effectiveness of current IPR protection**.[6] Unsurprisingly, while the quoted authors are in favour of less strict patent laws, innovating companies typically lobby for more IPR protection.

3.2.2 How should a global IPR system be designed?

The yardstick for evaluating IPR regimes is ultimately the well-being of people and not of an individual company. From a global perspective, this implies that a global IPR regime should serve the well-being of the entire world.

On the one hand, catching up in technology is key for catching up in per-capita income, especially in emerging and low-income economies (see Chapter 2). These positive effects from technology spillovers have to be weighed against the potential losses from lower rates of innovation because of lower incentives that may come with less IPR protection. However, lower innovation rates may not even materialise for three reasons:

- First, if the Boldrin and Levine (2013) results hold not only for the US but generally, the case for IPRs may be less strong than commonly assumed.
- Second, Eugster et al. (2018) find a positive effect of increased competition from emerging market firms on innovation.
- Third, when countries build on a Western company's knowledge – in fact many Chinese patents are extending on Western patents, often adding incremental changes to adapt a technology to local circumstances – the original innovator may also benefit from this. As we have seen before, global knowledge flows increasingly involve emerging economies in a bi- or even multi-directional way.

Regarding global IPR protection, the Agreement on *Trade-Related Aspects of Intellectual Property Rights* (TRIPS), is the relevant regulatory framework. If the above arguments on the positive effects of free(er) global knowledge flows, and the limited effectiveness of too strong patent laws are correct, it may well be that the current TRIPS agreement is too strict, as argued, for example by Boldrin and Levine (2013) and Baker, Jayadev and Stiglitz (2017). By contrast, many advanced countries are pressing for stricter rules and enforcement of IPR (see European Perspective 5.3).

EUROPEAN PERSPECTIVE 5.3

Intellectual property rights and European trade policy

Protection of IPRs is a key area of the EU's trade policy. In the words of the EU's trade policy website*, the EU "seeks to improve the protection and enforcement of intellectual property rights in third countries". Key elements are:

- A new revised "Strategy for the Enforcement of Intellectual Property Rights" in the Third Countries.

- Strong support of multilateral agreements, especially TRIPS.
- Inclusion of IPR chapters in bilateral trade agreements to "achieve similar levels of protection to that of the EU. Yet the EU does take into account the level of development of the country concerned".

* See https://ec.europa.eu/trade/policy/accessing-markets/intellectual-property/.

While it beyond the scope of this introduction to review the debate on TRIPS here in detail, two areas shall be highlighted where a free(er) flow of knowledge to developing countries might be particularly beneficial – health and environment. Fighting pandemics and reducing carbon emissions, both have high positive global repercussion effects. For both, timely and comprehensive access to new technologies is key.

4 The future of global intangibles

Intangibles have for a long time been dominating production in advanced countries. Increasingly, investments are also in intangibles, such as knowledge, and may change the way economies work (Haskel & Westlake, 2018).

With respect to the globalisation of intangibles, it appears that if there will be a fourth wave, commercial services, data, and knowledge will be the key drivers. Given their very specific features, the challenge for the emerging NGE is designing rules and regulations to deal with global intangibles in a mutually beneficial way. While there in no consensus on the details, most observers nevertheless agree that the current rules need to be made fit for purpose. To what extent this has best been done at the global, regional, or national levels is the subject of Chapter 7.

Recommended readings

For a general discussion of the rising role of intangibles, see Haskel and Westlake (2018). Baldwin (2019) argues the case for a new globalisation based on digitally-enabled services. The WTO's (2019) *World Trade Report* provides an in-depth analysis of the role of services in global trade.

Useful information and analysis can be found on the websites of World Intellectual Property Organisation (wipo.int), the World Trade Organisation (wto.org), and the United Nations Conference on Trade and Development (unctad.org).

Notes

1 See Baldwin and Forslid (2019) for an insightful analysis of the Indian service export industry.

2 Such a shape of the smile curve is not important for the argument here. For the case of inverted smile curve, e.g. in the automobile industry, see Chapter 2.
3 The role of labour-replacing versus labour-productivity enhancing new technologies is discussed in detail in Chapter 2.
4 Total patent applications include direct applications in the home country and under the Patent Cooperation Treaty (PCT). PCT is a treaty with more than 150 Contracting States, which makes it possible to seek patent protection in a large number of countries by means of a single application.
5 The discussion follows Ricardo Hausman from the Growth Lab of the Center for International Development at Harvard University, explaining key concepts of the Atlas of Economic Complexity in a number of highly recommended videos, available at https://atlas.cid.harvard.edu/key-concepts.
6 This classic argument for patents and technology policy needs a few qualifications in the reality of the NGE. First, as patents are public and often give detailed descriptions, a potential imitator can use them to invent something similar but distinct enough to not violate the patent. For this reason, companies often chose not to patent innovation that they find crucial. Second, especially for minor innovation, e.g. for processes that are complementary to a new product and its production, there is a tendency to have them all patented to make imitation more difficult or costly.

References

Acemoglu, D., & Restrepo, P. (2020).The wrong kind of AI? Artificial intelligence and the future of labour demand. *Cambridge Journal of Regions, Economy and Society, 13*(1), 25–35.

Arrieta-Ibarra, I., Goff, L., Jiménez-Hernández, D., Lanier, J., & Weyl, E. G. (2018). Should we treat data as labor? Moving beyond "free." *AEA Papers and Proceedings, 108*, 38–42.

Autor, D., Dorn, D., Katz, L. F., Patterson, C., & Van Reenen, J. (2020). The fall of the labor share and the rise of superstar firms. *The Quarterly Journal of Economics, 135*(2), 645–709.

Baker, D., Jayadev, A., & Stiglitz, J. (2017). Innovation, intellectual property, and development: a better set of approaches for the 21st century. *AccessIBSA: Innovation & access to medicines in India, Brazil & South Africa*, July, 1–90. http://cepr.net/images/stories/reports/baker-jayadev-stiglitz-innovation-ip-development-2017-07.pdf.

Baldwin, R. (2019). *The globotics upheaval: Globalisation, robotics and the future of work.* Oxford University Press.

Baldwin, R., & Forslid, R. (2020). *Globotics and development: When manufacturing is jobless and services are tradable.* NBER Working Paper 26731. National Bureau of Economic Research.

Boldrin, M., & Levine, D. K. (2013). The case against patents. *Journal of Economic Perspectives, 27*(1), 3–22.

Ebeke, C., Frie, J. M., & Rabier, L. (2019). Deepening the EU's Single Market for Services. IMF Working Paper 19/269. International Monetary Fund.

Eugster, J., Ho, G., Jaumotte, F., & Piazza, R. (2018). How knowledge spreads. *Finance and Development, 55*(3), 52–55.

Haskel, J., & Westlake, S. (2018). *Capitalism without capital: The rise of intangible economy.* Princeton University Press.

IMF. (2018). *World Economic Outlook.* April 2018. International Monetary Fund.

Fu, X., & Ghauri, P. (2021). Trade in intangibles and the global trade imbalance. *World Economy*, *44*(5), 1448–1469.

Krugman, P. R. (2020). Notes on Globalisation and Slowbalization, November. www.gc.cuny.edu/CUNY_GC/media/LISCenter/pkrugman/Notes-on-globalisation-and-slowbalization.pdf.

UNCTAD (2017). *World investment report 2017.* United Nations Conference on Trade and Development.

UNCTAD (2020). *World investment report 2017.* United Nations Conference on Trade and Development.

WTO (2019). *World trade report 2019.* World Trade Organisation.

6

GLOBAL MONEY AND FINANCE

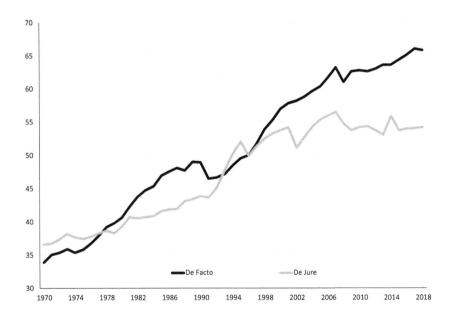

FIGURE 6.1 De Facto and De Jure Financial Globalisation.
Source: Own graph based on KOF Globalisation Index 2020 data. For a description of the index see Gygli et al. (2019).

From the 1970s until the great financial crisis (GFC) of 2008–2009 international finance globalised fast. Especially in the 1990s, global finance was rapidly liberalised. National monies became internationally convertible, mostly at market determined exchange rates, and cross-border banking and finance soared. However, over time the incidence of financial crises also increased, mostly in

DOI: 10.4324/9781003057611-6

emerging economies, but finally also affected advanced countries in the GFC. In consequence, re-regulation of global finance is back on the agenda (Figure 6.1). This chapter explores the workings of global money and finance, and the particular role of the design of the international monetary and financial system (IMFS) in the costs and benefits of globalising money and finance. It finishes with scrutinising the potential impact of digitalisation on the IMFS.

1 A very short history of global money and finance

Why do we need to talk about global money and finance? The simple and first answer is that we need an internationally accepted means of payments to conduct international trade, at least if we do not want to resort to barter trade.

In times before paper money existed – roughly until the end of the 19th century – all money was metallic. Consequently, there was only one money in which all transactions were made, gold. Hence, no exchange rates existed.[1]

With the emergence of nation states in the late 19th century, paper money was introduced. However, this money was fully backed by gold reserves and came with the promise of full convertibility into gold. As each country fixed the value of its paper money to gold, the exchange rates between their paper monies were also automatically fixed. A system of fixed exchange rates emerged – the *gold standard*. To ensure that the value of all monies was equal everywhere, complete freedom of capital movements had to be established. The core period of the gold standard between 1880 and 1914 was therefore also the first period of globalisation of capital.

In the interwar period, nation states became inward-looking, cross-border trade and finance were restricted, and the world economy disintegrated. Ultimately, economic disintegration culminated in the Second World War (WWII). Already in July 1944, before the end of WWII, the allied nations met in Bretton Woods, USA, to design the post-war international monetary order. The basic idea was to re-establish **fixed exchange rates** but without the shortcomings of the gold standard. The US dollar became the means of international payments. However, for most of the time that the *Bretton Woods System* (BWS) existed, cross-border capital mobility remained rather limited, as many nation states had capital controls in place. In 1971, the dollar came under attack because of high inflation in the US. As a result, the BWS was de facto abandoned and it gave way to market-determined exchange rates.

Flexible exchange rates stimulated the demand for some kind of insurance against exchange rate fluctuations. Among others, financial markets created the possibility to sell and buy currency not only 'on the spot' but also in advance on so-called future markets. Most currencies of advanced countries took the final steps towards full convertibility, also allowing the trade of foreign exchange in unlimited amounts for cross-border financial transactions. The Bretton Woods world of limited capital mobility gave way to the rapid globalisation of finance from the 1970s onward. In the 1990s and 2000s, free capital mobility and deregulated financial markets became the mantra of advanced countries. Eager to benefit from a globalising capital market, many emerging market economies also opened-up financially. Hence, de jure financial globalisation pushed cross-border finance even further.

While many countries moved to flexible exchange rates, Europe established a *European Monetary System* (EMS) of fixed exchange rates in 1979, reflecting its preference for fixed exchange rates to promote European integration. In 1999, the EMS gave way to the *European Monetary Union* (EMU), which combined unrestricted capital flows with irrevocably fixed exchange rates in the *Eurozone*, i.e., the countries which adopted the common currency, thus using only one common money, the euro.

In 2008–2009, the global financial system nearly collapsed. Shortly after the GFC, EMU came into rough waters. As a consequence, re-regulation of finance at the national, regional, and global levels is back on the agenda since then.

2 Global money and finance and the nation state

Only few countries can pay for imports with their own money. Under the BWS, the US had this privilege, and even nowadays the dollar is still dominating international invoicing. For such a country, imbalances of payments with the rest of the world can in principle be covered by printing money. To be sure, the euro's role in the global markets is increasing, and China has aspirations to make the renminbi an international currency. Yet, both have to take care, like most other nation states, about their *balance of payments* (BOP).

2.1 Understanding the balance of payments

The BOP of a country is, in its core, comparable to the balance of payments of an individual. From economic activities, you receive payments for working (wages) and investing (interest payments and dividends), from a pension or a study grant, and, if needed, from a loan. On the other hand, you make payments for your daily expenses, for investments, supporting relatives, and so on. If the received payments match the payments made, you enjoy a BOP equilibrium. If the inflowing payments exceed the outflows, you experience a surplus, which allows you to pile-up reserves. However, when your payment outflows exceed the inflows, you need to have enough reserves to finance your deficit. In case you do not have enough reserves, you may experience a BOP crisis. It forces you to either reduce your outflows, i.e., to spend less, or to increase your inflows, e.g. work longer hours. This is called a BOP adjustment. It is needed, especially when no creditor is willing anymore to lend you money.

A BOP for an individual would record the change in reserves from the difference of payment inflows and outflow. For a country, the BOP records inflows and outflows of foreign exchange (FX) to calculate the change (Δ) in FX reserves as shown by equation (6.1a):

$$\Delta FX\ Reserves = FX\ Inflow - FX\ Outflow \tag{6.1a}$$

$$\Delta FX\ Reserves = (+Exports - Imports) + (Capital\ Imports \\ - Capital\ Exports) \tag{6.1b}$$

$$\Delta FX\ Reserves = Current\ Account + Capital\ Account \tag{6.1c}$$

A country's BOP is recorded on a monthly, quarterly, and yearly basis to get timely information about the payments situation. However, like individuals, countries want to know more about where payments are coming from and where there are going to. This is where double-entry bookkeeping comes in. While on the left-hand side of equation (6.1b), we record the FX inflows and outflows to calculate the net change of reserves, on the right-hand side, we additionally record for what foreign exchange has been used or where it is coming from. Here we differentiate, grossly speaking, between trade and finance. Regarding trade, foreign exchange is earned by exports (hence they enter with a plus sign) and spent on imports (hence they enter with a minus sign). On the finance side, we differentiate between capital inflows and outflows.

However, in (6.1b) the labels exports and imports stand for a broader group of cross-border transactions that constitute the *current account* (CA): exports and imports of merchandise goods, which are recorded in the *trade balance*; exports and imports of services, recorded in the *service balance*; factor income (wages, profits, interest payments) received from or paid to abroad recorded in the *income balance*; and a *transfer balance*, which reports unrequited cross-border transfers, such as grants or contributions to international organisations. The *capital account* (KA) records all financial inflows and outflows, such as foreign direct investments, portfolio investments, and cross-border banking lending and borrowing. Hence, the balance of payments, i.e., the change of FX reserves, aka *overall balance*, is given by the sum of current account and capital account, as defined in equation (6.1c).

To get an idea of how the BOP is reported and what insights can be gained, Table 6.1 replicates a summary table on China's BOP. Usually, a BOP is reported in US dollars, but to put the developments into perspective we report the data in percentages of China's gross domestic product (GDP). The data show that the country's current account surplus was shrinking between 2014 and 2019. The trade balance remained positive but the surplus fell sharply in 2018. However, the service balance remained negative over the whole period, as did the income balance since 2015. The latter may have to do with repatriated profits of multinational companies operating in China.

Turning to the capital account, it should first be noted that International Monetary Fund (IMF) statistics speak of the *financial account*, while the term capital account is reserved for certain other activities that result in wealth transfers between countries but do not belong to the former ones, such as bequests. Mostly, the numbers are very small, in the case of China basically zero.[2] In this financial account (in our terminology the KA), we observe strong negative results in 2015 and 2016. This appears to be driven by a surge of China's outward overseas

TABLE 6.1 China Balance of Payments (in Percent of GDP), 2014–2018

	2014	2015	2016	2017	2018
Current account balance	**2.2**	**2.7**	**1.7**	**1.7**	**0.3**
Trade balance	4.1	5.1	4.3	4.0	2.9
Exports	*21.3*	*19.1*	*17.7*	*18.4*	*18.0*
Imports	*17.2*	*14.0*	*13.4*	*14.4*	*15.1*
Service balance	−2.0	−1.9	−2.1	−2.1	−2.2
Income balance	0.1	−0.4	−0.4	−0.1	−0.4
Current transfers	0.0	−0.1	−0.1	−0.1	0.0
Capital and financial account balance	**−0.5**	**−3.9**	**−3.6**	**0.9**	**1.0**
Capital account	0.0	0.0	0.0	0.0	0.0
Financial account	−0.5	−3.9	−3.6	0.9	1.0
Net foreign direct investment	1.3	0.6	−0.3	0.3	0.8
Foreign direct investment	*2.5*	*2.2*	*1.6*	*1.4*	*1.5*
Overseas direct investment	*−1.2*	*−1.6*	*−1.9*	*−1.1*	*−0.7*
Portfolio investment	0.8	−0.6	−0.5	0.2	0.8
Other investment	−2.6	−3.9	−2.8	0.4	−0.6
Errors and omissions	**−0.6**	**−1.9**	**−2.0**	**−1.8**	**−1.2**
Overall balance (=change in reserves)	**1.1**	**−3.1**	**−3.9**	**0.8**	**0.1**

Source: Own table based on Table 2 in IMF (2019: 51). A few numbers differ slightly from those reported by the IMF because of rounding errors.

investments, but also by high net outflows in the category "other investments". It seems that wealthy Chinese individuals and corporations tried to siphon money out of the country, partly in expectation of the devaluation of the renminbi in August 2015, and the continuous decline its value thereafter. Towards the end of 2016, the Chinese authorities imposed a number of capital controls to prevent these outflows. As can be seen from the 2017 and 2018 data, a turnaround has been achieved. To what extent this was due to the controls is another issue.

In principle, the current account and − in the new terminology − the sum of capital and financial account should give the overall balance, which indicates the change in official reserves. However, there is often a gap between what is reported to the authorities and the actual change in foreign reserves. For example, in 2016, based on reported data, the Chinese central bank would have expected a decrease in foreign reserves amounting to 1.9% of GDP. In fact, a reduction of about 3.9% was recorded. Since the sources of this gap are unclear, this amount is allocated to a balancing entry, tellingly called "errors and omissions".

2.2 Current account and capital account interdependencies

The definition of the BOP (6.1) shows that current account, capital account, and overall balance are closely interlinked. To understand the economics behind it, Table 6.2 illustrates three archetypical BOP positions. To start with, imagine a

TABLE 6.2 Examples of Balance of Payments Positions

$\varDelta$ Forex Reserves =	Current Account +	Capital Account
+50	+50	0
+5	+50	−45
+2	−30	+32

country running a current account surplus of 50. If this country does not engage in financial cross-border transactions, foreign reserves increase by exactly 50.

Does this make sense? First, piling up huge amounts of foreign reserves entails the risk of a declining value of the reserve currency, and second, the reserves could better be invested into interest-bearing assets or companies abroad. China is a case in point. When running huge trade surpluses in the 1980s, foreign exchange inflows were largely used to increase US-dollar reserves. In the 1990s, China started to invest in US government bonds and became one of the largest foreign US-bond holders. Later, China diversified its international investments geographically, and its sovereign wealth funds as well as Chinese corporations started to invest in companies abroad, not least to get access to foreign technologies. Such a case is shown in the second example. We conclude from this that a current account surplus typically goes hand-in-hand with a capital account deficit.

Vice versa, this implies that a current account deficit typically requires a capital account surplus. In case a country has enough foreign reserves, it could finance a current account deficit by running down the reserves. However, countries with access to international financial markets can finance the deficit with capital imports. In our example, the country has been able to attract a net inflow of 32, which even allows to increase foreign reserves a bit. As an example, take the US, which for most of the recent time has been running current account deficits. Because the US is considered a safe haven by international investors, it could easily finance the deficit by capital inflows. Likewise, developing countries with an 'investment grade' often use foreign finance for development investments.

In an interdependent world, some countries can only run current account deficits when other countries run a surplus. Subsequently, surplus countries ultimately finance deficit countries. Figure 6.2 shows the development of the US current account deficit and contrasts it with the sum of the current account surplus of China, Germany, and Japan, the major surplus countries in the world. In the first half of the 1980s, Germany and Japan were mainly financing the US deficit. In the 2000s, China (for which data is available only from 1997 onward) became an important source of funds, too (see also European Perspective 6.1).

With the euro crisis starting in 2010, financial flows to southern Eurozone countries dried up, and ultimately forced GIPS countries to run current account surpluses. As a consequence, the Eurozone as a whole started to run current account surpluses.

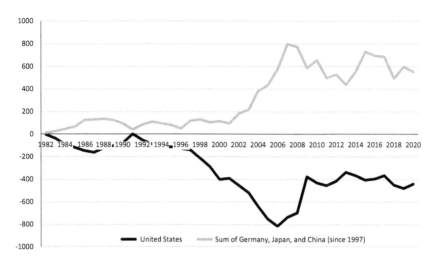

FIGURE 6.2 Current Account Balances (in Billion US$), 1982–2020.

Source: Own graph based on data from the IMF World Economic Outlook Database, October 2020. 2020 data are estimates.

EUROPEAN PERSPECTIVE 6.1

Current account imbalances in the Eurozone

Before the introduction of the euro in 1999, current account balances in the Eurozone were rather small. The arrival of the common currency reduced the

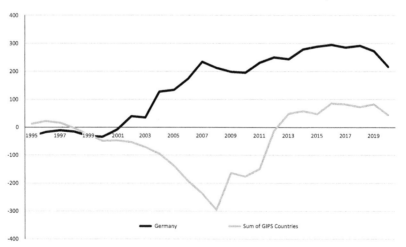

FIGURE EP 6.1 Current Account Balances in Billion US Dollar, Germany and the Sum of Greece, Italy, Portugal and Spain (GIPS), 1999–2020.

Source: Own graph based on data from the IMF World Economic Outlook Database, October 2020. 2020 data are estimates.

borrowing costs for southern European countries considerably, and induced an investment boom and fast growth in many of these countries. Imports soared and current account deficits increased. In the first half of the 2000s, Germany was the 'sick man of Europe', with an ailing economy, low imports, and a huge current account surplus. German banks channelled German savings to governments (especially Greece) and (real estate) investors in other southern European countries. The combined deficit of the so-called GIPS countries (Greece, Italy, Portugal, and Spain) became almost a mirror image of the German surplus, which in turn was the mirror image of lending from Germany to the GIPS.

2.3 What is behind current account imbalances?

From the very fact that a country's current account surplus requires deficits elsewhere, it is obvious that especially large imbalances can cause international tensions. For example, the huge surpluses of Germany in the 2010s, occasionally exceeding 8% of GDP, led to calls to reduce this surplus. Likewise, huge deficits are also causing concern as they may result in a payment crisis. What makes the political debate difficult, is that a current account imbalance simultaneously reflects two different circumstances: spending behaviour and competitiveness.

Consider **national spending behaviour** first. A current account surplus, such as in Germany, is ultimately the result of spending less than producing, which allows to export more than to import. Hence, a call to reduce a surplus is a request to spend and import more. Conversely, a current account deficit mirrors overspending. Hence, for reducing deficits spending reduction is required.

In economic terms, a country with a current account surplus saves more than it invests. Hence, it provides savings for the rest of the world, namely to deficit countries, which invest more than they save. If we differentiate between the private and public sectors, the so-called *macroeconomic accounting identity* says that the current account position reflects the excess of private savings over private investments, plus a government budget surplus, i.e., an excess of tax revenues over public spending, as indicated in equation (6.2)[3]:

$$Current\ Account \equiv \left(Private\ Savings - Private\ Investments\right) + \left(Taxes - Government\ Spending\right) \tag{6.2}$$

This accounting identity is very useful for understanding the sources of current account imbalances (see European Perspective 6.2). To put it in simple terms, a current account surplus (deficit) reflects:

- an underspending (overspending) of the private sector; or
- a government budget surplus (deficit); or
- both.

EUROPEAN PERSPECTIVE 6.2

Anatomy of current account balances in the Eurozone in 2007

What was behind current account imbalances in the Eurozone in 2007, the year before the open outbreak of the GFC? Let's consider three key countries to highlight the major differences.

Germany was running a CA surplus amounting to 6.9% of GDP. As the government budget was nearly balanced, the surplus mainly reflected an excess of private savings over investments.

Spain's deficit of 9.4% of GDP was the mirror image of an excess of private investment, especially into real estate, over private savings. In fact, this excess was even higher than the CA deficit because the government had a budget surplus of 1.9% of GDP.

By contrast, the enormous Greek CA deficit of 13.9% was the almost equally shared responsibility of an overspending public and private sector. It is noteworthy, though, that in 2010, when the real Greek fiscal situation was revealed, a government deficit of 11.2% of GDP was more than dominating the CA deficit of 10%.*

* All data is based on IMF, World Economic Outlook Database, October 2020.

Since a major part of the current account is trade in goods and services, **international competitiveness** is the second main factor behind a country's current account. Hence, calls for reducing a surplus are often taken as an attack on 'our export competitiveness'. Economists measure international price competitiveness by the so-called *real exchange rate*. We will discuss it in more detail in the next section.

3 Understanding exchange rates

Exchange rates connect national monies. Figure 6.3 depicts the development of the dollar–euro exchange rate, i.e., the price of one euro in US dollars. It shows substantial and often very volatile changes over time. If exchange rates move like this, they may have considerable effects on price competitiveness. Yet, on average, the euro seems to revolve over some kind of a long-term slightly upward trend, indicated here for illustrative purposes by a trend range around a simple trend line.

How to measure the exchange rate and its impact on price competitiveness? What are the major determinants of exchange rate developments? And what

FIGURE 6.3 The Dollar/Euro Exchange Rate, 1999–2020.
Source: Own graph based on data obtained from ECB Statistical Data Warehouse (https://sdw.ecb.europa.eu/). The rate shown is the ECB reference exchange rate (monthly average of observations through period). Data code: 120.EXR.M.USD.EUR.SP00.

happens if we do not allow the exchange rate to move by means of pegging it to another currency, as it has been the case of the BWS and EMS?

3.1 Nominal and real exchange rate

3.1.1 The nominal exchange rate

When speaking about the exchange rate, people typically mean the *nominal exchange rate*, i.e., the rate at which domestic money can be converted into foreign currency. The nominal exchange rate (e) is a relative price, defined as the price of a foreign currency in terms of the domestic currency. Equation (6.3a) illustrates this definition with a euro–dollar exchange rate of 0.8. This is the standard definition, and people in most countries understand exchange rates like this. Interestingly, maybe because the euro was introduced only in 1999, in the Eurozone the euro is mostly quoted as a foreign currency, as indicated in equation (6.3b), with 'w' being the inverse of 'e'.

$$e = 0.8€/1\$ \tag{6.3a}$$
$$w = 1/e = 1.25\$/1€ \tag{6.3b}$$

Figure 6.3, based on European Central Bank (ECB) data, also uses definition (6.3b). Hence, an increase in the dollar–euro rate (w) signifies a stronger euro and, thus, a weaker dollar (lower e). Conversely, a stronger dollar (higher e) implies a weaker euro (lower w).

When speaking about exchange rates it is therefore important to be clear which definition is being used. For example, an appreciation of the foreign currency (a higher e) makes our goods relatively cheaper and will thus tend to increase exports and lower imports. This is so, because our currency (w) is now cheaper. Conversely, an appreciation of our currency, makes our goods more expensive for foreigner and will thus lead to less exports and more imports.

3.1.2 The real exchange rate

While the nominal exchange rate influences how much people have to pay for foreign goods and services in terms of the domestic currency, it does not take into account the prices of these goods at home and abroad. Yet, for the decision to buy at home or abroad theses prices also matter.

The *real exchange rate* (RER) takes the prices at home and abroad into account. It can therefore provide information on price competitiveness of a country, as shown in equation (6.4a).

$$RER = \frac{e \star Foreign\ Prices}{Home\ Prices} = \frac{eP^\star}{P} = \frac{\frac{0.8\$}{1€} \star 5\$}{4€} = \frac{4€}{4€} = 1 \tag{6.4a}$$

Take the example of one product that is homogenous around the world, the Big Mac. If the sandwich costs 5\$ in the US and 4€ in the Eurozone, and the actual nominal exchange rate (e) is 0.8€/1\$, the US burger would cost a European also 4€. In this case we speak of **purchasing power parity** (PPP). The RER takes then a value of 1.

If the European price is higher, say 5€, European burgers would be 20% more expensive than American ones. A RER of 4€/5€, equalling 0.8 would indicate then a 20% overvaluation of the euro vis-à-vis the dollar, at least if we chose PPP in Big Macs as the benchmark for competitive exchange rates. Such a misalignment would be diagnosed whenever the nominal exchange rate is different from a *PPP exchange rate* that equates home and foreign prices. In our case, when a Eurozone burger cost 5€, the PPP rate would be achieved at $e_{PPP} = 1€/1\$$, a 20% higher price for the dollar. Or to put it the other way round, a 20% cheaper euro would make the Eurozone competitive again.

How to measure prices?

The Economist has famously introduced the 'Burger Standard' many years ago, to provide a simple and swiftly available indicator for exchange rate over- and undervaluation. However, price competitiveness of an economy concerns all goods that are tradable. Hence, instead of burger prices a measure of the average price level in economies should be employed. The consumer price index (CPI) is often used because it is available for practically all countries. However, it includes many non-traded goods such as housing rents, haircuts, and restaurant meals. A better alternative would therefore be a wholesale price index because everything that can be wholesaled can also be traded. Other often-used alternatives are

FIGURE 6.4 Nominal and Real Effective Exchange Rate of Eurozone Countries Against 19 Trading Partners, 1999–2020.

Source: Own graph based on data obtained from ECB Statistical Data Warehouse (https://sdw. ecb.europa.eu/). Data codes are NEER: EXR.M.E5.EUR.EN00.A, REER: EXR.M.E5. EUR.ERP0.A. NEER and REER are measured as monthly averages with 1999 Q1 = 100.

indices of unit labour costs and producer prices (PPI), which give a good indication of production costs, and thus price competitiveness.

Development of competitiveness over time

The real exchange rate, calculated with price or cost indices, is more difficult to interpret than the Burger Standard. Hence, indices are calculated to show price or cost developments starting from a base year with a value set at 100.[4]

Figure 6.4 shows the development of the Eurozone's price competitiveness from 1999 to 2020 vis-à-vis 19 major trading partners. This is the so-called *real effective exchange rate* (REER), which is calculated as a weighted average against major trading partners (rather than vis-à-vis one trading partner only). The REER shown in the graph is based on producer prices. For comparison, the figure also includes the weighted average of the nominal exchange rates vis-à-vis these 19 countries, the *nominal effective exchange rate* (NEER). For reading the graph, note that the ECB data is defined as such that an increase means an appreciation of the euro in both nominal and real terms (like w in definition (6.3b)). A higher REER means therefore a loss in price competitiveness.

These REER developments provide some important insights:

- The REER follows closely the NEER developments. Hence, as the euro lost value shortly after its introduction in 1999, this resulted in an almost one-to-one improved price competitiveness. Likewise, the later rise of the euro until the GFC directly caused a loss in competitiveness.

- After the GFC, Eurozone price competitiveness improved by more than movements of the nominal exchange rates suggest. In particular, during the euro crisis, inflation in the Eurozone remained below that of their major trading partners.
- The development of the REER reveals how difficult it is to make a judgement about purchasing power parity, and thus about price competitiveness. If the Eurozone had had PPP with its trading partners in 1999, then we would still diagnose a price advantage in 2020. For this, the interpretation speaks that the Eurozone had a 2% current account surplus in 2020. By contrast, in 2003 and 2005 the CA was nearly balanced when the REER was close to 100. This suggests that PPP could be around the index number of 100, probably with an error margin of some 3%–5% or so.

For a quick check of changes in competitiveness, one can use the *relative version* of the RER, which is quite handy. Equation (6.4a) can easily be transformed into a version using percentage rates of change (g) as shown by equation (6.4b).[5]

$$g_{RER} = g_e + g_{P\star} - g_P \tag{6.4b}$$

The interpretation is straightforward. A country gains in price competitiveness when:

- the value of the foreign currency increase (a higher e, implying a depreciation of the home currency);
- foreign inflation increases;
- home inflation decreases.

Just consider three cases with real-world significance:

- If domestic inflation equals foreign inflation, price competitiveness is entirely driven by the nominal exchange rate. The case is important because inflation rates are often very similar in many advanced countries.
- Inflation differentials do not need to cause competitiveness problems if the exchange rate adjusts accordingly. For example, a 2% higher inflation at home can be compensated with a 2% depreciation of the domestic currency. As we will see below, exchange rate theory posits that in the long-run exchange rates will be driven by inflation differentials, and hence, restore competitiveness.
- If domestic exceeds foreign inflation, by say 2%, and the exchange rate does not change, home will suffer a 2% loss in price competitiveness. The case is of particular relevance in case exchange rates are (irrevocably) fixed (see European Perspective 6.3).

EUROPEAN PERSPECTIVE 6.3

Price competitiveness within the Eurozone

As all member countries have adopted the euro, there are no exchange rates within the Eurozone. As a consequence, differences in inflation rates directly influence price competitiveness. Especially in the period from 1999 to 2010, German prices increased in this period by only 11%, while they rose in Spain by 39%, in Greece by 37%, in Portugal by 35%, in Ireland by 25%, and even in France by 21%.* Germany became hypercompetitive within the Eurozone, while especially southern Eurozone countries increasingly faced competitiveness problems. As a consequence, the current account balance of Germany improved, while it deteriorated in the other countries.

* Own calculations using the GDP deflator as a measure of inflation as reported by the IMF World Economic Outlook database.

When exchange rates are free to move, there is no guarantee that price competitiveness is ensured, especially in the short run. As exchange rates can have an enormous impact on a country's competitiveness, it is useful to understand the basics of exchange rate theories.

3.2 A brief introduction to exchange rate theories

What determines the value of a currency? If exchange rates are allowed to move freely, they are market-determined **flexible exchange rates**. Hence, exchange rate moves reflect changes in the supply and demand for the foreign currency. From BOP accounting we know where supply and demand is coming from: from export and import of goods, services, and factor services, and capital imports and exports, to mention only the major items.

Economists advocate two exchange rate theories, depending on the type of the cross-border activities. Cross-border trade reacts to differences in prices across countries. Arbitrage will thus drive the exchange rate until *purchasing power parity* is reached. However, finding out about price differences, ordering, and finally delivering takes time. The full impact on the exchange rate may thus only be felt after some time. Trade is therefore considered a **long-run determinant**.

By contrast, financial transactions react fast to the smallest differences in returns on assets, which nowadays are arbitraged away in a fraction of a second, enforcing *interest rate parity*. Differences in asset returns are thus a major **short-run determinant**.

The development of an exchange rate over time can therefore be viewed as the interaction of finance-driven short-run movements and trade-driven long-run developments. To illustrate this, consider the period from approximately 2005 to 2008, when the euro appreciated sharply against the dollar. This implied a loss of price competitiveness for the Eurozone, which at some point will impact on the exchange rate and bring it back to a position where price competitiveness is more or less restored. Such a position may be somewhere in the shaded range, indicated in Figure 6.3. However, as discussed before, to determine which exchange rate (range) is in line with price competitiveness is quite difficult and requires more than calculating a simple trend, as we have done in the graph for illustrative purposes. In fact, we need some more theoretical backup.

3.2.1 The long run: purchasing power parity

In the long run, no country can forever be more expensive than another. Absent of trade restrictions, arbitrage processes would set in, and ultimately equalise the prices across countries. This is stated by the famous *law of one price* (LOOP), which defines purchasing power parity, namely that the domestic prices are equal to the foreign prices after converting them into domestic currency:

$$P = eP \star \tag{6.5}$$

The LOOP is a long-run proposal. If goods and services are relatively more expensive, exports will shrink and imports rise, thus ultimately increasing the value of the foreign currency until PPP is restored at an equilibrium exchange rate level e_{PPP}:

$$e_{PPP} = P/P \star \tag{6.6a}$$

The PPP theory as formulated above is quite strict in demanding full price equalisation. In reality, a myriad of trade costs, ranging from transportation costs to the cost for dealing with different languages to trade barriers exist.

Rather than this *absolute version*, a *relative version* of PPP exchange rate theory focusing on rate of changes can accommodate these concerns. The relative version simply posits that in the long run the foreign exchange rate follows the **inflation differentials**:

$$g_e = g_P - g_P\star \tag{6.6b}$$

The predictions are then straightforward. Two countries that have the same inflation rates should see their exchange rate being stable in the long run. Countries with relatively higher inflation will see the value of their currency falling by the same percentage point as the inflation differential. Economists therefore call inflation differentials 'the fundamentals'.

The relative version of the PPP theory helps to get an idea of the long-run directions an exchange rate may take. The rising trend for the euro value vis-à-vis the dollar, reflects to some extent that US inflation has exceeded inflation in the Eurozone. Again, while it is difficult to determine a PPP exchange rate exactly, the range indicated by the shaded area in Figure 6.3 may give a first idea where a PPP-compatible exchange rate could lie.

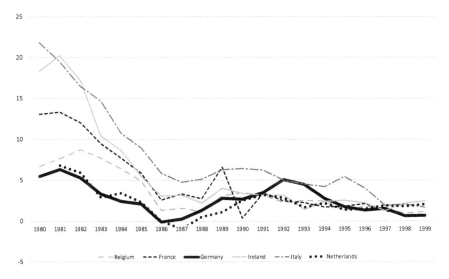

FIGURE 6.5 CPI-Inflation Convergence of Five Original EMS Member Countries, 1980–1999.

Source: Graph based on CPI data obtained from IMF World Economic Outlook Database, October 2020.

The relative version of the PPP theory of exchange rates has an important implication under **fixed exchange rates**. With fixed rates the exchange rate change g_e is zero. Equation (6.6c) then implies that in the long run, home and foreign inflation rates will converge:

$$g_P = g_{p^\star} \tag{6.6c}$$

The key reason for this convergence is that relatively higher inflation makes a country less competitive. This can lead to higher unemployment, and thus to a downward pressure on wage and price increases, and vice versa. Two examples illustrate the relevance of this mechanism:

- When inflation surged in the US in the late 1960, European countries imported inflation from the US because the US was the dominant economy in the BWS.
- In Europe, the creation of the EMS in 1979 brought inflation convergence of member countries. Germany became the anchor country whose low inflation rates the other countries 'imported' (see Figure 6.5).

3.2.2 The short run: interest rate parity

In a world of unrestricted capital flows, financial investors look for the highest returns for their investment. Thus, if domestic interest rates (i) are lower than foreign rates (i*), capital flows to the high interest rate country. This results in an appreciation of the foreign currency, i.e., a depreciation of the domestic currency.

However, investing abroad in foreign currency carries a currency risk: the sum invested abroad may be worth less when returning it home if the foreign currency loses value in the meantime.

Unrestricted arbitrage equalises the returns on investment at home and abroad. Yet, the return on an investment abroad needs to take into account the currency risk. This is stated by the *Uncovered Interest Parity* (UIP) condition:

$$i = i^* + \frac{e^{expected} - e}{e} \tag{6.7a}$$

Table 6.3 illustrates the implication of the UIP with some simple cases. In case 1, investors expect the value of the foreign currency not to change. Now assume a US bank (Foreign) would offer a 6% interest rate on a deposit, and a European bank (Home) only 4%. This would lead to an outflow of funds from Europe to the US. To attract funds, European banks raise interest rates, while US banks lower rates until interest rate parity is reached at, say 5%.

In case 2, investors believe that the dollar appreciates by 3%, e.g. from the current 0.8€/1$ to 0.824€/1$ (the price of a euro would then fall from 1.25 to 1.2136 dollars). A European investor who wants to make a 1,000$ deposit in the US now pays 800€ for buying 1,000$. When she exchanges the sum back after

TABLE 6.3 Cases Illustrating the Uncovered Interest Parity Condition

Case	Home Interest Rate $=$	Foreign Interest Rate $+$	Expected Appreciation of Foreign Currency	Country Risk Abroad $-$	Interpretation
1	5%	5%	0%	0%, or risk-neutral investors	Domestic interest rate equals foreign interest rate when no change of the exchange rate is expected
2	8%	5%	3%	0%, or risk-neutral investors	Home has to pay higher interest rates to keep capital at home when investors expect the value of the foreign currency to rise
3	1%	5%	−4%	0%, or risk-neutral investors	Home can pay lower interest rates as capital flows in from abroad when investors expect the value of the foreign currency to fall
4	6%	5%	3%	2%	Investing abroad is viewed as riskier than domestic investing. This allows lower interest rates at home
5	2%	1%	0%	−1%	A "convenience yield" allows a foreign safe haven to pay lower interest rates

one year, she receives 824€ for the invested sum, exactly 3% more. Add this to the 5% interest payment, and the dollar deposit offers a return of 8%, which European banks have to match.[6]

Case 3 showcases an expected dollar depreciation of 4%. A dollar deposit would thus have an expected return of only 1%. This allows Eurozone banks to pay lower interest rates, namely also 1%.

The key practical lesson from this is that interest rate differentials reflect exchange rate risks. Countries, whose currencies are expected to fall typically have to pay higher interest rates, and vice versa.

However, currency risks are not the only risks of an investment abroad. The foreign banking system may be fragile, exposing investors to losses in case of bankruptcies. Likewise, there may be a risk that the country introduces capital account restrictions that makes it impossible to return the invested sum home, or there might even be the risk of outright expropriation. If country risks abroad exceed those at home, this constitutes a *country risk premium*, which allows the home country to pay lower interest rates as indicated in case 4. While equation (6.7a) is correct whenever country risks are zero or investors are risk-neutral, equation (6.7b) gives the UIP when investors are risk averse.

$$i = i^* + \frac{e^{expected} - e}{e} - \text{Country Risk Premium} \tag{6.7b}$$

With respect to country risk, the US is special. It is considered by many investors as a safe haven. US treasury bonds are amongst the most favoured assets, especially in times of global financial instability. Jiang, Krishnamurthy and Lustig (2018) argue that international investors accept to forgo a sizeable return to own these assets, which they call the 'convenience yield'. It is essentially a negative country risk that allows the US treasury to pay lower interest rates. This situation is illustrated in case 5. In a similar vein, Germany is viewed as a safe haven since the outbreak of the Eurozone crisis, which allows Germany to issue government bonds with lower – at times even negative – interest rates.

What does arbitrage in financial markets imply for the exchange rate? With a bit of algebra, the UIP condition can be rearranged and solved for the exchange rate:

$$e_{UIP} = \frac{e^{expected}}{\left(1 + i - i^* + \text{Country Risk Premium}\right)} \tag{6.8}$$

The interpretation is straightforward. The foreign currency appreciates (e increases) in the following cases:

- An appreciation of the foreign currency is expected. This leads to higher net capital exports, the demand for the foreign currency increases, and thus its value. Exchange rate expectations can become a self-fulfilling prophecy.
- A decrease of domestic interest rates.
- An increase of foreign interest rates.

- A decrease of the country risk premium, either because it is getting less risky to invest abroad or riskier to invest at home. The GFC is a case in point: US treasury bonds became a safe haven, the convenience yield increased, and the dollar appreciated in foreign currency markets.

Under **fixed exchange rates**, full capital mobility implies interest rate convergence. Interest rates will either align fully as indicated by equation (6.9a), or partially if investors are risk averse (6.9b).

$$i = i^*$$ (6.9a)

$$i = i^* - \text{Country Risk Premium}$$ (6.9b)

Europe is again an interesting case in point. In 1992, the EU Single Market came into effect and capital became fully mobile. For members of the EMS, interest rates started to converge. Figure 6.6 shows the development of interest rates on 10-year debt securities. Already one year before the introduction of the euro in 1999, all interest rates of the initial member – Greece became a member only in 2002 – have almost fully converged (German rates are indicted by the bold black line). Earlier, some doubts about final membership in the Eurozone of the southern European countries, Italy, Spain, and Portugal, kept interest rates in these countries higher. Moreover, in the EMS, exchange rates of the mentioned countries were allowed to vary within a broader band after the EMS-crisis of 1992–1993.[7]

3.3 How useful are exchange rate theories?

Both theories, PPP and (risk adjusted) UIP provide valuable insights into how international monetary systems work, and why occasionally they can be subject to malfunctioning or financial crises, as discussed in the next sections.

However, using these theories for predicting exchange rates has not been very successful. In an influential article, Meese and Rogoff (1983) show that the simple prediction that tomorrow's exchange rate is the same as today's performed better than models that relate to macroeconomic variables like interest rates and prices.

A look again at the dollar–euro exchange rate in Figure 6.3 indeed reveals that exchange rates 'wander around extensively', as econometricians would put it. Yet, over a longer period of time exchange rates revert to the fundamentals. In fact, research has shown that the longer the time horizon of the prediction the better the theories work, i.e., over time, fundamental factors will become more relevant. In the long-run, exchange rates cannot ignore fundamental factors like price competitiveness altogether.

4 International monetary systems

When nation states create their own currency, they ultimately have to decide how to link their money to the monies of all other countries. Alternatively, one could create one global money for all countries. An intermediate solution is to

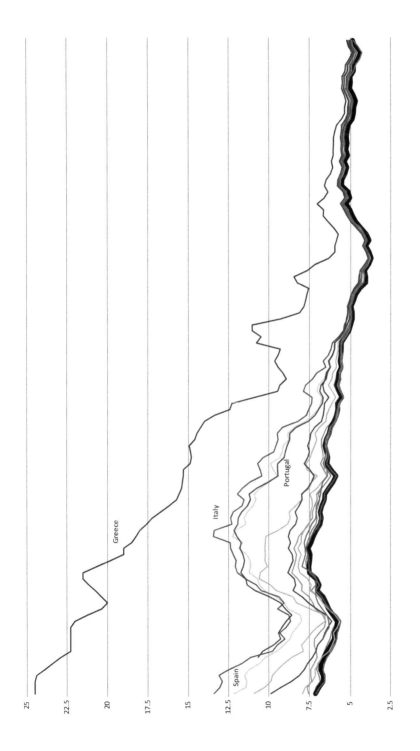

FIGURE 6.6 Interest Rate Convergence on 10-Year Debt Securities in EU12, 1993–2002.

Data source: European Central Bank: https://sdw.ecb.europa.eu/. Interest rates statistics: long-term interest rate for convergence purposes.

create a regional money for a group of countries, like the Europeans did with the introduction of the euro.

The design of monetary system has far-reaching consequences for both, the workings of the global economy and the well-being of nations and their citizens. A well-designed monetary system can as much promote a healthy global order as a poor designed or poorly managed monetary system can ultimately lead to global disorder, as the breakdown of the gold standard in the 1930s has demonstrated. In the following, we therefore scrutinise the workings of different international monetary systems.

4.1 Key elements of international monetary systems

International monetary systems need to address four key issues (see Table 6.4):

- **Convertibility**. Can national currencies be exchanged into other currencies? While today's major currencies are fully convertible, other currencies are often only convertible for certain purposes like trade, but not for cross-border financial transactions, i.e., they lack *capital-account convertibility*.
- **Exchange rate system (ERS)**. Are exchange rates fluctuating depending on demand and supply, or is the value of national currencies fixed against each other?
- **Liquidity system**. How to finance international transactions? Under the gold standard, this was, of course, gold. In the BWS, it was the US dollar. The current system is dominated by flexible exchange rates between the major currencies, which can all be used for international payments. However, the dollar is still the dominant currency for international invoicing.
- **Adjustment mechanism**. How to deal with BOP surpluses and deficits? Do both deficit and surplus countries have to adjust? After all, we have seen that one country can only have a deficit when another runs a surplus. Alternatively, some systems rely on asymmetric adjustment in deficit countries.

Historically, the gold standard was, after the interwar period, replaced by the BWS. Today we have a parallel of different monetary arrangements, all with their specific design and adjustment mechanisms. While these arrangements differ in detail,[8] the key differences are between flexible and fixed exchange rate systems. A special case are currency unions, which we discuss with special reference to the EMU.

4.2 The gold standard

Under the gold standard, the value of all currencies is fixed to gold. In consequence, they are also fixed against each other. The gold standard features automatic and symmetric adjustment. This means that a deficit country must ship

TABLE 6.4 Key Elements of International Monetary Systems

Key Elements	Gold Standard	Bretton Woods System	Current System		
Convertibility	Yes	US dollar: Yes Europe: 1958 Japan: 1964	Yes		
Exchange rate system (ERS)	*Fixed ERS:*	*Fixed ERS:*	**Parallel of several ERS:** *Flexible ERS:*	*Pegs:*	*Currency unions:*
	Currencies pegged to gold	Currencies pegged to US dollar	Among major international currencies	Pegs to anchor currencies or regional fixed ERS	Regional common currency areas, like EMU
Liquidity system	Gold	US dollar and SDR	Several international currencies	Anchor currency or synthetic currency	Common currency
Adjustment mechanism	Automatic & symmetric	Discretionary & asymmetric Devaluation as exemption	Automatic & symmetric	Depending on type of peg	Wage and price flexibility

gold to the surplus country. Since the gold standard requires that national money is fully backed by gold reserves, the deficit country has to reduce money supply, while the surplus country has to increase it. This way, it is hoped that in the deficit country, prices fall and restore price competitiveness, while in the surplus country higher money circulation raise prices. As a consequence, BOP imbalances on both sides should disappear.

Unfortunately, the gold standard can undermine itself. In the 20th century with the emergence of labour movements on the one hand, and oligopolistic industries on the other, wages and prices became more downward rigid, respectively. The price adjustment mechanism failed to work quickly enough for deficit countries. High unemployment emerged, especially after the Great Depression of 1929. Conversely, surplus countries were confronted with an immense inflow of gold, and hence drastic increases in money circulation and prices. This 'golden straitjacket' turned out to be too rigid to deal with extreme events, such as the Great Depression. It asked for enormous adjustments that run counter to the interests of labour, which became more powerful through labour unions. It has therefore been argued that the gold standard finally cracked because of overburdening of the political limits of the young democracies in Europe in the early 20th century (Eichengreen, 2019; Polanyi, 1944).

4.3 The Bretton Woods System

Under the BWS, all countries fixed their currencies to the US dollar, which in turn was fixed to gold. By pegging all currencies to the dollar, the value of all currencies against each other were also automatically fixed. However, to avoid the problems of the gold standard, the BWS allowed for exchange rate adjustments. Nevertheless, devaluations were considered as exemptions and had to be agreed upon by the newly created IMF to forestall competitive devaluations. Moreover, the IMF could assist countries with payments problems with balance-of-payments credits.

The adjustment burden was asymmetrically placed on deficit countries. The US had a special status, though. It had to run BOP-deficits, as this was the major mechanism to bring US-dollar liquidity into the international system. In fact, the US overfulfilled this task by far in the 1960s, and flooded the world with dollars. With high inflation, the US deficits increased further and led to speculation on a devaluation of the dollar. Dollars became for sale, and central banks in Europe and Japan had to buy these dollars with their own currencies to stabilise their exchange rates. Like under the gold standard, money supply in these countries increased drastically, and ultimately caused *imported inflation*.[9] In consequence, many countries cut their link to the dollar in 1971, and the BWS of fixed exchange rates was officially terminated in 1973.

4.4 Flexible versus fixed exchange rates

Between the major global currencies, US dollar, euro, and yen, exchange rates are flexible. While many other countries also opt for market-determined exchange rates, along with some developing economies, especially Europe has shown a strong preference for stable exchange rates amongst EU member countries. This resulted in the creation of the EMS of fixed exchange rates in 1979 (see European Perspective 6.4).

EUROPEAN PERSPECTIVE 6.4

A brief history of the EMS

The termination of the BWS in 1973 left a vacuum for European countries who continued to have a strong preference for stable exchange rates amongst their member states, as a means to promote European integration.

An immediate response was the *Snake*: the Europeans limited the variation of their bilateral exchange rates to 4.5%. Like a snake all European currencies followed the same trend against the US dollar, usually led by the Deutschmark. This informal arrangement paved the way for the European system of fixed exchange rates. The EMS, going into effect in 1979, is essentially a regional variant of BWS, but without the dominant position of one currency. Instead, an artificial currency, the European Currency Unit, named ECU, has been created as reserve currency. But like in the BWS, readjustments of parities are possible only upon joint agreement to avoid competitive devaluations.

While the EMS worked in principle, it often required realignments of currencies to restore competitiveness. In particular, southern member countries often had substantially higher inflation rates than the northern ones, notably Germany. In 1992–1993, several exchange rates came under speculative attacks, which ultimately helped to bring the euro into existences (see Section 6).

EMS still exists as EMS II, as EU member countries outside the Eurozone must keep their currencies stable relative to the euro for two years before they can adopt the euro.

What are the major differences between flexible and fixed exchange rate regimes in principle, and thus their major benefits and costs?

4.4.1 Benefits and costs

Flexible exchange rates promise **automatic and symmetric adjustment**. If a country is *heading* towards a deficit, it will see the demand for its currency falling, and thus its value depreciating. This increases price competitiveness and eliminates the deficit. A surplus country will see the opposite happening. Moreover, as the foreign exchange market sets the price to clear the market, i.e., to equate supply and demand, market-determined exchange rates promise that the BOP is always balanced. Hence, there are – at least in theory – no payments problems.

In practice, the situation can be more complicated. For example, to balance supply and demand it may be necessary that a currency value has to fall so drastically that it will inflict substantial damage on the economy. Instead of a payment crisis, a currency crisis would occur. Alternatively, a country can be swamped with capital inflows, thus appreciating its currency. A loss in international competitiveness could be the consequence. Hence, **volatile exchange rate movements** are often viewed as a major disadvantage of flexible exchange rates.

The European **preference for stable exchange rates** is largely driven by the wish to deepen economic integration, particular intra-EU trade. The fear is that volatile flexible exchange rates, occasionally driven by speculation, could hold back trade, tourism, and other cross-border activities. The downside is that substantial BOP imbalances can occur. How to adjust to this? While the details depend on the design of the peg, the adjustment burden often falls on the deficit countries, and may require currency devaluations and/or spending reductions. In other words, the adjustment mechanism can be discretionary and asymmetric, especially if countries unilaterally peg their currency to a major currency like the US dollar. By contrast, in the EMS, decisions to adjust parities are taken jointly – and a devaluation of your currency means a revaluation of the surplus countries' currency against the same currency basket.

The second key difference is that fixed exchange rates come with a **loss in policy autonomy**, as a look back at our exchange rate theories reveals.

Purchasing power parity theory suggests that in the long-run, inflation rates converge under fixed exchange rates. By contrast, flexible exchange rates allow countries to have 'the right on their own inflation rate'. Is this an advantage or a disadvantage? As discussed before,

- in the BWS, countries suffered from *imported inflation* from the US;
- in the EMS, member countries that had high inflation rates in the 1970s and early 1980s, however, *imported price stability* from Germany, the EMU anchor country. As with flexible exchange rates there would have been no need for monetary discipline, and this is seen by many observers as an advantage of the EMS.

Interest rate parity suggests that under fixed exchange rates the central bank has no **monetary autonomy**. Interest rates are determined by foreign interest rates. By contrast, flexible exchange rates allow national central banks to set interest rates in a way that is best for the national economy. This argument is famously summarised in the so-called *impossible trinity*, aka the *monetary policy trilemma*. The trilemma posits that a country can only chose two of following three:

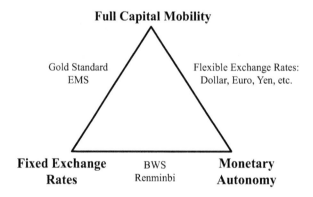

FIGURE 6.7 The Monetary Policy Trilemma: Chose Two, Only Two.

fixed exchange rates, monetary autonomy, and full capital mobility (Figure 6.7). This leaves three policy options:

- Choosing fixed exchange rates, like in EMS or the gold standard, requires giving up monetary autonomy. To be sure, the EMS still allows devaluations, and is less strict than the gold standard, nevertheless, central banks lack control over their interest rates, as long as capital is fully mobile.

- Opting for fixed exchange rates and limited capital mobility, like in the BWS, allows to keep exchange rates stable and still control interest rates. China is another case in point. As long as the country restricts capital mobility it can keep both exchange rates and interest rates under control.
- Flexible exchange rates allow to reconcile capital mobility with monetary autonomy.

4.4.2 The cost of losing monetary autonomy

How bad is it for a country to forgo monetary autonomy? Does it really pose a problem? To understand the issue, it is important to recall the role of monetary policy. Central banks use interest rates to steer the business cycle and control inflation. Hence, when inflation is too high, they increase rates to reduce spending and ultimately the rate of price-increases. Conversely, in a recession they reduce interest rates to stimulate demand and thus economic activity. The crucial point is, then, whether or not the interest rate that a country has to accept, is in line with the country's needs.

If all members of a fixed exchange rate system are in the same economic situation, losing monetary autonomy is no problem. If all countries are hit by a recession, all national central banks lower the interest rates, which is good for you as your country is also in a recession. This is the case of a **symmetric shock**.

If, however, something happens to you that does not happen to the others, the loss of monetary autonomy can cause serious economic hardship. This is called an **asymmetric shock**. For example, in the early 1990s, Finland was hit seriously by the economic collapse of the former Soviet Union. Finland exports were heavily concentrated on the Soviet Union and fell drastically. Unemployment in Finland, formerly almost non-existent, increased to two-digit levels. However, Finland was at that time not a member of the EMS and could use its currency, the Finish markka, as an **automatic stabiliser**. With the loss of its major export market, the value of the markka fell sharply, thus making Finland price competitive again, redirecting exports to western Europe, and recovering quickly.

In sum, the loss of policy autonomy can impose high costs in case of asymmetric shocks. A country may have to go through a prolonged period of unemployment until wages and prices fall enough (or rise less than in the other countries) to restore competitiveness. By contrast, flexible exchange rates offer a quick fix: a depreciating currency increases price competitiveness immediately. However, most fixed exchange rate systems, including the EMS allow for exchange rate adjustments, which can mitigate the problem. The case is, however, different when exchange rates are irrevocably fixed, like in the case of a currency union.

4.5 Currency unions

Why should countries trash their own currencies and adopt a common currency? Economists like Robert Mundell, Ronald McKinnon, Peter Kenen, and others developed a theory of an *optimum currency area* (OCA) in the 1960s. It argues that the benefits of forming a currency union (CU) should exceed the costs. Only then a monetary union is mutually beneficial, and, ultimately, sustainable.

4.5.1 The benefits and costs of a common currency

Several benefits of a common currency are obvious. Citizens of the 19 countries which have adopted the euro, enjoy travelling within the Eurozone without the need to exchange money to purchase goods and services abroad. More generally, the main benefits are:

- reduced transaction costs for exchanging money;
- eliminated exchange rate risks;
- as a consequence of the points above, trade is promoted, thus helping companies to realise economies of scale; and
- as a common currency makes it easier to compare prices in different countries, more competition and thus lower prices are expected.

Clearly, the more integrated a group of countries is, i.e., the more they trade, the more workers cross borders, the more cross-border banking and finance takes place, the more beneficial it is to use the same currency. Figure 6.8 illustrates the argument that benefits increase with the degree of integration. Hence, the curve reflecting benefits is upward sloping.

Unfortunately, currency unions also create costs. When countries are using the same currency, they cannot use their own monetary policy and lose monetary autonomy. In a monetary union there is only one currency and hence only a single **one-size-fits-all monetary policy**. Similar to the previously

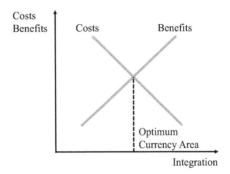

FIGURE 6.8 The Optimum Currency Area.

discussed fixed exchange rate regimes, this is no problem as long as all members are undergoing similar economic developments, i.e., when they are exposed to **symmetric shocks**. A good example is the financial crisis of 2008–2009, which affected all countries of the Eurozone. The single response by the ECB helped all member countries alike. However, if countries are exposed **to asymmetric shocks**, a single monetary policy does not fit all needs. Countries in a recession need lower interest rates, while those in an economic boom need higher interest rates, and just an average rate is of too little help.

It is reasonable to assume that business cycles of economies that are more integrated are also more synchronised. Hence, the more integrated the member countries, the lower the costs from not having an own monetary policy. Hence, the costs curve slopes downward when the degree of integration increases.

Given this reasoning, it is clear that an OCA is one where the benefits of a single currency outweigh the costs, as indicated in Figure 6.8. Hence, assessing whether or not a CU is an OCA, requires a judgement on the degree of integration, and thus, the potential exposure to asymmetric shocks.

The EMU offers a showcase for the OCA theory. We can apply a few criteria to make a judgement in comparison to the US, the other major CU:

- **Trade integration**. The more countries trade, the higher the benefits. Moreover, the economies of countries that trade a lot with each other are more likely to go through the same business cycle. Intra-European trade is indeed very high, though falling short of intra-state trade in the US. However, the criteria is largely fulfilled, though at varying degrees from country to country.
- **Labour mobility**. If one country of a CU suffers from unemployment and others do not, workers could move across countries. Hence, labour market integration could compensate for a lack of symmetry in a CU. In fact, in the US, labour mobility across states is quite high. By contrast, not least because of language barriers, in the Eurozone it is low and not sufficient to deal with severe asymmetric shocks.
- **Similar economic structures**. If countries are very similar, for example, by having similar industries, they are more likely to be hit by symmetric shocks. By contrast, if a CU comprises agriculture-based economies as well as manufacturing-based economies, the likelihood of asymmetric shocks is higher. Here the balance is more on the side of Europe, though not entirely, as will be seen soon.

What do these criteria jointly tell us about the EMU project? In the run-up to the EMU, economists tried to identify the presence and importance of asymmetric shocks for the initially proposed 11 member countries. In an influential paper, Bayoumi and Eichengreen (1993) identified two subgroups: a "Core Europe" of northern member countries and a "Club Med" of southern member countries.

The analysis implied that a CU with all 11 members would be an asymmetric EMU and not an OCA.

Nevertheless, the EU went ahead with the single currency project for all EU members. For sure, forming two currency unions for each of the symmetric subgroups, or simply excluding some EU members was politically not acceptable. The choice was therefore to go ahead with the project or abandon it. One reason to go ahead was the hope that adopting a single currency would increase economic integration and contribute to more symmetry.[10] This is the argument of an endogenous OCA: a CU will evolve over time into an OCA.

In sum, EMU was not a clear case for an OCA at the time the euro was adopted. What are the costs of creating an asymmetric currency union, and what are potential ways of dealing with an asymmetric EMU?

4.5.2 The costs of an asymmetric currency union

To understand the costs of having an asymmetric CU, consider that one country is hit by an asymmetric shock. The central bank cannot help this country with lower interest rates because it has to set the rates for the average of all member countries. This is the loss of monetary autonomy we already talked about in the context of a fixed exchange rate system. However, in a CU, the key difference is that a devaluation is not possible.

Absent of an own currency, lowering wages and prices relative to other member countries, is therefore the only way left to increase price competitiveness. This is called an **internal devaluation**. However, in modern economies prices and wages are often rather downward sticky. It can thus take a long time to bring about an internal devaluation. The costs of having an asymmetric CU are therefore in terms of a high and long-lasting unemployment in case substantial asymmetric shocks occur.

This analysis suggests that an asymmetric CU could become an OCA if the process of an internal devaluation is fast. For this, **labour market flexibility** plays a key role. The faster workers accept lower wages, the more rapidly the adjustment process works. Hence, many EMU member countries, notably Germany in the 2000s, introduced far-reaching labour market reforms. The OCA line in Figure 6.9 visualises this trade-off between symmetry and labour market flexibility. It indicates the minimum combinations of symmetry and labour market flexibility needed for having an OCA.

To understand this Figure, consider first the example of the US. The various US states differ a lot in their economic structures, with some states concentrating on agriculture, others on heavy industry, or on new technologies. Hence, asymmetric shocks are likely to occur. However, since labour markets in the US are rather flexible, making it easy to hire and fire workers, most economists would locate the US on the right-hand side of the OCA line.

Where to locate EMU in this space? Before the start of the EMU, many economists have pointed to labour and product market rigidities in many potential

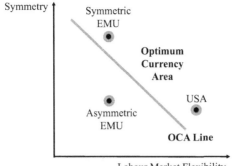

FIGURE 6.9 The Trade-Off between Symmetry and Labour Market Flexibility in a Currency Union.

Source: Own elaborations, closely based on the symmetry-flexibility diagram by De Grauwe (2014: 74).

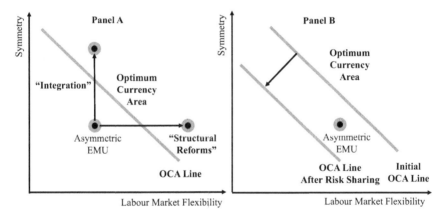

FIGURE 6.10 Policies for Turning an Asymmetric EMU into an OCA.

Source: Own elaborations based on the symmetry-flexibility diagram by De Grauwe (2014: 127–131).

member countries, as well as low labour mobility. If we accept this judgement, everything depends on how symmetric EMU is. Hence, we have indicated a symmetric EMU in the graph above the OCA line, and an asymmetric EMU below the OCA line.

If the EMU of the original 11 member countries was indeed an asymmetric CU, as suggested before, was it not premature to create the EMU? And if yes, what would be needed to turn an asymmetric CU into an OCA? Figure 6.10 illustrates three key policy measures graphically.

First, as illustrated in Panel A, EMU members can embark on **structural reforms**, which is the political term often employed for measures meant to make labour markets more flexible. Second, also illustrated in Panel A, one can try to

increase integration, for example by promoting the single market for goods, services, and – nowadays – increasingly digital services, as well as to promote labour mobility across EU member countries. However, the argument comes with a caveat. As the example of the US shows, more integration can also lead to more regional concentration of industries (Krugman, 1991), and thus to less symmetry.

Third, **risk sharing** amongst member states can turn an asymmetric CU into a functioning OCA. This is illustrated in Panel B. If member countries assist each other financially in case of asymmetric shocks, an OCA will be more beneficial than otherwise. Hence the OCA line shifts downwards. **Public risk sharing** typically involves fiscal transfers. This could be done by direct fiscal transfers through a joint fiscal budget or a joint unemployment insurance system. The US, for example, has a federal unemployment insurance system and can accommodate large fiscal transfers to ailing states. In other words, public risk sharing constitutes some kind of a fiscal union. By contrast, in the EMU any kind of a fiscal union has been excluded by the *Maastricht Treaty* of 1992, and a 'transfer union' is still controversial today (see European Perspective 6.5).

Private risk sharing could substitute – at least partly – for a lack of public risk sharing. Integrating the financial markets of a CU would allow some burden sharing. Banking market integration would in particular be helpful in this respect. Banks in countries that are doing well could then provide finance to ailing economies, where the banks are often in a bad shape.

In sum, a CU is no panacea. In fact, ill-designed common currencies can become politically explosive, especially when an asymmetric currency area relies too heavily on internal devaluations via wage and price flexibility with limited risk sharing. The cost of not meeting the OCA criteria will then ultimately be felt in national labour markets, and result, as earlier under the gold standard, in political tensions that may even risk the break-up of a CU. EMU has been experiencing this risk after 2010 when the euro crisis erupted (see Section 6).

EUROPEAN PERSPECTIVE 6.5

Public risk sharing in the EMU

When the euro was envisioned in the Maastricht Treaty of 1992, it was clear that the appetite for risk sharing, or even a full-fledged fiscal union was very low, if not nil. The Maastricht criteria, the conditions for joining the Eurozone, were thus minimal and geared towards avoiding burden sharing.

The famous fiscal criteria that limited government budget deficits to 3% of GDP and government debts to 60% of GDP were meant to ensure never having to be in a position to take joint responsibility for individual countries' debts. Moreover, the criteria were the counterpart of the non-bailout rule that prohibit the ECB to finance member states' deficits and debts by printing money.

> Given the limited willingness for joint burden sharing in EMU countries, the success of the EMU project relied heavily on (i) creating a true single market, which eventually turns an incomplete EMU into an OCA, and (ii) promoting labour market flexibility, which in many countries has been lacking.

5 Understanding global financial markets

Until the GFC, financial globalisation often outpaced other cross-border activities. International finance became somewhat detached from the real economy. It is therefore useful to recall its initial key function, namely, to finance international transactions, including temporary payment imbalances. Its second key function is enabling diversification. Investing across countries should – in principle – reduce risks. In practice, an increasing incidence of financial crises in the recent decades points to inherent risk in international finance, often depending on the form international finance takes. In this section, forms, functions, and risks of foreign finance are reviewed.

5.1 Forms of foreign finance

In finance the key differentiation is between equity and debt finance. In international finance, equity can be a **foreign direct investment** (FDI) or a **portfolio investment**. As discussed in Chapter 4, an equity investment is considered to constitute an FDI if more than 10% of the capital of a foreign company is acquired. Otherwise, it is considered as portfolio equity investments.

Regarding debt finance, there are, first, **portfolio bond investments**, either in sovereign or corporate bonds. The next major item is **cross–border banking**, namely cross-border loans and deposit taking.[11] These activities are either conducted with non-banks in the so-called retail bank market with firms and households, or with other banks in the so-called *interbank market*, aka *money market*. Lending and borrowing between banks used to be quite common. If a bank transfers money for a customer to another bank, it may be short of cash, while the other bank is awash with it. To solve the temporary liquidity problem, the receiving bank can lend the transferring bank the needed sum. For this lending, money market interest rates for different maturities are being charged (overnight, one month, three months, one year). The rates are quoted, for example as *LIBOR* (London Interbank Offered Rate) or *EURIBOR* (Euro Interbank Offered Rate).

The BOP statistics also report an entry for 'other sectors', which covers the financial cross-border activities of financial intermediaries, like insurances, mutual funds, or hedge funds. Finally, there are the **foreign exchange markets** as the mirror image of all cross-border transactions plus the foreign exchange interventions of central bank, as recorded in the official reserve balance.

5.2 Integration of financial markets

How integrated are financial markets across borders? Measuring this is more difficult than it seems at first glance (see Baele et al., 2004). A first benchmark is the law of one price, which is the base for **price-based measures** of financial integration. Comparable assets should have the same price. Hence, more integration means less price dispersion.

Measuring price (or interest rate) convergence is, as can be seen from the uncovered interest rate parity condition, not easy because exchange rate risks, which are not directly observable, complicate this task. Within the Eurozone where exchange rates do not exist anymore, this is straightforward.[12] Already before the introduction of the euro in 1999, interest rates on government bonds started to align closely, suggesting closely integrated Eurozone sovereign bond markets. Likewise, money markets in the Eurozone appeared to be fully integrated before the GFC. Corporate bond and equity market integration is more difficult to assess because of credit and business risks, respectively. Yet, for the Eurozone before the GFC, the consensus view was that corporate bond markets were quite integrated, while integration of equity markets was increasing.

To arrive at such judgements, economists use two additional measures. First, they look at **quantity-based measures**, such as cross-border trading of assets. Second, they employ a so-called **news-based measures**. The idea is that in an integrated market, asset prices should react similarly to common news.

In contrast to the abovementioned markets, the retail banking market in the Eurozone has remained largely segmented. As argued by Kleimeier and Sander (2007), the occasionally observed convergence of interest rates can give a misleading picture, as the same prices for not fully comparable loans and deposits would not reflect correct arbitrage. The authors argue looking instead at news-based measures, such as co-movement of interest rates in response to monetary policy changes, as well as at quantity-based measures, such as increased cross-border activities. Based on such indicators, the authors found that retail banking markets remained segmented in the Eurozone, however, in some markets, such as corporate loans, some signs of increasing integration could be observed. Nevertheless, the GFC, and in particular the euro crisis, has led to a severe disintegration of Eurozone banking markets.

5.3 The benefits and costs of global finance

Why should we care about financial integration? The simple answer is that it has benefits and costs.

To start with the benefits, international finance has two main functions. The first main function of finance is to channel funds from those having surpluses to those lacking funds. As such, finance should direct funds to their most productive uses. This means that countries with abundant capital will finance countries will less savings as compared to investment opportunities. For example, and as discussed in Section 2, Germany when in a recession in the mid-2000s, provided savings for booming countries in the Eurozone. Capital-abundant countries typically feature low interest rates, while in countries that lack savings, higher interest rates are being paid to attract more capital. Arbitrage by means of capital movements will equalise interest rates across countries. The law of one price will thus ensure an **optimal global allocation of capital** as it goes to those countries where it yields highest returns. This is the first key benefit of foreign finance.

The argument comes, however, with a caveat, known as the **capital paradox**. On the assumption that poor countries are facing capital scarcity, capital should flow from rich to poor countries. In fact, historically it has on aggregate often been the opposite way (Lucas, 1990). For example, advanced countries as a group have been running huge current account deficits, especially in the first decade of the 21st century, peaking in 2008 at $672 billion, while emerging markets and developing economies were running a combined surplus of $581 billion in that year. Hence, poor countries were financing the rich. More recently, the situation of the advanced countries reversed, but the combined current account of the poorer countries has not shown high deficits, which indicates that capital is not flowing in a significant way to them as a group. Some countries are exemptions, receiving capital on a net base. But this implies that for many other poor countries, capital continues to flow upward, mainly to safe havens in advanced countries.[13]

The second major benefit of global finance is to allow for **global portfolio diversification**. Investors can thus enjoy an improved risk-return trade-off. Especially exchanging assets with different risk profiles across countries allows for so-called **intra-temporal consumption smoothing**: Consider you hold stocks from both European companies and Russian gas companies. As a European this helps you to keep your consumption up in case gas price increases hit the European economy because you gain as a holder of Russian gas stocks. Conversely, Russian investors benefit from holding European stocks as they do better in case of drastically falling gas prices.

The increasing incidence of financial crises, especially after the break-down of the BWS and with the liberalisation of capital movement, reveals that capital mobility comes with **risks and costs**:

- Capital mobility can lead to a **loss of policy autonomy**, especially when a country has pegged it exchange rate. While the impossible trinity, as discussed in Section 4, suggests that flexible exchange rates allow for policy autonomy, recent research has been raising doubts on this proposition. We will return to this issue in the concluding Section 7.
- Foreign finance can increase the vulnerability to **sudden stops**. As long as lenders are confident about the prospects of a country, finance is often available in abundance. Bad news, leading to a loss in investor confidence, often result in an abrupt stop of the flow of finance. What makes this so risky is not the stop as such, but its suddenness.

- Foreign finance often reveals a high **procyclicality of financial flows**: Access to finance is easy in good times but difficult, if not impossible, in bad times.
- Foreign finance is often subject to **crisis spillovers and financial contagion**. A typical example is the common lender problem. If an investor makes losses in a crisis country, he may reduce his lending to other countries, even if nothing has changed there.

The above discussion suggests that riskiness depends crucially on the form of foreign finance:

- Equity finance is typically less risky that debt finance. Equity owners participate in losses, thus allowing a more equal burden sharing. Moreover, equity finance is much less procyclical than debt finance, and often even contra-cyclical. For example, when the currency of a crisis country depreciates, it is cheaper to produce for exports in this economy, which may attract FDI.
- Portfolio and bank finance exhibits a high procyclicality in times of crises. Especially bank loans tend to be the first to dry up and often turn negative because of repayments. Hence, the risks are typically higher when countries resort to short-term rather than long-term borrowing.
- Borrowing in foreign currency is much more dangerous than borrowing in own currency. The reason is that the value of debt measured in home currency increases when the home currency gets weaker. Many financial crises, especially in developing countries, often go hand-in-hand with drastic currency depreciations. For example, a 50% loss of value of the home currency will lead to a doubling of the debt measured in domestic currency. This can easily lead to widespread bankruptcies and a sharp deepening of a crisis. Borrowing in foreign currency has therefore been dubbed as "original sin" (Eichengreen & Hausmann, 1999: 3), especially of countries that do not have the "exorbitant privilege" to borrow in their own currency.[14]

In sum, the benefits of foreign finance have to be weighed against its costs. Especially, many emerging and developing economies have experienced devastating financial crises that have dwarfed the benefits of foreign finance, in particular, when it came in the form of foreign-currency-denominated debt rather than FDI. Moreover, the experience with the GFC has led to a reevaluation of foreign finance, and thus its regulation.

6 Understanding financial crises

What are financial crises? In a comprehensive database of past financial crises, Laeven and Valencia (2020) differentiate currency crises, sovereign debt crises, and banking crises. However, as their dataset shows, many crises are twin or even triple crises. For example, a sovereign debt crisis can trigger a cut-off of the country from international finance, thus leading to a currency crisis. A banking crisis – a widespread bankruptcy of banks – can have similar effects. However, causality can also run the opposite way. A speculation against a currency that results in a severely reduced exchange rate can ignite a sovereign debt and/or a banking crisis, especially when governments, corporations, or banks are highly indebted in foreign currency.

What distinguishes financial crises from ordinary recessions, is that the negative impact on the economy is often both more severe and lasts much longer. Twin or triple crises are especially malign. The main reason is that the economy will only go back to normal once the balance sheets of all economic actors – governments, banks, corporations, and households – are sufficiently restored to allow a return to normal pre-crisis spending behaviour.

The focus here is on currency crises, though keeping in mind the interlinkages with sovereign debt and banking crises. First, the major currency crises of the 1980s and 1990s are discussed. They were mostly characterised by a speculative attack on a fixed exchange rate, yet provide valuable lessons for understanding current financial crises. Second, the GFC is reviewed, which was not a currency crisis but had fall-outs for the external financial situation of many countries. Finally, the euro crisis is scrutinised, which – by some politicians and observers – has not been viewed as a currency crisis, but as a sovereign debt crisis of some countries. The alternative interpretation is that it indeed was – or even still is – a crisis of the currency union as it involved speculations on the break-up of the Eurozone.

6.1 Three generations of currency crisis

Currency crises are diverse in both causes and effects. A now classic theoretical distinction is between first-, second-, and third-generation currency crisis models, which – to some extent – match with the major currency crises of the past 40 years.

Most of these crisis events originated in a speculation against a fixed exchange rate. The mechanics of such a speculation are fairly simple. If you expect that a currency will have a lower value tomorrow, you sell it today at the still high and fixed exchange rate. When the currency is devalued in the future you can exchange it back with a profit. For example, (just think of the EMS around 1990) assume the fixed exchange rate is two French Francs (FF) per Deutschmark (DM). If you expect a parity of 3FF per DM tomorrow, you exchange 1000FF into 500DM today. Once your expectations have materialised and the Franc is devalued, you exchange the 500DM at the new rate back into 1500FF, thus realising a 50% profit on the invested sum.

It is easy to see from this simple example that with full capital mobility, speculations on a currency devaluation can become massive if many investors bet on it. But even if capital controls are in place, the non-legal version 'capital flight' is often sufficient to ignite a currency crisis.

6.1.1 First generation currency crises and the developing country debt crisis of the 1980s

First-generation currency crisis models highlight the role of macroeconomic policies in producing outcomes that are inconsistent with maintaining a fixed exchange rate. In this sense, many currency crises originate from excessive government deficits.

As discussed in Section 2, such deficits can be behind high current account deficits, which need to be financed by capital imports. Moreover, printing money to finance the deficit leads to high inflation – and in presence of a currency peg – to a loss in price competitiveness. Once foreign creditors and/or citizens realise that the peg may not be sustainable, foreign finance dries up and capital flight increases. The country may not be able to finance its current account deficit anymore. The currency crisis assumes full form.

The developing country debt crisis of the 1980s is very much a showcase of a first-generation crisis. The crisis ignited when Mexico declared in August 1982 that is had no more foreign reserves to service its foreign debts. Mexico, like other developing countries, mostly in Latin America but also countries like Nigeria and the Philippines, had borrowed in US dollars from international banks to finance government deficits, partly used for investment projects, in particular for developing new oil fields, which had become profitable after the two oil price shocks in the 1970s.

The situation went sour when the US embarked in 1981 on a strict anti-inflation policy. This led to double-digit interest rates, a sharp appreciation of the dollar, and ultimately to a drastic fall of oil and other commodity prices on world markets. As a consequence, dollar-denominated interest payments rose sharply at a moment when dollar inflows from selling commodities dried up. As the payments problems of the countries became visible, international banks tried to withdraw funding. This *sudden stop* pushed many countries close to a default.

To avoid defaults, the affected countries asked the IMF for stand-by credits to mitigate the payment problems. In return, the IMF arranged adjustment programs by means of conditioning the payment tranches on implementing a set of policies to terminate the currency crisis, known as *IMF conditionality*. The most important policy conditions are:

- **Expenditure reduction policy** conditions ask for reducing domestic spending, in particular by reducing government deficits.
- **Expenditure switching policy** conditions often require a devaluation of the currency.[15] Citizens will then buy more domestic goods, the current account deficit shrinks, and less foreign capital is needed.

The difficulty with this approach was that the required adjustments in the debtor countries were so severe that the economies almost collapsed. The reason was that all creditors wanted to withdraw funding at the same time, while insisting on a pay-back of the short-term loans. As the IMF's own funds were too limited to fill the gap, the challenge for the IMF was to 'convince' banks to continue lending to the countries. The IMF therefore conditioned IMF stand-by credits to the countries on financing contributions from the involved banks. What banks called 'forced lending', eventually rescued these banks, as some major players were involved with more than 100% of their own capital. Ultimately, forced lending avoided a first potential major crash of the world financial system after WWII.

However, one round of forced lending was followed by another. While the situation of the concerned countries hardly improved, banks won time to repair their balance sheets. Finally, the situation was resolved through debt relief measures in 1990 under the Brady Plan, named after US treasury secretary Nicolas Brady, that led to debt reductions after a 'lost decade' from the point of view of the debtor countries.

6.1.2 Second generation crises: the EMS crisis of 1992–1993

In 1992–1993, the EMS was hit by a major crisis. What happened? Over time the EU had liberalised capital markets, finally culminating into the European Single Market. However, when capital is fully mobile, investors can gain from speculating on a devaluation of a fixed exchange rate. Such situations occurred in 1992–1993.

In contrast to first-generation crises, the speculative attack occurred despite sound macroeconomic environments in the attacked countries. The key trigger is the belief that **a country will not defend its currency** in case the parity will be attacked. In such a case, a currency crisis can occur at any time and can affect in principle any country with a fixed exchange rate.

Why should an EMS country not be willing to defend the fixed parity? Before unification in 1990, Germany was not only the largest but also the dominant economy in the EMS. With capital now flowing freely within the EU, Germany de facto set the interest rates in the EMS. After unification, the German economy began to overheat, and the Bundesbank pursued anti-inflationary policies. Interest rates increased to nearly 10%.

Such high interest rates were not in the interest of all EMS countries. Many of them were struggling with recessions and high unemployment rates. Especially in the UK, the high interest rates were holding back a badly needed recovery. In 1992, investors such as George Soros, the owner of a large London-based hedge fund, started to make a bet that when under pressure, the British government would prefer devaluing the pound rather than continue suffering from high unemployment. Like in our introductory example of a speculation, Soros exchanged large amounts of British pounds into Deutschmark. This was felt as a pressure on the pound in European currency markets. Other investors followed his example until the Bank of England was running out of Deutschmark and unable to keep the pound at the fixed level. The pound was devalued, and, eventually, Britain left the EMS.

The lessons were learned quickly. With perfect capital mobility, any fixed exchange rate can in principle be attacked. This, of course, is easier when potential victims are more vulnerable. Hence, the currencies of southern EMS countries with high unemployment and competitiveness problems became the main targets of the next speculative attacks in 1993. The crisis was resolved by temporary suspensions of the attacked currencies from EMS, and a later return into the EMS with a lower parity.

What are the lessons learned for the future of monetary arrangements in Europe?

- First, the EMS crisis taught the Europeans that fixed exchange rates in the presence of open capital markets can create speculative attacks very sudden and at any time, even when macroeconomic fundamentals are sound. Hence, the system is vulnerable.
- Second, the British solution of moving to flexible exchange rate was a no-go on the continent.
- Third, restricting capital movement was no option as the single market had just been created, and border controls in many countries had been removed by the Schengen agreement.

However, there was another 'corner solution': irrevocably fixed exchange rates. If one only makes clear that exchange rates will never be changed again, any speculative attack will fail, and thus never occur. Hence the Europeans started to take seriously what they had already agreed upon in 1992 in the *Maastricht Treaty*, i.e., to create a single currency. Once a country has joined the EMU, there is no pre-defined way out. Attacks on individual countries will therefore never happen again – or so goes the saying.

6.1.3 Third generation currency crises: the Asian crisis of 1997

The key lesson from the EMS crisis was that an attack on a fixed exchange rate in an environment of free capital movements can be successful. Asian countries, which often had pegged their exchange rates to the US dollar and opened up financially in the 1990s, were the next targets.

In August 1997, the Thai Baht was attacked. Thailand had been running high current account deficits, peaking in 1996 at 8.1% of GDP. Unlike in the 1980s debt crisis, behind this deficit was not a government deficit but private investments that exceeded private savings. As investments promote future growth, investors were not very worried about the high current account deficits and continued to provide finance. However, increasingly these investments went into real estate, which do not easily generate foreign exchange to repay the borrowed money. Another weakness was a loss in price competitiveness. This loss was not excessive, but as exports began stagnating while imports continued booming, financial markets started expecting a devaluation of the Thai Baht. Finally, the speculative attack commenced.

Thailand first tried to defend the currency by deploying reserves, but soon realised it had to increase the interest rate to keep capital in the country. However, as Thai companies and banks were highly indebted, higher interest rates caused a sharp economic contraction. Finally, Thailand stopped defending the currency and the value of the Baht almost halved. As Thai companies and banks had borrowed extensively in foreign currency, the economic contraction deepened even further. Creditors rapidly withdrew funding, and Thailand experienced an economically devastating capital account reversal. In 1996, the country received on a net base US$19.5 billion. In 1998, the year after the crisis ignited, the net outflow amounted to US$14.1 billion.

Other countries in Asia with fixed exchange rates and open capital markets came soon under scrutiny as well, the crisis became contagious and spread to countries like Malaysia, Indonesia, Korea, and the Philippines, thus leading to the *Asian crisis*.

How was the crisis solved? While the IMF advised to resort to traditional expenditure switching and expenditure reduction policies, several countries felt uneasy with it. For example, Thailand increased – against the advice from the IMF – government spending to stimulate the economy. Malaysia opted for imposing temporary capital controls, while keeping the IMF completely out. Additionally, Asia had good luck. With the global economy booming, driven by the electronics industry in which most of these countries specialised, the recovery of most countries was fast.

In sum, the **third-generation currency crisis** model argues that economies can be pushed from a good into a bad equilibrium. Bankruptcies and banking crisis are often the outcome of an attack on the currency. A loss in confidence can lead to severe currency and economic crisis, which is ultimately self-validating, and largely independent of fundamental economic factors. As a saying, ascribed to US economist Guillermo Calvo, goes "it was a big punishment for a small sin".

6.2 The great financial crisis 2008–2009

Strictly speaking, the GFC was not a currency crisis but a banking crisis that crossed borders. It was not even a global banking crisis but essentially a transatlantic affair, originating in and affecting cross-border banking between the US and Europe.

Most observers locate the origin of the GFC in the US mortgage market. Low interest rates and ample availability of funds in the early 2000s led to a boom in the housing market. Mortgages were given without sufficient screening of borrowers' solvency. Moreover, often borrowers bought houses only to sell them later at a higher price. This led to a very classical speculative bubble that could burst at any time. This happened when interest rates were gradually increased and housing prices started falling in 2006. Homeowners could not service their mortgages, and the value of the houses were not sufficient as a guarantee anymore.

Normally one would expect some mortgage lenders to go bankrupt, causing some disruptions in the US economy, but not much more. However, deregulated cross-border banking and the existence of a 'shadow banking system' of other financial intermediaries, made all the difference. 'Subprime', shaky and insecure mortgages, were securitised and sold in bundled packages from the original lenders to investors everywhere in the world, but in particular to US and European financial institutions. Packaging and re-packaging of these *asset-backed securities* (ABS) was complicated and opaque. Nevertheless, most of these vehicles received Triple-A ratings from rating agencies. ABS offered high returns and provided the illusion of a safe asset. Most importantly they helped international banks to engage in regulatory arbitrage, i.e., to use these assets and other activities abroad to exploit differences in national regulations to reduce capital requirements. The idea is that the less capital is held as equity, the more can be invested in loans or other interest-bearing assets. European banks used the US market especially in this respect by simultaneously lending to and borrowing from it, while flying under the radar of national regulators.

When the subprime bubble burst, the risks in the balance sheets of banks and financial intermediaries were very unclear. However, as they were gradually uncovered, one financial institution after the other faced problems. Given the deep interlinkages in the markets, one domino after the other fell, with the collapse of Lehman Brothers in September 2008 being the ultimate event that started the financial meltdown. Banks started to distrust each other. As a consequence, the interbank market where banks lend each other money to avoid short-term liquidity problems, collapsed both nationally and internationally. This can push even healthy banks into bankruptcy.

The US government finally arranged support programs for banks by buying assets via the *Troubled-Asset Relief Program* (TARP). European governments stepped in rescuing banks, creating 'bad banks', and giving extended or even unlimited guarantees to bank depositors to avoid bank runs. Moreover, national central banks stepped in to provide banks with sufficient liquidity in order to operate normally again.

However, even this was not enough, as mainly European banks that had borrowed on US markets in dollars were unable to obtain dollars to meet their obligations. As the ECB cannot print dollars, the *US Federal Reserve Bank* (Fed) created *swap lines*, under which the ECB could borrow dollars directly from the Fed and lend them to European banks. It should be noted that there was not a shortage of foreign reserves on the side of the ECB or other major central banks. As such it was not a currency crisis. Rather, it was a global shortage of US-dollar liquidity to which the Fed reacted.

In sum, the GFC led to a severe fall-out on the global real economy. European banks have still not recovered fully from the GFC. This has led policymakers to reconsider national and global regulation of global finance in general, and global banking in particular. We will return to this in the concluding section of this chapter.

6.3 The EMU crisis

In 2010, the euro crisis ignited when Greece revealed that its government debts exceeded the limits set by the Maastricht criteria, by far. Soon after this, other countries with high or increasing debts, in particular Ireland, Portugal, and Spain came into the focus of financial markets, which became increasingly un-willing to finance the government debts of these countries. Interest rates for re-financing public debt and deficits skyrocketed and pushed these countries close to a situation where they would have been unable to re-finance their debt and had to default.

Sovereign debt default within the Eurozone was a no-go for European policy-makers at the time. However, honouring public debts was not simply an ethical issue. Many European banks, which had just hardly survived the GFC, were holding large amounts of Greek government bonds or claims in banks in other affected countries. A Greek default would have triggered a second and probably even more devastating banking crisis after the GFC. Rescue programs for coun-tries were arranged, which essentially rescued the European banking system.

6.3.1 Crisis narratives

All this stirred up a debate whether the Eurozone was merely witnessing the sovereign debt crises of some member countries or whether it was a crisis of the EMU:

- The **profligate country narrative** stresses fiscal profligacy of some prob-lem countries, mostly in southern Europe. While this diagnosis was true for Greece, with respect to most other countries it is not convincing. In many countries deficit and debts increased only after the GFC, partly because they rescued banks (especially Ireland), and partly because the burst of the credit bubble ended economic booms and pushed economies into deep recessions (especially Spain).
- The **Eurozone crisis narrative** stresses that speculations on exits of mem-ber countries from EMU are key.

If we take the second argument seriously, how do such speculations emerge? A group of prominent economists has proposed a **consensus narrative**, which points to some key mechanics in the workings of EMU, which contributed signif-icantly to the crisis (Rebooting Consensus Authors, 2015). Recall that Germany was suffering from low growth in the 2000s, while many southern countries were enjoying a boom. Germany and other northern countries financed the cur-rent account deficits of the south. This situation changed drastically when in 2010 the risks of lending to governments and the private sector became visible. Investors and banks stopped financing the south abruptly. This *sudden stop* ignited a *doom loop*, which deepened the problems of the affected countries rapidly.

The doom loop can be triggered from a standard sovereign debt crisis originating in overspending (like Greece), or from a banking crisis, e.g. when governments rescue banks and their debts increase in consequence (like Ireland). In either case, deteriorating government finances make it more difficult and costly to obtain finance. Thus, government debt loses value. Another specific feature of the Eurozone is that banks hold debts of their own government. Here the doom loop sets in. The falling value of government bonds worsens the banks' financial situation, more banks need to be rescued with government money, sovereign debts increase further, bank problems deepen, and so on. Figure 6.11 illustrates this.

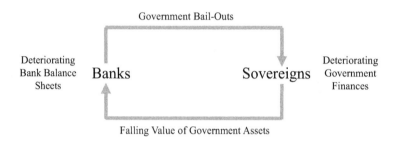

FIGURE 6.11 The Doom Loop in the Eurozone.

As a consequence, speculations on country exits from the Eurozone emerged. Lending to these countries dried up or lenders asked for higher interest rates to compensate for higher country risks. However, higher interest rates lead to higher government deficits and debts, thus making an exit even more likely. As we have learned from the EMS crisis, it is very difficult to stop such a speculation. Moreover, the 3rd generation crises have taught us that even a small sin can lead to big punishments and push countries from a good to a bad equilibrium.

This situation left policymakers basically with three options:

- First, trying to contain the crisis country-by-country with financing packages and adjustment conditionality. As it turned out, the effects of the various rescue packages between 2010 and 2012 were often short-lived and speculations soon increased again (Figure 6.12).
- Second, letting EMU exits happen. However, this is easier said than done. Re-introducing a national currency that does not exist anymore may at best be possible at a much lower value. A country that has borrowed extensively in euro, will see its debts ballooning – and creditors will eventually face huge losses. As Eichengreen (2010) has put it, this could cause "the mother of all financial crises".
- Third, market participants must be convinced that a strong enough lender of last resort will do "whatever it takes to preserve the euro". After ECB president Mario Draghi announced this famously in 2012,[16] exit speculations have dried up and interest rates have fallen rapidly (Figure 6.12).

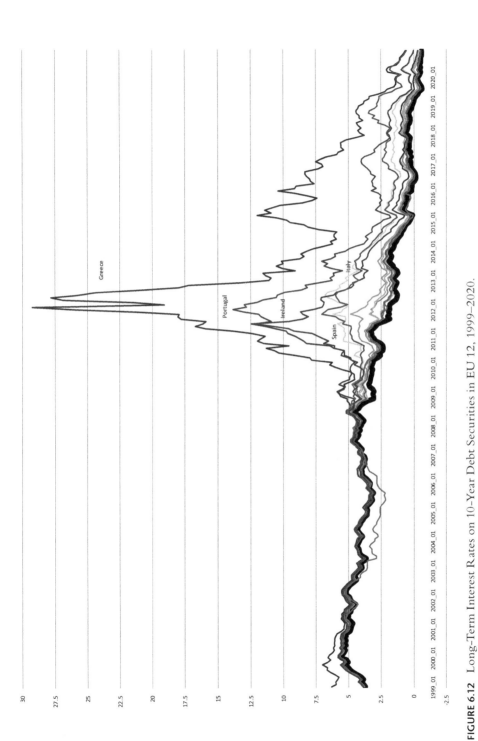

FIGURE 6.12 Long–Term Interest Rates on 10–Year Debt Securities in EU 12, 1999–2020.

Data source: European Central Bank: https://sdw.ecb.europa.eu/. Interest rates statistics: Long–term interest rate for convergence purposes. German rates are indicated by the bold black line.

6.3.2 How to make the euro sustainable?

The ECB has effectively stabilised the Eurozone and provided breathing space to build the structures necessary to create a stable and sustainable currency area. What is needed to make the Eurozone more crisis-resilient in the future?

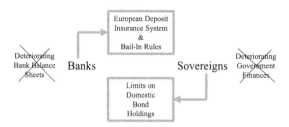

FIGURE 6.13 Disrupting the Eurozone Doom Loop.

A first key issue is to **disrupt the doom loop**. As Figure 6.13 illustrates, two things are important:

- Banks should replace national government bond holdings by a mixed port-folio of Eurozone sovereign bonds and/or a single European safe asset.
- A joint *European Deposit Insurance System* (EDIS) can avoid the collapse of a bank overburdening a sovereign government.[17] EDIS is by many observers seen as the final element of the EU *Banking Union*, which already has established single banking supervision and a single resolution mechanism. The latter features bail-in rules to make equity and bond holders participate in case of a bank failure.

Disrupting the doom loop requires some kind of **risk sharing** amongst member countries, as we have discussed it in Section 4. It is essential for turning an asymmetric EMU into a more crisis-resilient OCA. Next to EDIS, other discussed **public risk sharing** instruments are:

- A joint European unemployment insurance.
- A *European Stability Mechanism* (ESM) to provide temporary funding for countries suffering from asymmetric shock. As the ESM, as it stands at the time of writing, bases lending on policy conditions, it is highly controversial. It is for this reason that Italy has, for example, strongly rejected the idea to provide financial support to countries severely affected by the Covid-19 pandemic via the ESM.
- Issuance of joint bonds, so called 'Eurobonds', as a single European safe asset, e.g. for financing long-term European infrastructure projects. While most northern members oppose joint debt issuance in general, in reaction to the

Covid-19 pandemic a €700 billion joint debt-financed programme, named *Next Generation EU*, has been launched. As it is understood to be an exceptional programme, the future of Eurobonds remains to be seen.

However, the less member countries are willing to accept public risk sharing, the more **private risk sharing** through financial markets is required. In this respect, not only is completing the Banking Union essential, but also building a Capital Markets Union.[18]

In sum, the creation of the euro turned out to be one of the most ambitious social experiments ever. To make it sustainable in the presence of continuing asymmetric shocks, however, requires a minimum of solidarity within Europe and the Eurozone.

7 The future of global money and finance

In a speech at the 2019 Annual Meeting of Central Banks in Jackson Hole, USA, the governor of the Bank of England, Mark Carney,[19] remarked about the challenges of the international monetary and financial system: "…most fundamentally, a destabilising asymmetry at the heart of the IMFS is growing. While the world economy is being reordered, the US dollar remains as important as when Bretton Woods collapsed". His data illustrates this by contrasting the United States' 15% share of global GDP and 10% of world trade, with the 50% share that the dollar has in global trade invoicing, and a two-third dominant share in official FX reserves, in global security issuance, and in emerging economies' external debt, respectively.

For the NGE, this raises the question whether the emerging multipolar world will in future be matched by a multipolar IMFS, in which euro, pound, renminbi, and other currencies play a more important role. In his speech, Carney also suggested that a 'Synthetic Hegemonic Currency' (SHC), constructed as a basket of Central Bank Digital Currencies (CBDC), could help overcome the dollar dominance.

7.1 The dollar dominance

The dollar dominance can restrict national policymakers' policy options. In this respect, two major arguments challenge the conclusion of the impossible trinity that flexible exchange rates can reconcile monetary autonomy with capital mobility. The first argument highlights the dominant dollar invoicing, which limits the efficacy of devaluations.[20] The second argument highlights results from empirical studies, which show that monetary conditions in countries with floating exchange rates are influenced by foreign monetary conditions, notably interest rates in the US. Rey (2015) has therefore argued that flexible exchange rates are not sufficient to guarantee monetary autonomy. Economies would thus face not a trilemma but a dilemma to choose between monetary autonomy and capital mobility.

The dollar hegemony also makes the world dependent on dollar liquidity, which can only be provided by the Fed. In the GFC, the US reserve bank established swap lines to allow the ECB and the Swiss National Bank to directly borrow dollars for some time. In 2013, the swap lines were made permanent and included major advanced countries. However, emerging economies are not included, and have to approach the IMF when in need of foreign currency. This partly changed in March 2020, when as a side-effect of the Covid-19 pandemic, bond and equity markets in the US came briefly under severe pressure. As a consequence, investors drastically reduced their exposure to emerging markets and created a severe dollar shortage there. In response, the Fed established temporary swap lines for Brazil, Korea, Mexico, and Singapore, as well as for Australia and the Scandinavian non-Eurozone countries.

7.2 What role for digital currencies?

Digital currencies may or may not change the way the IMFS works. Digital currencies are, at the time of writing, basically proposals, with details remaining to be seen. Only cryptocurrencies, like Bitcoin, are yet to be fully established. However, given the volatility of their value, they are more like a speculative asset than a means of payments that can contribute to solving global liquidity problems.

Other private issuers have therefore launched the idea of *stable coins*. Unlike free-floating bitcoins, the value of stable coins is linked to a currency and backed by reserves in this currency. The reader may feel reminded of fixed exchange rates, and their advantages and disadvantages. A fixed value, e.g. against the US dollar could make such stable coins a handy means of payments for US citizens. It potentially saves them substantial transaction costs as compared to traditional payment methods. Moreover, they would avoid exchange rate losses from a fluctuating value against the base currency.

Facebook's proposed 'Libra' (now called 'Diem') is different in that it is intended to be tied to a basket of major advanced countries' currencies. While this may help Libra to become a global digital currency, it exposes the holder to exchange rate risks, namely to value changes to the holder's home currency vis-à-vis the basket.

However, there is a major drawback of private stable coins that we know from fixed exchange rate systems. The peg can be challenged. A speculation against Libra and other stable coins could easily lead to a full depletion of the backing reserves, resulting in huge losses for those who hold the private digital currencies. The main reason is that there is no lender of last resort, and this makes private digital currencies vulnerable at any time. For this major reason, central banks and financial regulators are indeed very sceptical, and it is far from clear whether such private digital currencies will see the light of day. And if they do, it might only happen under tight regulation (Table 6.5).

However, the advantages of digital currencies have caught the attention of central banks around the world (see BIS, 2020). CBDCs could provide the same

TABLE 6.5 Typology of Digital Currencies

Issuer	Private			Public	
Type of Digital Money	Cryptocurrencies	Stable Coins		Central Bank Digital Currency (CBDC)	Synthetic Hegemonic Currency (SHC)
Example	Bitcoin	National digital currency	Global digital currency "Libra"	Digital € or $	Digital "SDR"
Means of payments	Yes	Yes	Yes	Yes	Maybe
Remuneration	No	No	No	Maybe	Maybe
Volatility	High	Fixed value against one currency	Fixed value against a basket of currencies Volatility against home currency	Fixed value against the issuing Central Bank's currency	Fixed value against a basket of currencies Volatility against home currency
Provision of global liquidity	No	Depending on the currency peg	Yes	Yes	Yes
Lender of last resort	No	No	No	Yes	Yes

benefits to users as private stable coins, but without the risk of a severe loss of value, because the central bank acts as the lender of last resort always. Hence, CBDCs will always be superior to private digital currencies.

How CBDCs should be designed is a topic of intense research efforts and discussions. The design also impacts on possible negative side-effects. While it is beyond the scope of this introduction to go into details that do not yet exist, three major issues shall be highlighted:

- Will private households be allowed to hold accounts directly at the central bank? In this case, CBDCs constitute 'reserves for all' (Niepelt, 2020) and compete with depositing money in commercial banks. Alternatively, such accounts could be mediated by a bank or a fund. However, BIS (2020) argues that this would not constitute a CBDC, as the end-user would not hold a claim on the central bank, but on a commercial bank.[21]
- Should reserves for all receive interest payments? If yes, they would simultaneously constitute a means of payments and a financial asset.
- Should non-residents be allowed to hold national CBDCs, i.e., should they be internationally traded?

Regarding the impact of internationalising national CBDCs, Ferrari, Mehl and Stracca (2020: 8) argue that the global use will intensify international spillovers of shocks in a quantitatively significant way, through a kind of "super charged uncovered interest rate condition". According to the authors, these spillovers can be mitigated by imposing holding limits on transactions by foreigners, and by adjusting the remuneration rates to be more flexible. Nevertheless, they caution that a global CBDC could increase asymmetries in the international monetary system by reducing monetary policy autonomy in foreign economies. Hence, introducing a CBDC early-on could give rise to first-mover advantages.

If CBDCs will come, they will surely first be introduced by national central banks, such as the US Fed or the ECB. China has already started experimenting with it. As such, CBDCs can also be a step towards gradually replacing the dollar-dominated IMFS by a multipolar one, reflecting the multipolar character of the NGE.

Last but not least, there is Carney's proposal of a SHC. However, it is unclear how it should look like and in particular, who would be allowed to use it other than central banks. The more restrictive the selection, the more it would be something like the already existing *Special Drawing Rights* of the IMF, the artificial basket currency by which central banks settle payments in a digital form. More radical proposals hark back on the Keynes plan, proposed at the Bretton Woods Conference in 1944, suggesting taxing trade surplus and deficits symmetrically (see, e.g., Varoufakis, 2016).

7.3 Quo Vadis?

From all these arguments, it follows that the policy debate of the future of the IMFS may revolve around three major issues:

- Should, or will capital movements be somewhat restricted to allow more policy autonomy?
- Should or will key players, such as the Eurozone and China make more efforts to increase the role of their currencies in global financial markets, possibly with the help of CBDCs?
- Will the IMFS finally create a synthetic world currency that allows both smoother creation of global liquidity and more symmetric adjustment processes?

Whatever route the IMFS will take, these three avenues, or combinations thereof, will be key in shaping an IMFS for a multipolar NGE. In the meantime, prudential regulation of global finance remains a key issue (see Chapter 7).

Recommended readings

For a more detailed coverage, the reader may consult classic textbooks like Daniels and Hoose (2017) or Krugman, Obstfeld and Melitz (2018).

For an in-depth coverage of the history of globalising capital, including a discussion of digital currencies, see Eichengreen (2019). De Haan, Oosterloo and Schoenmaker (2015) provide a useful introduction to European financial markets and institutions, and De Grauwe (2014) is a classic text on monetary unions, which is updated regularly.

The websites of the International Monetary Fund (imf.org) and the Bank of International Settlements (bis.org) are useful sources for recent analyses of issues in international finance.

Notes

1 To be more precise, it was a world of *bimetallism*, with a certain role for a gold-to-silver exchange rate. See Eichengreen (2019) for a detailed discussion.
2 Often the official reserve balance is also defined as a part of the financial account. In this case, the current account (plus the 'new' capital account) by definition equals the financial account.
3 In macroeconomic textbooks, the macroeconomic accounting identity is typically derived based on the definition of the GDP. This identity links domestic spending behaviour to net exports, thus ignoring the net income balance with the rest of the world. To link the current account with domestic spending, our accounting identity is therefore based on the Gross National Income (GNI), which includes net factor payments. This is why we speak here of 'private' instead of 'domestic' savings. The interested reader may consult an international economics textbook for details of deriving equation (6.2).
4 The choice of the base year is a crucial one. In the best case, we select a year in which two economies were close to a PPP situation, but it is very difficult to make that judgment with sufficient confidence.
5 Mathematically, converting an absolute version into the relative one is a logarithmic transformation. A multiplication becomes a plus and a division a minus when converting level data into rates of change, i.e., growth rates.
6 This is only approximately true because it ignores that the interest payments received from abroad are also in dollars and, hence, their expected value is also higher when we expect a higher dollar. An exact statement of the UIP includes therefore a term that covers currency gains or losses on the interest payments. However, the term is often very small, especially when interest rates and expected exchange rate changes are not very high. Hence, equation (6.7a) is a good approximation. Professional investors, of course, will include the interaction term in their calculations.
7 The EMS crisis is discussed in more detail in Section 5.
8 The IMF has adopted a classification system based on the flexibility of exchange rate arrangements. All countries are classified by this system in the IMF's Annual Report on Exchange Arrangements and Exchange Restrictions.
9 This has already been discussed in Section 3 and is basically what equation (6.6c) posits.
10 Rose (2000) made the point, based on an empirical study of currency unions, that adopting a common currency boosts trade by a factor of three. Subsequent studies contested these results, and 'shrunk' the common currency effect. Bayoumi and Eichengreen (1992) also caution that a common currency could lead to a more synchronised business cycle, thus turning an asymmetric CU into a symmetric one.
11 Note that the term cross-border banking also covers 'multinational banking', i.e., the creation of subsidiaries and branches, including mergers and acquisitions abroad. These activities are classified as FDI. McCauley (2014) points out that after the GFC, banks increasingly shifted from cross-border banking to multinational banking.

12 For a detailed discussion, especially from a European perspective, see De Haan, Oosterloo and Schoenmaker (2015), which informs this short section. The interested reader should also consult the ECB's regular reports on 'Financial Integration in Europe'.

13 Data is based on the IMF World Economic Outlook Database, October 2020.

14 In a recent study, Hofmann and Park (2020) point to a high risk for emerging economies emanating from a US dollar appreciation. One reason is that US dollar-denominated debts have almost doubled since the GFC, now amounting to above 9% of the GDP of this group. A second reason is that despite the fact that the countries have in recent years gone some way to develop local currency sovereign bond markets, a foreign ownership rate of about 20% since approximately 2013 has not decreased the vulnerability.

15 In principle, higher tariffs could also lead to expenditure switching. However, asking for more trade restrictions would not have been in line with the IMF statutes.

16 Speech by Mario Draghi, President of the European Central Bank at the Global Investment Conference in London, 26 July 2012. Available at: https://www.ecb.europa.eu/press/key/date/2012/html/sp120726.en.html.

17 For a detailed and insightful discussion, see Schoenmaker (2018).

18 The discussion of the Capital Markets Union is beyond the scope of this introduction. For an explainer, see: https://ec.europa.eu/info/business-economy-euro/growth-and-investment/capital-markets-union/what-capital-markets-union_de.

19 The speech is available in the website of the Bank of England: https://www.bankofengland.co.uk/-/media/boe/files/speech/2019/the-growing-challenges-for-monetary-policy-speech-by-mark-carney.pdf.

20 See Adler et al. (2020) for a recent in-depth discussion.

21 This possibility is sometimes called a 'synthetic CBDC'. It should, however, not be confused with Synthetic Hegemonic Currency, as proposed by Carney (2019).

References

Adler, G., Casas, C., Cubeddu, L. M., Gopinath, G., Li, N., Meleshchuk, S., Osorio Buitron, C., Puy, D., & Timmer, Y. (2020). *Dominant currencies and external adjustment.* IMF Staff Discussion Note, SDN 20/05 International Monetary Fund, July.

Baele, L., Ferrando, A., Hördahl, P., Krylova, E., & Monnet, C. (2004). Measuring European financial integration. *Oxford Review of Economic Policy, 20*(4), 509–530.

Bayoumi, T., & Eichengreen, B. (1992). *Shocking aspects of European monetary unification.* NBER Working Paper 3949, January. National Bureau of Economic Research.

BIS (2020). *Central bank digital currencies: Foundational principles and core features.* Report 1. Bank for International Settlements.

Carney, M. (2019). *The growing challenges for monetary policy in the current international monetary and financial system.* Jackson Hole Symposium 2019, August. https://www.bankofengland.co.uk/-/media/boe/files/speech/2019/the-growing-challenges-for-monetary-policy-speech-by-mark-carney.pdf.

Daniels, J. P., & Hoose, D. D. (2017). *Global economic issues and policies* (4th ed.). Routledge.

De Grauwe, P. (2014). *Economics of monetary union* (10th ed.). Oxford University Press.

De Haan, J., Oosterloo, S., & Schoenmaker, D. (2015). *Financial markets and institutions: A European perspective* (3rd ed.). Cambridge University Press.

Eichengreen, B. (2010). The Euro: Love It or Leave It? Voxeu.org. May. https://voxeu.org/article/eurozone-breakup-would-trigger-mother-all-financial-crises.

Eichengreen, B. (2019). *Globalizing capital: A history of the international monetary system.* Princeton University Press.

Eichengreen, B., & Hausmann, R. (1999). *Exchange rates and financial fragility*. National Bureau of Economic Research Working Paper 7418, November. National Bureau of Economic Research.

Ferrari, M., Mehl, A., & Stracca, L. (2020). *Central bank digital currency in an open economy*. ECB Working Paper 2488, November. European Central Bank.

Gygli, S., Haelg, F., Potrafke, N., & Sturm, J.-E. (2019). The KOF globalisation index – revisited. *Review of International Organizations, 14*(3), 543–574.

Hofmann, B., & Park, T. (2020). The broad dollar exchange rate as an EME risk factor. *BIS Quarterly Review*, December 13–26.

IMF (2019). *People's Republic of China. 2019 Article IV Consultation*. IMF Country Report No. 19/266. International Monetary Fund.

Jiang, Z., Krishnamurthy, A., & Lustig, H. (2018). *Foreign safe asset demand and the dollar exchange rate*. NBER Working Paper 24439. National Bureau of Economic Research.

Kleimeier, S., & Sander, H. (2007). *Integrating Europe's retail banking market: Where do we stand?* CEPS Reports in Finance and Banking. Centre for European Policy Studies.

Krugman, P. R. (1991). *Geography and trade*. MIT Press.

Krugman, P. R., Obstfeld, M., & Melitz, M. (2018). *International economics. Theory and policy* (11th ed.). Prentice Hall.

Laeven, L., & Valencia, F. (2020). Systemic banking crises database II. *IMF Economic Review, 68*, 307–361.

Lucas, R. E. (1990). Why doesn't capital flow from rich to poor countries? *American Economic Review, 80*(2), 92–96.

McCauley, R. (2014). De-internationalizing global banking? *Comparative Economic Studies, 56*(2), 257–270.

Meese, R. A., & Rogoff, K. (1983). Empirical exchange rate models of the seventies: do they fit out of sample? *Journal of International Economics, 14*(1–2), 3–24.

Niepelt, D. (2020). Reserves for all? central bank digital currency, deposits, and their (non)-equivalence. *International Journal of Central Banking, 16*(3), 211–237.

Polanyi, K. (1944). *The great transformation*. Farrar & Rinehart.

Rebooting Consensus Authors (2015). *Rebooting the Eurozone: Step 1 – Agreeing a crisis narrative*. Voxeu.org. November. http://voxeu.org/article/ez-crisis-consensus-narrative.

Rey, H. (2015). *Dilemma not trilemma: The global financial cycle and monetary policy independence*. NBER. Working Paper 21162, May, Revised February 2018. National Bureau of Economic Research.

Rose, A. K. (2000). One money, one market: the effect of common currencies on trade. *Economic Policy, 15*(30), 9–45.

Schoenmaker, D. (2018). Building a stable European deposit insurance scheme. *Journal of Financial Regulation, 4*(2), 314–320.

Varoufakis, Y. (2016). Imagining a new Bretton Woods. Project-Sydicate.org. May. https://www.project-syndicate.org/commentary/imagining-new-bretton-woods-by-yanis-varoufakis-2016-05.

7

GOVERNANCE IN THE NEW GLOBAL ECONOMY

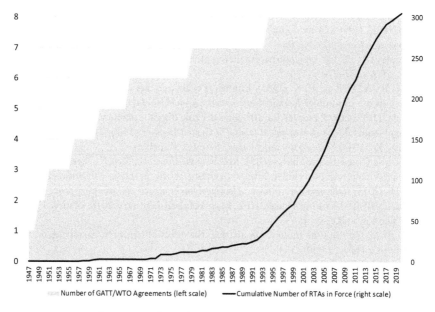

FIGURE 7.1 Cumulative Number of Multilateral and Regional Trade Agreements (RTAs), 1947–2020.

Data sources: For regional trade agreements: WTO, Regional Trade Agreements Information System (RTA-IS), for GATT/WTO agreements: Evenett and Baldwin (2020b).

The crossing of national borders is the fundamental character of international economic activities. In consequence, does a closely integrated global economy need global governance, or is it sufficient that nation states regulate their economic relations with the rest of the world based on national reasonings? While

DOI: 10.4324/9781003057611-7

there are advocates for the extreme positions, in reality we find a parallel of national, regional, and global governance in the global economy. This does, however, neither mean that the present division of governance is the most appropriate one, nor that one approach is best suited for all cross-border activities. Rather, some areas, like climate change or a pandemic, require a global approach while some spillovers could be better regulated or contained by national measures. This chapter discusses these issues, first in more principal terms and then in the context of the major existing global and regional institutions that deal with economic globalisation (Figure 7.1).

1 Global governance for a global economy?

1.1 The globalisation paradox

How much global governance is needed? Harvard professor Dani Rodrik (2011) argues that a political trilemma exists, which forces policymakers to make a choice between hyper-globalisation, national self-determination, and democratic politics, because they can only achieve two of the three at the same time (Figure 7.2).

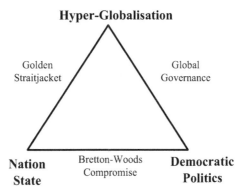

FIGURE 7.2 Rodrik's Political Trilemma: Pick Two, Any Two.
Source: Graph based on Rodrik (2011: 201).

The basic argument for the existence of a globalisation paradox is that **full** economic integration, dubbed as hyper-globalisation, limits the policy space at the national level. In such a 'flat world' nation states are under the discipline of a fully globalised market – the 'golden straitjacket'. For example, under full capital mobility, low tax rates can lure capital into tax havens, and restrict the fiscal policy space of other nation states. Hence, democratic elections may change little to nothing when it comes to actual policy choices. Thus, unrestricted globalisation can be in conflict with democratic mass-politics. According to Rodrik, there are three options:

- The choice of hyper-globalisation and national governance, which runs counter to democratic politics when nation states are unable to deal adequately with the consequences of global integration.

- The choice of hyper-globalisation and democratic politics, which requires democratically legitimised global governance.
- The choice of national self-determination and democratic politics, which requires limiting full economic integration to regain policy space.

Rodrik posits that it is unlikely that nations will surrender sufficient parts of their sovereignty to supranational institutions. If the capacity of nation states to deal with hyper-globalisation is limited, this will ultimately undermine their democratic legitimisation. Hence, Rodrik argues against an **excessive** globalisation that threatens economic and social stability.

The political trilemma is widely debated and has both been criticised and modified. With a bit of oversimplification, we may differentiate three views:

- The so-called **neoliberal view**, which highlights the benefits of globalisation. In this view, there exists at best a dilemma between globalisation and national sovereignty. This limitation of the policy space of the nation state is often viewed positively, even, as markets then discipline policymakers.
- A **differentiating view**, which argues that the choice between two of the three alternatives depends on the problem at hand. While issues that are truly global, such as climate change or a pandemic, are best addressed by global cooperation, other policy areas might better be addressed at the national level.
- A **sweet spot view**, which argues looking for intermediate solutions rather than thinking of the trilemma in terms of 'corner solutions'.

To be fair, Rodrik is aware of all these arguments and has framed the trilemma against the extreme case of a flat world of hyper-globalisation. This should not necessarily be understood as a description of the current state of the world. Rather, the trilemma is best understood as reminding us of narrowing policy options when pushing too far forward with flat world policies.

Clearly, in some areas, like global finance, we are closer to a flat world than in others. Whether or not the trilemma allows sweet spots depends very much on the issue at hand. Moreover, if we are not bound by corner solutions, it may be possible to manage the trade-offs and reconcile them with democratic politics (see European Perspective 7.1).

EUROPEAN PERSPECTIVE 7.1

The EU and the political trilemma

The European Union (EU) as a supranational institution is an interesting application of the political trilemma. While it functions to some extent by means of inter-governmental decision making (elected governments decide jointly in the European Council), it is far from perfect, and democratic legitimisation could clearly be enhanced, e.g. by strengthening the directly elected EU parliament. Yet, the EU offers more democratically legitimised supranational decision-making for the highly integrated European economy than any other supranational body.

Is the EU, which explicitly transfers sovereignty of nation states in some narrowly specified areas, for example in trade policies, better equipped to deal with the trade-offs of Rodrik's trilemma? Benoît Cœuré, a former member of the Executive Board of the *European Central Bank*, responds to Rodrik's trilemma as follows:

> … the European experience shows that these trade-offs are manageable. A variant of globalisation could be based on a parsimonious framework of international rules which leaves room for manoeuvre for national governments. In fact, the principle of subsidiarity which is firmly anchored in the Treaty on European Union can be interpreted as a regional attempt to solve Rodrik's "political trilemma". It aims to ensure that decisions are taken as closely as possible to the citizen and that action at European level is only taken if the objectives cannot be properly achieved at national, regional or local level.*

* Cœuré, B. (2017). Sustainable Globalisation: Lessons from Europe. Speech at the Workshop "Financial Globalization and Its Spillovers – Monetary and Exchange Rate Policy in Times of Crises", Special Public Event "25 Years after Maastricht: The Future of Money and Finance in Europe", Maastricht, 16 February. Available at: https://www.ecb.europa.eu/press/key/date/2017/html/sp170216.en.html.

The key message that can be derived from the political dilemma, formulated in a 'continuous version' that allows for sweet spots, is that nation states face three major open issues in dealing with globalisation:

- What effects on democratically legitimised politics will nation states face when globalising without sufficient global governance? Section 1.2 looks at the trilemma's **golden-straitjacket option** by reviewing the recent evidence regarding the impact of globalisation on democratic politics and political stability.
- How much national sovereignty must be shared at a federal or global level to keep a democratically legitimised policy space? Section 1.3 discusses the pros and cons of the **global governance option**.
- What policies areas are still best being addressed at the national level? Section 1.4 dissects the **compromise option** for nation states in a globalised economy.

1.2 Globalisation and politics: a globalisation backlash?

If free global markets would benefit all – at least after losers from globalisation are compensated sufficiently – there would be no conflict between global economic integration and democracy. This contrasts with the recent rise in populism in many advanced countries, which is often viewed a threat to democracy that has emerged as a consequence of an 'unmanaged' hyper-globalisation. The link between globalisation and a populist globalisation backlash is best understood as a two-step process: First, globalisation must be associated with 'pains', and second, these pains must lead to a politically relevant backlash against democracy.

1.2.1 Globalisation pains

The past three decades of globalisation have lifted millions of people out of poverty, notably in Asia and especially in China, where a new global middle class is emerging. On the other hand, in many advanced countries, the income of the poor and even the middle class has been almost stagnating, while the top 1% in advanced countries were able to increase their incomes substantially, at least until the great financial crisis (GFC).[1] Since all this happened in the era of rapid globalisation, the link between the loss of well-paid (manufacturing) jobs in rich countries due to competition from emerging economies is quickly made.

Standard trade theory suggests that jobs losses in one industry will be over-compensated by the creation of new jobs in other industries. Hence, in the long-run workers will find jobs in the expanding export industry (see Chapter 3). However, a much-debated study (Autor, Dorn & Hanson, 2016) for the US documents lasting negative effects from the offshoring of manufacturing jobs to China. These effects were found to be concentrated on local labour markets, where little adjustment takes place. In consequence, too few new jobs have been generated for those replaced, unemployment has been rising, and lifetime income has been falling.

However, trade globalisation is not the only culprit. New technologies also bear considerable responsibility for job and income losses, especially amongst less-skilled workers in advanced countries. A study by the International Monetary Fund (IMF, 2017) investigates the causes of the global fall of labour shares in income. It reports that in advanced countries the income share of labour has fallen by some 4% points between 1993 and 2014. About half of this fall is attributed to technological advancements, while participation in global value chains (GVCs), as well as financial integration, has played a much smaller role.[2] The study also decomposes the impact according to skill levels and reveals that technology was the relatively more important factor in "hollowing-out the middle class" in advanced countries. This result can also be reconciled with the effects of automating tasks by robotisation, which impacts negatively on labour shares, as argued by Acemoglu and Restrepo (2018).

The situation has been aggravated with the GFC that has pushed especially advanced countries into a long-lasting recession. In Europe, and especially in the Eurozone, the situation has been deteriorating for several countries even more due to the Eurozone crisis. Whereas in a high-pressure economy the fallout of structural changes can somewhat be cushioned by increasing employment opportunities, the twin shock of globalisation and financial crises easily results in deep and permanent negative effects on income and economic security for many people.

In sum, we can identify three major sources of an increased economic insecurity, especially for low- and medium-skilled people in advanced countries: globalisation via a relocation of jobs, technology via robotisation of jobs, and the economic fall-out of financial crises after the GFC.

1.2.2 From globalisation pains to a globalisation backlash?

Are the dark sides of globalisation causing a backlash against globalisation, such as an increase in populist and nationalist sentiments that threaten political stability?

Globalisation pains do not necessarily lead to a rise in populism. In fact, much depends on how policy reacts to these challenges, by preempting or at least cushioning their impact. In a study on populism, Eichengreen (2018: x) conjectures:

> The history recounted here suggests that populism is activated by the combination of economic insecurity, threats to national identity, and an unresponsive political system, but that it can be quelled by economic and political reforms that address the concerns of the disaffected.

What holds back such responses? The argument of economists that losers from globalisation can be compensated from the overall gains of trade is true in principle, but often missing in reality. In fact, policy responses are a matter of political choice. Clearly, some cultures are less inclined to cushion structural change than others. Just think of the US in contrast to Scandinavian countries with their generous welfare systems. Moreover, adequate policy responses can be limited by available resources relative to the size of an economic shock. Especially, the effects of financial crisis shocks can be so dramatic that even massive policy interventions will not be sufficient to avoid a deep and long-lasting recession.

Recent research has shown that the rise of economic insecurity in the aftermath of long-lasting financial crises contributes to the rise of populism. In a historical study for the period 1870–2014, Funke, Schularick and Trebesch (2016) show that recessions induced by financial crises have increased the vote share of far-right parties on average by 30%. Similar results for the Eurozone crisis also speak in favour of this backlash mechanism, pointing again to the important role of cross-border finance and financial instability (see European Perspective 7.2).

EUROPEAN PERSPECTIVE 7.2

Financial crisis and the rise of populism in Europe

In a recent study using regional data across Europe, Algan et al. (2017) find that voting for anti-establishment parties, especially populist ones, has increased in the aftermath of the GFC. Likewise, trust in national and European political institutions has suffered as well. The authors conclude that "crisis-driven economic insecurity is a substantial determinant of populism and political distrust" (2017: 309).

In the Eurozone, where fiscal austerity has been enforced in southern member countries that suffered from a sovereign debt crisis, this has constituted a 'policy straitjacket' for dealing with the impact of globalisation, in particular the 'China shock'. Guiso et al. (2019) show that for western European members of the Eurozone, this straitjacket effect explains three quarters of the higher share of populist parties as compared to the non-Eurozone countries. In other words, the lower the discretion of countries to deal with globalisation in financial crises times, the higher the support for populist parties.

1.3 What role for global governance?

The political trilemma implies that global governance can – in principle – reconcile integration-driven economic efficiency with democratic politics, and thus be instrumental against a backlash to democracy or globalisation. It is therefore tempting to argue that global interdependencies always necessitate global governance. An obvious case for global governance is climate change. Global warming is a global problem, and to be regulated efficiently, a global climate compact involving all emitters of carbon dioxide (CO_2) is clearly the first best solution. In other areas, however, it is not always obvious whether global governance is needed, or even desirable.

The basic rationale for global coordination are spillover effects from one country to another jurisdictions. Such (external) effects can in principle be negative or positive. However, almost all economic decisions and activities create spillovers. For example, high investments in education in China in the past decades have helped the country to upgrade its production and export structure, moving from agriculture to clothing exports to assembling iPhones, and beyond. The subsequent inroads China has made in the clothing and electronics industry has had dramatic repercussions in many advanced countries. Is therefore massive investment in education already a policy that needs to be coordinated globally? Clearly, everybody would disagree. What, then, about government investments in research and development (R&D)? Again, most observers would lodge these policies into the realm of national sovereignty – as long as it is about basic research in government laboratories and universities. But what if R&D support goes as a subsidy to companies? Cases in point are European subsidies to Airbus and US support to Boeing through government agencies. Both policies have been found by the World Trade Organisation (WTO) to violate global trade rules.

The first two examples demonstrate that the simple existence of spillovers is not sufficient to make the case for global governance. It is therefore important to think clearly about when global governance is needed and when not. Rodrik (2020) has developed a number of criteria to judge the cases for and against global governance. We largely follow the very useful logic of his arguments (though not all arguments in detail) in our discussion below.

1.3.1 The cases for global governance

A clear case for global governance is given when cooperation avoids a loss of global welfare (or creates welfare gains) that would (not) occur if countries act in their own self-interests. This, in essence, is the key message of the famous **prisoner's dilemma**, analysed in a game-theoretic approach developed by Nobel laureate John Nash. Cooperation makes each actor better-off than pursuing individual interests in isolation.

Put simply, the prisoner's dilemma is the outcome of a 'game' in which two prisoners are held in isolation and each is made an offer to be released if they accuse the other. The offer is 'designed' in a way that whether or not the accomplice confesses, either prisoner is better-off by confessing. However, if both confess, both are sentenced to long years in prison. By pursuing one's individual self-interest, one harms oneself and the other prisoner. If, on the other hand, both were to pursue a cooperative strategy of 'not confessing', they would have to be released after a short time. The prisoners face the dilemma because they have to decide under complete uncertainty about the other's decision. If they could and would communicate, this 'Nash equilibrium' could be trumped by a cooperative solution, e.g. by a binding and enforceable agreement in advance 'not to talk'. In fact, this is why members of criminal gangs, such as the Mafia, often get away without conviction.

With respect to cross-border activities, two major cases can lead to a prisoner's dilemma situation, where cooperation offers superior solutions: global public goods and (avoidance of) beggar-thy-neighbour behaviour.

Global public goods are an obvious case for global coordination. Public goods are **non-rival** and **non-excludable**. Both features distinguish them from private goods. For example, a sandwich is clearly a private good. It is rival because if you eat it, nobody else can eat it anymore; and it is excludable, as you will only get it after paying for it. By contrast, sunny weather is non-rival. There is no less sunshine for others when you sunbathe, and nobody can be excluded from enjoying the nice weather.

Global climate is a clear case of a global public good. If all countries would agree to limit greenhouse gas emissions, nobody will be excluded from the benefits, and there is no rivalry as the climate benefits for one country will not reduce the benefits for another country. Hence, with a global climate agreement, the world would be better off. But will the world reach such an agreement?

Consider a world of small countries where each country makes only a small contribution to climate change, but the sum of all small countries' emissions is responsible for climate change. A small country has now an incentive not to pursue costly greenhouse gas abatement policies when others are providing the **global common**. Following self-interests in isolation, a world of small countries would decide against climate policies, and make the world as whole – and ultimately each of them – worse off. This situation can only be overcome by a global agreement that rules out free-rider positions. Climate protection is thus a clear case for global governance, especially if there is no enlightened large country that would take the lead in its own interest.

Other examples for global commons are global health policies to contain pandemics, coordinated stimulus packages against a global economic slump, such as after the GFC, or cooperative regulatory efforts to promote global financial stability.

The second case for global governance based on the prisoner's dilemma, is to avoid so-called **beggar-thy-neighbour policies** that were most notorious in the 1930s in the aftermath of the Great Depression when countries tried to protect their economies against foreign competition with higher tariffs or lower values of their currencies.

To make the case of a beggar-thy-neighbour policy, the countries must be large enough to have an impact on the other country. If, then, one country decides in isolation to restrict imports by means of tariff, it can make gains at the expense of the other country. If the other country has the same incentives, it will also be protectionist and retaliate. Trade shrinks and countries forgo gains from trade. Clearly, the cooperative solution of keeping borders open is superior.

What are the gains that countries hope for? If it comes to tariffs and subsequent trade wars, it should be recalled that restricting imports from a more efficient source causes no gain at all, to the contrary, it makes import more expensive. The argument therefore relates only to large countries that can overcompensate these losses by their impact on reducing import prices.[3] Second, in the 1930, high unemployment made it tempting for policymakers, and often rewarding in political terms, to 'support' local producers – be it with tariffs or by means of currency devaluations to reduce imports and increase exports. This led to so-called competitive devaluations in the 1930s, when all countries devalued their currencies to increase (net) exports. However, when all countries devalue, no country achieves improvements, and jointly, they suffer from a 'currency war'.[4]

How, then, to reach a cooperative equilibrium? First, countries can learn from the past and refrain from beggar-thy-neighbour policies. Second, they can resort to global governance, i.e., using formal cooperation-enhancing or cooperation-enforcing institutions. This route has been taken after World War II (WWII). The *General Agreement on Tariffs and Trade* (GATT) was created to restore global trade and avoid trade wars. The *Bretton-Woods* System (BWS) tried to put a hold on competitive devaluation with a system of fixed exchange rates, where devaluations were seen as an exemption that must be agreed to by the *IMF*.

A special case of a beggar-thy-neighbour policy occurs if the world is asymmetric, for example with one large and many small countries. The large country can always gain from not cooperating and, thus, has no incentive to cooperate. Interestingly, a non-cooperative outcome is not so much found with respect to tariffs, probably because even large countries do not value such gains very highly relative to other policy objectives. Instead, Rodrik (2020) points to two cases:

- the case of a cartel, where only one or a few actors can exercise power, for example monopolies in rare minerals; and
- the case of pure tax havens, understood as financial jurisdictions that attract re-domiciling companies for the only reason of obtaining these tax revenues.

In both cases, other countries cannot easily retaliate. Especially regarding taxation, larger countries that have to fund a lot of domestic infrastructure and current spending, cannot afford to reduce the tax rate to a level offered by small tax havens. Consequently, they will not engage in tax competition. Being a tax haven is, therefore, an option that is available only for a few small countries from whom cooperation cannot easily be expected. Hence, this is a very strong case for global governance.[5]

Finally, we can make the case for global governance even when cooperative behaviour is superior, i.e., no prisoner's dilemma exists. A case in point is free trade. Rodrik (2020) reminds us that free trade is not a global public good is the sense described above – at least if one subscribes to the standard trade theory insights that free trade is beneficial for each small individual country, and countries thus have no incentive to be protectionist. However, even if the cooperative free trade solution is superior from the individual country's point of view, the cooperative solution may not materialise because of information and coordination errors. One possible reason could be a lack of mutual trust. Hence, providing transparency is a key task of the WTO.

Another possible rationale for having such an institution is to protect countries with bad domestic governance from hurting themselves and hence, others. Obviously, such 'beggar-thyself policies' are quite frequent for a variety of reasons. They range from a misunderstanding of 'how the world works', to a deliberate use of such policies to favour interest groups within a country, or to please populist sentiments in order to win political support. Examples are trade wars against selected countries, anti-migration policies, misguided austerity policies, financial under-regulation, bad tax systems, and many more.

In sum, there are three strong cases for global governance:

- Prisoner's dilemma cases where coordination creates welfare gains that would not emerge from pursing individual self-interests, such as global climate and global health policies.

- Beggar-thy-neighbour policies, which can induce 'a race to the bottom', e.g. trade wars, competitive devaluations, regulatory competition, and asymmetric beggar-thy-neighbour policies, such as those pursued by pure tax havens.
- Cases in which superior cooperative solutions are in the 'enlightened' self-interest of a country, but information and coordination errors require institutions or mechanisms to help the cooperative solution to materialise.

1.3.2 Ambiguous cases for global governance

From our introductory examples of spillovers, we have seen that not everything that creates a spillover requires global governance. How should we decide what to leave to the discretion of national policymakers and what needs global coordination? Again, we follow Rodrik (2020), identifying three cases that speak in favour of national decision-making:

- **The spillover does not create a global inefficiency**. For example, national education policies or general R&D spending make the world better-off, as they contribute to global knowledge.
- **The spillover creates a global inefficiency, but the domestic economy bears the direct costs**. Consider, for example, a ban on imports of goods produced with forced labour. The country that bans the imports will then pay with higher import prices for its higher moral standards and values.
- **The policies that create spillovers are mainly introduced for domestic reasons**. Education policies, R&D spending, as well as industrial and regional policies fall into this category, whenever they aim at strengthening the domestic economy rather than enriching the economy at the expense of the others. However, here the devil is in the detail. Industrial policies, especially, are often a major cause of trade policy conflicts nowadays.

In sum, we have seen that in some areas the case for global governance is strong, while in others it is not so clear cut. This does, however, not mean that cooperation is not useful or desirable. Rather, the task is to identify for what issues coordination is needed and most helpful, and how deep this cooperation should go.

1.4 The nation state in the global economy

The nation state is still the core unit of decision-making in the global economy. It can transfer sovereignty to supranational bodies if it wishes so, or reclaim it. EU enlargement and Brexit are the obvious examples. Why and when are nation states willing to hand-over sovereignty to supranational institutions? One set of reasons has been discussed before, and points to areas in which global regulation is superior to national regulation. But global regulation also comes with costs: one-size-fit-all solutions can be bad fits if preferences about these rules and regulations differ across countries. According to an influential theoretical model by

Alesina and Spolaore (1997, 2005), the optimal size of a political union can be derived by weighing the benefits of integration against the costs that accrue to citizens because of heterogenous preferences.

The benefits of integration often increase with size. The classic example is that larger markets allow for economics of scale, which reduce not only the costs of producing goods for the domestic market, but also enhance competitiveness in global markets. This has been a key argument for the European Single Market from its inception onward.

However, countries often differ in preferences. Regarding private goods, like cars or clothing, citizens make their own choices. This is why we observe national differences in what clothes people wear and what cars they drive. However, the provision of public goods such as schooling, healthcare, defence, etc. is typically the task of the nation state. Thus, these public goods should also reflect the preferences of the citizens.

The major lesson from these considerations is that a balance needs to be struck between efficiency and scale on the one side, and catering for heterogeneity on the other side. Large countries may be very efficient in economic terms, but small countries may have an edge in catering for their citizens' preferences. However, large countries have developed ways to deal with heterogeneity, namely federalism. For example, the US is a single market with one currency, but individual states have leeway in providing some public goods, or regulating how to deal with drugs, weapons, etc.

Many EU member states are federal states as well, and in the EU itself the principle of subsidiarity is key. It says that what can be regulated at the lowest level, should be delegated to that level. This way it should be ensured that the benefits of size are obtained without regulating against the preferences of the EU citizens (see European Perspective 7.3).

EUROPEAN PERSPECTIVE 7.3

Is Europe an optimal political area?

In a recent paper, Alesina, Tabellini and Trebbi (2017) explore whether Europe is an optimal political area, thus trying to shed empirical light on the theoretical questions asked by Alesina and Spolaore (1997, 2005).

The authors start by noting that majority of Europeans are in favour of EU decision-making in key areas such as fighting terrorism, promoting peace and democracy, protecting the environment, or dealing with migration from outside the EU. However, in terms of key cultural traits they found fundamental differences in the original EU-15 countries, which have not converged by any important measure between 1980 and 2009. To quote the authors:

> On the contrary, between 1980 and 2009 Europeans became slightly more different in their attitudes toward trust, values such as appreciation of hard work or obedience, gender roles, sexual morality, religiosity, ideology, the state's role in the economy, and related economic issues. We show that these traits evolved over time and are not immutable national characteristics. Both Northern and Southern European countries became more secular, but the former at a faster rate than the latter, so cross-country differences increased.
>
> However, the authors also show that preference heterogeneity and cultural diversity are up to ten times as large within each member state than between them. Hence, if individual member states can handle these differences, why not the EU? Moreover, the authors posit that the problem is not cultural differences at such, but rather, that these relatively small differences are vastly amplified by other cleavages, such as national identity and language. If this is so, working on developing a European identity relative to national identity may be most important for a well-functioning EU.
>
> (Alesina, Tabellini & Trebbi, 2017: 171)

That said, it does not mean that everything that is subject to common EU policies really belongs there, and conversely, some areas regulated at national level might better be allocated at the EU level. Consider, for example, the dramatic increase of asylum seekers from Syria in 2015, labelled as the 'migration crisis'. It revealed the lack of a common border protection and policy in the presence of free mobility within the EU's Schengen area. The inherent contradiction between national control in and within a supranational territory ultimately resulted in a (temporary) re-erection of national borders.

In sum, the decision of what should be allocated to the national or to the supranational level will remain a key issue of governance in the new global economy (NGE).

1.5 Multilateral, regional, and national governance

The governance of cross-border movement of goods, services, capital, labour, knowledge, etc. is multi-layered, with national, regional, and global regulations overlapping. In many cases, national sovereignty is restricted by commitments at the global, regional, and – increasingly – at the bilateral level.

The major difference between multilateral and regional (as well as bilateral) agreements is that the former are non-discriminatory, treating all countries alike, while the latter are discriminatory and preferential, treating members and non-members differently.

Most regional agreements focus on trade and trade-related issues. Hence, the recent proliferation of regional and bilateral agreements competes with the multilateral trade system. However, the WTO rules allow countries, under certain conditions, to form or join a regional or bilateral trade agreement. Basically all WTO member countries are also members of one or more of the – at the time of writing – 305 regional and bilateral trade agreements. These agreements typically override WTO rules. However, increasingly, these agreements are deeper in the sense that they often regulate cross-border issues in more detail than multilateral agreements. Arguable, the EU represents the world's deepest regional integration scheme, comprising a single market with uniform rules and regulations as well as a single currency.

Regional and bilateral agreements can thus be complementary to the multilateral system, as they allow deeper forms of integration than the multilateral system provides. Our discussion of the role of nation states suggests that the more preferences differ across countries, the less deep integration is meaningful. Consequently, the more countries involved, the less likely a good match of preferences. Hence, it may make sense to have a parallel of regional and global arrangements. Moreover, as argued by the former Director General of the WTO, Pascal Lamy (2020: ix), "preferential trade agreements could create a dynamic reform process leading to more, not less, global integration."

However, regional agreements can also become a substitute – if not a threat – to the multilateral system. For example, regional clubs could set and dominate the global rules, or large countries could aim at substituting the multilateral system by means of a multitude of bilateral agreements.

In Section 2 the governance of the multilateral trading system is discussed. Section 3 reviews the economics and politics of preferential agreements, and Section 4 exhibits the key elements of governance of global finance.

2 The multilateral trading system

Do we need a multilateral trade system with internationally accepted rules, overseen and enforced by an institution like the WTO? After all, if free trade is in the interest of each country, there is no reason to expect a prisoner's dilemma that calls for cooperation. Rather, acting in one's own enlightened self-interest would be enough to ensure free trade and cooperative behaviour. However, as discussed before, for containing beggar-thy-neighbour policies and to overcome information and coordination failures, a more secure alternative is to resort to global governance by creating institutions, such as GATT. While GATT was basically a **contract** between member countries, its successor, the WTO, is an **organisation** that oversees whether members play according to the rules and provides information on compliance, hence contributing to solve information and coordination problems.

2.1 The basic principles of the multilateral trading system

GATT had been established in 1947 as a **contract** between 24 signatory states. This contract is based on a few basic principles.

The first one is the **most-favoured nation (MFN)** principle.[6] It ensures that all countries are treated alike, thus establishing a non-discriminatory trading system. The principle demands that a 'favour' to one member must be extended to all others. A favour in the context of trade is typically a lower tariff. Note that this language is based on a mercantilist view that considers more and cheaper imports as a threat, rather than something that a country does in its own interest, as free traders would argue.

The second principle demands **reciprocity**. The favour extended to one country should be matched by a **comparable concession** from that country. Again, this reflects mercantilist thinking: if our country opens its market as a concession, it will demand more market access to that country as well. To negotiate comparable concessions is a highly complex task, as it is usually not about comparable concessions in the same industry but across industries. For example, a country with a (comparative) advantage in agriculture may wish better access to the foreign food market, while the other country wants market access for its automobile industry. To determine what is acceptable, trade negotiators need to feed back with stakeholders at home, of which some are winners and others are losers. Here, and only here, the basic insight of Ricardo's principle of comparative advantage applies: a deal is better than no deal, i.e., opening up delivers efficiency and welfare gains. Trade negotiators have the difficult task to weigh these overall gains against the distributional consequences inside their societies.

The third principle demands **binding concessions**. Once an agreement is reached, no backsliding is allowed. In the classical disciplines of trade policies this means no tariff increases, no new quotas, and no new export subsidies.

These three principles lead almost automatically to **multilateral trade negotiations**. To illustrate this, consider that the US wants to negotiate a better access to the Japanese automobile market, and Japan agrees provided that the US lowers tariffs for Japanese electronics. Now the MFN principle comes in and demands that Japan open its automobile market to all other car exporters as well, while the US must extend the tariff reduction on electronics to all other countries. Hence, lower MFN tariffs are introduced. However, this is not the end of the story, as the US and Japan would now demand reciprocity from all other electronics and automobile exporters, respectively. Their offers will most likely cover many different industries. As a consequence, ultimately all countries and all industries will be involved in trade negotiations. Such talks are best organised in multilateral meetings, earlier labelled 'GATT-Rounds', and since the establishment of the WTO in 1995, as 'WTO Ministerial Meetings'. When successfully concluded, these rounds determine new sets of MFN tariffs as well as other trade regulations, which are binding until a new agreement in the next round is accomplished.

Table 7.1 gives an overview of the trading rounds since 1947. Most strikingly, after large initial tariffs cuts only little progress was made until 1967. European countries and Japan were reluctant to open up their economies because they were still reconstructing their economies after WWII. Even after 1967, Japan was still

TABLE 7.1 Multilateral Trading Rounds since 1947

Negotiation Round	Countries	Average Tariff Cuts
1st round 1947	23	26%
2nd round 1949	13	3%
3rd round 1951	38	4%
4th round 1956	26	3%
5th (Dillon) round 1960–1961	26	4%
6th (Kennedy) round 1964–1967	62	37%
7th (Tokyo) round 1973–1979	102	33%
8th (Uruguay) round 1986–1994	123	38%
WTO Doha round 2001–?	157	no agreement

Source: Based on Evenett and Baldwin (2020b: 25).

considered relatively closed. Hence, the next GATT round started in Tokyo, and finished with severe average tariff cuts.

Both the Kennedy and the Tokyo Round changed the design and outcome of the negotiations. With the Kennedy Round, the cumbersome item-by-item negotiations were replaced by a formula approach that became instrumental in engineering larger tariff cuts. The approach requires an average tariff cut for all industries, but leaves room for more protection for sensitive industries, as long as the average target is met. With respect to outcomes, other trade policy instruments became the target of trade liberalisers. The Kennedy Round finished with provisions on anti-dumping measures, and the Tokyo round targeted other non-tariff barriers. However, the following Uruguay Round (UR) became the most ambitious trading round ever, bringing several new items under the umbrella of the world trading system.

2.2 From GATT to the WTO

To understand what was achieved in the UR and why the results are such that the appetite for a new agreement is almost nil, even after more than 25 years, we need to briefly go back to the situation that the UR sought to address. Three major issues stood out:

- Many developing countries were highly protectionist and exempted entirely from reciprocity requirements.
- A protectionist backlash emerged in the 1980s. A grey area protectionism employed new instruments like 'voluntary export restraints' and 'orderly marketing arrangements', such as the infamous 'Multifibre Agreement' (MFA) that imposed export quotas on developing countries. Moreover, an increasing (mis-)use of anti-dumping and countervailing duties was observed, which unlevelled the previously levelled playing field again.[7]

- Agricultural markets in advanced countries had remained relatively closed, especially the European common agricultural market, but also the rice market in Japan, and sugar market in the US.

The UR addressed these and a number of other new issues. The most important results are:

- The landmark achievement of the UR was the establishment of the WTO as an institution to oversee the trading rules of the multilateral rules-based system. Hence, the WTO became more powerful than the GATT, thus strengthening all multilateral disciplines and making market access more secure.
- Grey area measures, such as certain forms of voluntary export restraints, had to be phased out. In particular, the UR terminated the MFA, which was first converted into the Agreement on Textile and Clothing (ACT), which finally expired on January 1, 2005.
- So-called **special and differential treatment** provisions were established. They allow developed countries to treat developing countries more favourably than other WTO members and not to demand full reciprocity.
- Liberalisation of the agricultural sector, especially by converting European quotas into equivalent tariffs which were scheduled to be reduced over time.
- An agreement on trade-related intellectual property rights (TRIPS).
- An agreement on trade in services (GATS).
- An agreement on trade-related investment measures (TRIMs).

The UR achieved these results in a **single undertaking** and created a multilateral agreement that went far beyond traditional trade policies.

2.3 The structure of the WTO

The WTO is governed by member countries' government representatives by consensus decisions in the *Ministerial Conference* (see Figure 7.3). Three major bodies handle the major tasks of the WTO. The *General Council* oversees trade in goods (GATT), trade in services (GATS), and trade-related intellectual property rights (TRIPS). The latter are new multilateral disciplines introduced by the UR. Further, the UR introduced the *Trade Policy Review Body* and the *Dispute Settlement Body*, which also report to the Ministerial Conference. The former documents and analyses member states' trade policies in regularly published trade policy reviews. Hence, they play an important role for the information function of the WTO by providing transparency on trade policies. The latter's task is not to pass judgements, but to settle disputes between members based on clearly-defined rules. This, of course, can limit the national sovereignty, when member states respect the rulings of the Body. If not, the Body can give the complaining side the permission to retaliate. This way, it is hoped to make a rules-based multilateral trading system more effective and predictable.

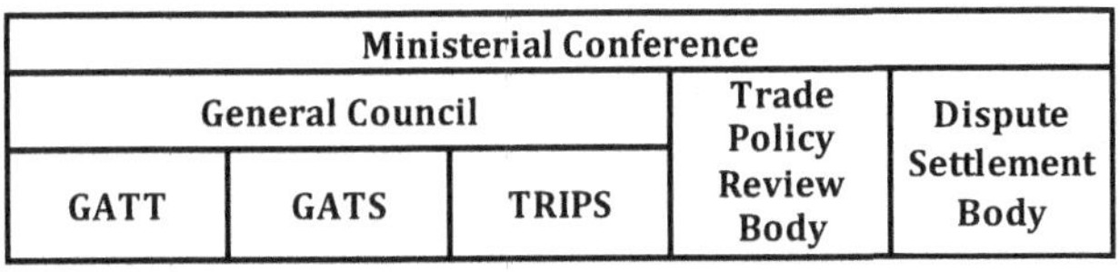

Ministerial Conference				
General Council			Trade Policy Review Body	Dispute Settlement Body
GATT	GATS	TRIPS		

FIGURE 7.3 The (Simplified) Structure of the WTO.

2.4 The future of the WTO

Why has no new agreement been reached since 1993, and is, therefore, the WTO still fit for purpose? Three major groups of issues stand out: (1) old unresolved controversies, (2) new, difficult to tackle issues, and (3) the bridging between different capitalist systems in an emerging multipolar world. The old unresolved issues are:

- Many developing countries consider the markets for their agricultural exports as too closed, and argue that the advanced countries have neither delivered fully on the expectations raised in the UR, nor made sufficient offers yet.
- The TRIPS agreement has made access to technology more expensive, especially for developing, non-innovating countries. A particular case in point are patents on pharmaceuticals. This has been revealed by the dispute on the production of generic AIDS medicines by countries like Brazil, India, and South Africa, which led to demands from the US government to honour US patents. While the TRIPS agreement allows the production of generics in case of public health emergencies, it was only in 2001 with the launch of the Doha Round, that such emergencies were clearly defined to include the AIDS epidemic. Many observers, however, view the current regulations as still harmfully impacting public health, especially in poor countries that do not have an own pharmaceutical industry.
- Advanced countries are dissatisfied with the protection of intellectual property rights in some developing economies, notably China.
- The dispute settlement mechanism has been criticised, predominantly by some US administrations, unwilling to accept the Body's rulings. The conflict culminated in 2020 when the Trump administration rejected the nomination of new judges.

A non-exhaustive list of new and often difficult to tackle items, which potentially call for multilateral regulation includes

- rules and standards to facilitate global value chain trade,
- rules and standards for trade in data,
- incorporating environmental standards in trading rules,
- incorporating labour standards in trading rules,

- rules for trade in knowledge and intellectual property rights, and
- dealing with behind the border policies, such as subsidies and government procurement.

The last point also relates to the challenge of dealing with different economic systems in a multipolar world. The Chinese version of state capitalism with an important role of government guidance and financial support is challenging the Western view, which has informed and dominated the development of the multilateral system in the past. Opening up has been seen as key to spur productivity and growth via international competition, with the paradigm of a level playing field guiding the multilateral trade agenda. The new key players, however, insist more or less openly on actively using **industrial policies**. This already has changed the stance of advanced countries towards interventionist policies, and will require new answers on how to deal with the substantial differences in policy approaches in a multipolar world.

How can the world trading system respond to these challenges?

- First, initiating a new WTO Round, aiming at resolving and balancing the open issues in a new single undertaking.
- Second, aiming at less ambitious multilateral agreements, which re-focus on what a multilateral trading system should and can deliver. In other words, identifying a new denominator concerning the very purpose of the WTO (Evenett & Baldwin, 2020b).
- Third, delegating the new 'deep' issues to agreements at the regional or bilateral level (see below).

The first route has so far led to an impasse, and it is not clear how this type of multilateralism can be revived in a multipolar world without a hegemon to champion it. If this assessment is correct, the alternatives left are re-focused multilateralism or discriminatory regionalism. We return to this issue after the discussion of regional agreements.

3 Regional trade agreements

Regional trade agreements (RTAs) are discriminatory, and thus preferential agreements[8] that treat members better than non-members. Hence, they violate the MFN principle. Nevertheless, the WTO rules allow exemptions if a number of criteria are met.[9] Above all, the agreements should liberalise trade among the RTA members, and shall not erect new barriers with the formation.

In December 2020, 305 RTAs have been in force. Especially in the 2000s, the (cumulative) number of RTAs in place increased rapidly, as can be seen from the yearly numbers of new notifications to the WTO in Figure 7.4. As the notifications concern goods, services, and accessions to an RTA, there is some overlap.

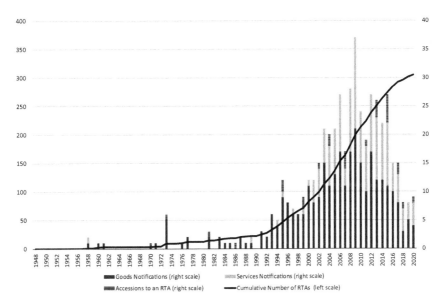

FIGURE 7.4 Evolution of Regional Trade Agreements, 1948–2020.
Source: Own graph inspired by WTO graph at http://rtais.wto.org/UI/charts.aspx#. Data are
retrieved from Regional Trade Agreements Information System (RTA-IS).

Hence, the sum of all notifications is higher than the sum of all RTAs. Moreover,
not all notifications resulted (already) in an RTA in place.

3.1 Forms of RTAs

RTAs can take different forms with different levels of integration:

- A **Free Trade Area** (FTA) is the least demanding agreement. In most cases,
  abolishment or lowering of trade barriers is agreed upon. A key issue is that
  FTAs require detailed **rules of origin** to avoid third-party exports from
  entering a country under preferential tariffs, e.g. by taking advantage of a
  lower external tariff by the partner country.
- A **Custom Union** (CU) can avoid the rules-of-origin problem by agreeing
  on **common external tariffs**. While this avoids expensive import controls,
  a consensus on a uniform tariff structure is often difficult to reach, especially
  when countries differ in development levels and economic structure. For example, a developing country may wish to protect its infant electronics industry, while the RTA partner prefers to import cheap electronics from third
  countries. By contrast, if countries share economic interests, like the six European countries that founded the European Steel and Coal Community in
  1950, the nucleus of the later EU, an agreement may be reached more easily.

- A **Single Market**, like the EU Single Market created in 1992, comprises not only free movement of goods and services but also of capital and labour. Moreover, a single market requires the approximation of regulation to create a level playing field.
- An **Economic Union** aims at establishing common economic policy making, such as a common fiscal policy or a single currency, e.g. the Euro, introduced in 1999.
- A full-fledged **Political Union**, probably as a federal union, thus creating a nation state.

The most common form of an RTA are FTAs, which focus on reducing standard trade barriers. Typical examples are the (former) North American Free Trade Agreement (NAFTA), ASEAN Free Trade Area (AFTA), and many more. We therefore start with discussing the economics and politics of a classic FTA.

3.2 The economics of preferential trade liberalisation

The classic theory of preferential trade liberalisation holds that regional trade liberalisation is not simply a partial liberalisation, which is just a bit less welfare-increasing than a global one. Rather, it can actually be welfare-reducing. Hence, forming an FTA can be a bad idea.

To illustrate this, consider three countries, South, Middle, and North, which all produce bananas. South is the most efficient and cheapest producer, North the most expensive one, and Middle in-between. Without any tariffs, North would import bananas from South. Now consider that North protects its banana industry with a prohibitive tariff, such as the country only consumes bananas expensively produced at home. If the country now forms an FTA with Middle, it starts importing relatively cheaper bananas from Middle. Consumers in North will benefit from this **trade creation**. But what if the tariffs had not been prohibitive before joining the FTA, such that North imported bananas from South? Forming an FTA now with Middle could provide the new partner with a price advantage. North will switch from cheap South bananas to less-efficiently produced Middle bananas. This **trade diversion** will not only hurt South, but also consumers in North, who now buy from a less efficient source.

The key insight of the theory of preferential trade liberalisation is that an FTA is only beneficial if trade creation exceeds trade diversion. Economists therefore investigate these effects in detail when evaluating the welfare effects of an FTA. Without going here into the details of such an evaluation, there are four useful rules of thumb to check whether an FTA 'tends' to be favourable (see also European Perspective 7.4):

- If the FTA is large and involves many countries, it is more likely that the least-cost producers in most industries are part of it. Hence, trade diversion is less likely. Clearly, the largest FTA is the multilateral trading system that comprises the whole world where no trade diversion is possible.

- If the cost differences between intra-regional and extra-regional suppliers are small, the negative welfare effects may be negligible. This is often true in major industries across advanced countries. By contrast, in agriculture, this condition is often not met.
- If tariff were high or even prohibitive, and is then cut sharply by forming the FTA, substantial trade creation effects are more likely to dominate trade diversion.
- If the FTA pursues an 'open regionalism' that aims at low external tariffs, this might mitigate or avoid trade diversion effects.

EUROPEAN PERSPECTIVE 7.4

Is the EU a favourable trading bloc?

The EU can serve as an illustration of the listed bullet points. It is a very large trading bloc and has least-cost suppliers in many industries, such as the automobile industry. Moreover, in such industries cost differences are often small and trade between members and non-members is thus often characterised by intra-industry trade.

There are exemptions, though. For one thing, there is agriculture, where producers outside the EU often have a comparative advantage, e.g. because of climatic reasons in tropical products or because of vast availability of land. Another example are labour-intensive industries such as clothing. The difference between the two sectors is that in agriculture, the EU is highly protectionist, while trade restrictions on clothing imports are low and have been reduced. Hence, trade diversion in agriculture is much more likely than in clothing.

In sum, most observers agree that the EU is on balance trade creating while there is some trade diversion in sensitive and highly protected sectors.

In the policy world, however, the economic argument of trade creation versus trade diversion is not always decisive for forming or joining an RTA.[10]

- First, forming an RTA is not driven only, or even predominantly, by economic considerations. The formation of the EU has been foremost a project to bring peace and stability to the region. This was the driving factor for signing the Treaty of Rome in 1957, and is also key for the EU's eastern enlargement process. Geopolitics are a key driver of many other RTAs as well.
- Second, policymakers typically emphasise other economic aspects than net welfare effects from trade creation and trade diversion. In particular, 'market access' is a major argument in the political sphere.
- Third, in the context of today's global value chains, which are often regionally concentrated, RTAs support cross-border value chain trade, which can

bring huge efficiency gains. For example, the formation of AFTA in 1992 has been understood by Asian policymakers as an attempt to send a signal to international investors to locate their production networks in the region.

- Fourth, RTAs are increasingly viewed as instruments that go beyond what can be achieved at the multilateral level, especially as there has been no substantial new multilateral agreement since 1993.

The last two arguments especially have contributed to the rise of so-called deep trade agreements.

3.3 Deep trade agreements

Regional agreements are increasingly going beyond removing obvious trade restrictions, such as tariffs and quotas. Many new deep trade agreements (DTAs) aim at

> establishing five 'economic integration' rights: free (or freer) movement of goods, services, capital, people, and ideas. DTAs also include enforcement provisions that limit the discretion of importing governments in these areas, as well as provisions that regulate the behaviour of exporters.
>
> *(Mattoo, Rocha & Ruta, 2020: 3)*

Figure 7.5 illustrates these developments. The measures labelled 'WTO+' are those already covered by the WTO mandate but where the RTA goes deeper

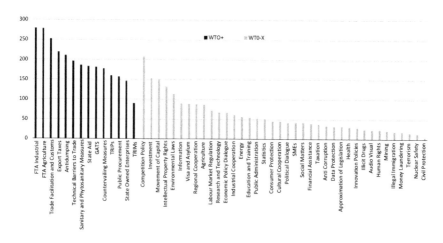

FIGURE 7.5 Number of Policy Areas Covered in Preferential Trade Agreements Within (WTO+) and Outside (WTO-X) the WTO Mandate, 1958–2015★.

Source: World Bank, Deep Trade Agreements Data Set DTA1: information by trade agreements. Retrieved at: www.datatopics.worldbank.org/dta/table.html.

★ Notified at WTO. For a detailed description of the policy areas and a discussion of the classification see Mattoo, Rocha and Ruta (2020).

than WTO regulations. Especially areas where the debate at the WTO level are at an impasse play a big role here, notably intellectual property rights and government subsidies (labelled state aid in the figure). Increasingly new issues, labelled 'WTO-X', are also on the agenda of these agreements. Especially measures aiming at creating a level playing field, such as competition and investment measures, and rules for dealing with labour and environmental standards, are of increasing importance in DTAs.

Arguably, the EU is the deepest of all DTAs, with its single market for goods, services, capital, and labour as a core element, but also including common regulations in many other areas, ranging from competition policy to labour, environment and safety standards, and, last but not least, a common currency.

Another important step towards DTAs have been the mega-regional trade agreements, initiated by the Obama administration. Best knows are the controversial *Transatlantic Trade and Investment Partnership* (T-TIP) between the US and the EU, and the *Transpacific Partnership* (TPP) between the US and a select number of Pacific countries. Both agreements aimed at creating a level playing field to facilitate global value chain production and trade, and also to include some measures especially regarding labour and environmental standards. In doing so, they went beyond what would have been attainable at the multilateral level. Yet, they also had a very strong geopolitical intention by strengthening the transatlantic cooperation via T-TIP, and containing China by excluding the country from TPP.

Both agreements met with fierce critique. T-TIP received criticism in the civil society in Europe because it had been negotiated in secrecy, intended to establish an 'Investor-State-Dispute-Settlement' mechanism, which would use arbitration fora that could seriously impair national sovereignty rights, and a general assessment that business interests have trumped the interests of consumers and workers. The Trump administration put the T-TIP on hold, and in 2019 the EU decided to consider the agreement as obsolete. Instead, the EU has in the meantime focused on negotiating DTAs with many other countries and regions (Canada, Vietnam, Japan, Singapore, Australia, New Zealand, Mexico, Mercosur).

TPP was most controversial in the US. After the Trump administration withdrew from TPP, the agreement has been re-negotiated and concluded as *Comprehensive and Progressive TPP* (CPTPP), which features many innovative rules for dealing with global value chains, as well as labour and environmental rights.

Furthermore, in 2020 the *Regional Comprehensive Economic Partnership* (RCEP) negotiations have been concluded. RCEP is a regional Asia-Pacific RTA that includes China. However, most observers see RCEP more like a somewhat extended FTA rather than a DTA.

3.4 The perils of deep trade agreements

Regional initiatives, especially DTAs, go beyond what can be achieved at the multilateral level. In this sense, they can be complementary to the multilateral trading system. However, differences in the agreements of a country or a trading bloc with its various partner countries is inherently discriminatory.

What can often be observed is that civil society representatives lobby in favour of including conditions regarding human, environmental, and labour rights into RTAs, thus using the lever of the partner countries' business interests to promote these rights abroad. Regional agreements, thus, often face a debate whether negotiators have been strict enough, or rather bowed to business interests and/or the sheer economic power of negotiation partners (see European Perspective 7.5).

EUROPEAN PERSPECTIVES 7.5

The EU–China comprehensive agreement on investment (CAI)

On 30 December 2020, the EU has concluded with China a comprehensive agreement on investment. According to first information from the EU Commission,

> China has committed to a greater level of market access for EU investors than ever before, including some new important market openings. China is also making commitments to ensure fair treatment for EU companies so they can compete on a better level playing field in China, including in terms of disciplines for state owned enterprises, transparency of subsidies and rules against the forced transfer of technologies. For the first time, China has also agreed to ambitious provisions on sustainable development, including commitments on forced labour and the ratification of the relevant ILO fundamental Conventions.*

The CAI has met two lines of critique. First, from the point of view of the incoming Biden administration, a joint US-EU dealing with China would have been preferred. Second, the provisions on dealing with human and labour rights, have been criticised as too vague and non-enforceable. In contrast, Rodrik** argues that the EU should not attempt to export its system and values by negotiating very narrow commitments, and thus limiting it freedom to pursue policies to safeguards its values. Most recently, by the time of final editing this book, the CAI has been put on hold by the EU.

See: http://trade.ec.europa.eu/doclib/press/index.cfm?id=2233.
*** See: http://www.project-syndicate.org/commentary/what-the-europe-china-investment-treaty-can-and-cannot-achieve-by-dani-rodrik-2021-01.*

An alternative, suggested by Rodrik (2017), is defining the basic 'traffic rules' in the multilateral system, while nation states or regional blocs like the EU, treat – within these rules – all countries alike. For example, if countries wish to protect labour or environmental standards, e.g. by means of a social anti-dumping policy or a border carbon adjustment tax, they could do so on the basis of the MFN principle rather than treating countries differently, and imposing rules based on their relative negotiation powers in RTAs.

However, are such traffic rules in line with current WTO rules, or rather, can we expect such rules to be included in future WTO agreements with the consent of all major players in the emerging multipolar world? In other words, could such rules be part of a revitalisation of a re-focused multilateral trading system as discussed in Section 3?

4 The governance of global money and finance

The governance of global money and finance has been evolving along monetary and financial integration – occasionally shaping it but at times also lagging behind. The rise of flexible exchange rates from the 1980s onwards has held the promise of national monetary independence and less need for global governance. However, as discussed in Chapter 6, this promise has not been kept fully. Recurrent financial crises, including the GFC and also the dominance of the US dollar in the international monetary and financial system (IMFS) are pointing to the need for global cooperation.

4.1 International financial institutions

The core international financial institutions are the so-called Bretton-Woods twins, the *IMF* and the *International Bank for Reconstruction and Development* (IBRD), commonly known as the *World Bank*.

The original key functions of the IMF were linked to the needs of the *Bretton-Woods System* (BWS) of fixed exchange rates (see Chapter 6). The IMF provided balance-of-payments financing in case of a shortage of foreign exchange. After the breakdown of the BWS in 1973, most advanced countries switched to flexible exchange rates. Yet, many developing countries kept their currencies linked to major currencies, mostly the US dollar. Hence, the IMF's major clients became developing countries. A particular game changer was the Asian crisis in 1997. Asian countries were dissatisfied with both the efficacy and the intrusiveness of IMF assistance and conditionality. After the crisis was resolved, these countries started to pile up currency reserves to become independent of the IMF. Since then, the Fund has been changing towards an institution providing macroeconomic advice and to develop IMF-supported policy programs in a more consensual way, as it has been recognised that 'program ownership' by national government is a key success factor.

In more general terms, and in its own words from its website at www.imf. org/en/about:

> The IMF's primary purpose is to ensure the stability of the international monetary system—the system of exchange rates and international payments that enables countries (and their citizens) to transact with each other.

The Fund's mandate was updated in 2012 to include all macroeconomic and financial sector issues that bear on global stability.

Hence, today, the IMF plays a major role by means of its expertise gathered from close surveillance of global financial stability at the country, regional, and global levels.

The World Bank basically provides long-term finance and advisory services to middle-income and low-income countries, and – if need be – assists with co-ordinating responses to regional and global challenges, such as natural disasters, reconstruction after wars, or health pandemics. Similar tasks are also performed by *Regional Development Banks*, such as the *Interamerican Development Bank*, the *Asian Development Bank*, the *African Development Bank*, and the *European Bank for Reconstruction and Development*.

Another key player is the *Bank for International Settlements* (BIS), located in Basel, Switzerland. Established in 1930, its original purpose was to act as the bank of the central banks. Given the challenges to financial stability, its mission today includes also "to serve central banks in their pursuit of monetary and financial stability and to foster international cooperation in those areas". The BIS is best known, for the *Basel Committee on Banking Supervision* (BCBS), which is setting global standards for the prudential regulation of banks, in its present version aka *Basel III*.

Though by definition not an international institution, the *US Federal Reserve Bank* (Fed), is playing a key role in the IMFS. As discussed in more detail in Chapter 6, the dominance of the US dollar can in times of crisis lead to severe dollar shortages. This happened in a dramatic way during the GFC and again in March 2020 in the midst of the Covid-19 pandemic. The Fed reacted in the joint interest of the global financial system by providing direct dollar credits, so-called *swap lines*, to major central banks, which they in turn could pass on to banks and corporations in urgent need of US dollars.

The meetings of the *G7*, the group of seven major advanced countries, and the *G20*, the larger group of 20 leading advanced and emerging economies, also provide fora for global policy cooperation. The *G20*, for example, has also estab-lished in 2009 the *Financial Stability Board* (FSB) to monitor the stability of the global financial system, and give recommendations to the *G20*.

When listing the G7 and G20 as key players in international cooperation, one should bear in mind that in the policy world, cooperation typically means only **col-laboration**, for example by exchanging and sharing information, and discussing important issues of common interest. By contrast, **coordination** typically refers to formally agreed policy actions to reach superior outcomes for all. Such policies often involve multinational institutions as well (Agénor & Pereira da Silva, 2018: 22).

4.2 Global governance in global money and finance

In Section 1.3, we have discussed in more general terms that not all spillovers justify global governance. Why and when do we need policy collaboration or even coordination in the area of global finance?

To illustrate the point, consider that the Fed increases interest rates to cool down the US economy. Spillovers may lead to rising interest rates in other countries as well. Does this already make the case for coordination? Four arguments speak against it:

- First, modern central banks argue that they do not target the exchange rate but **domestic policy objectives**, like inflation rates or employment. In fact, if all spillovers of monetary policy would be subject to demands for coordination, no independent monetary policy would be possible.
- Second, policymakers might be able to **contain the impact of spillovers with national policies**. For example, the classic result of the 'monetary policy trilemma' posits that a flexible exchange rate enables a country to use its monetary policy even under full capital mobility, to reach its domestic objectives.
- Third, **spillbacks can promote cooperative behaviour in the country's self-interest**. For example, if the decision of the Fed to raise interest rates would push so-called 'systemic middle-income countries' into financial crises with negative spillbacks on the stability of the US banking system, the Fed may take this into account when making interest-rate decisions.[11]
- Fourth, even if we can make the case for coordinated policies, there can be **disagreement on the desirable coordinated policy**. For example, in the 1980s, the call for coordinated fiscal policy between the US and the EU meant a joint fiscal impulse to bring the world economy back to full employment. In the Eurozone after 1999, fiscal policy coordination has been understood as restraining fiscal policy to limit sovereign debts. Moreover, even within societies there is often deep disagreement about policy objectives and instruments, which makes it even more difficult to reach an agreement on coordinated policies.[12]

What, then, are cases for global coordination?

- The strong case for coordination is when the **impact on other countries is severe and cannot easily be contained**. Consider, as an example, the interest rate increases to two-digit levels in the US in the early 1980s. This contributed significantly to the debt crisis of developing economies that had borrowed internationally short-term and in US dollars.
- Another strong case is given when **coordination delivers superior outcomes.** For example, the IMF (2020) has estimated that a coordinated infrastructure investment programme in response to the Covid-19 pandemic would increase global real gross domestic product (GDP) by about 2% by 2025, as opposed to 1.2% for a programme when countries act alone.
- While cooperative behaviour may emerge already from the self-interest of countries, this insight requires a lot of exchange of information and coordination among all players. Therefore, **using the expertise of international institutions** is often essential.

- Finally, given deep global financial interdependencies, **ensuring global financial stability** is a strong candidate for global coordination (see below).

4.3 The quest for global financial stability

In the presence of free capital flows, ensuring financial stability may require international regulation. Schoenmaker (2011) argues that a financial stability trilemma exists. In his view, national supervision of integrated financial systems is a threat to the stability of global and national financial systems (Figure 7.6).

The Euro crisis is a case in point. European financial market integration increased rapidly after the introduction of the common currency. As regulation and supervision, especially of banking, had remained national, this helped igniting a doom loop, where failing large European banks were rescued at a national level, thus contributing to sovereign debt crises (see Chapter 6). Since then, at the global level Basel III has been developing new coordinated rules for banking and the FSB has been created. In the EU, a banking union with single supervision and regulation is developing.

The key aim of international supervision is to preempt regulatory arbitrage by financial institutions. Moreover, it is important to use coordination to avoid spillovers from regulatory differences. For example, when some countries introduced blanket guarantees for bank deposits to avoid bank runs, this attracted large amounts of deposits from other countries, rendering the banking system in these countries even more vulnerable.[13]

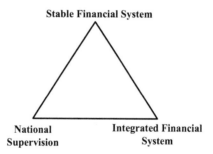

FIGURE 7.6 The Financial Stability Trilemma.
Source: Based on Schoenmaker (2011).

4.4 The future of governance in the IMFS

Recent research has highlighted a dollar dominance in the IMFS. If this problem is considered severe enough, even flexible exchange rates may not be sufficient to isolate a country from shocks emanating from the dominant economy. Countries may then only have the choice between policy autonomy and capital mobility. Rey (2015) has therefore argued that a **policy dilemma** exists (see also Chapter 6).

This argument implies that regaining policy autonomy could require limiting international capital mobility. In this respect, the old idea of Nobel laureate James Tobin to put a small tax on international capital movements has gained prominence. The charm of a *Tobin tax* is that a fraction of a percentage point discourages short-term capital flows, while leaving long-term investments largely unaffected.

However, while most advanced countries shy away from outright restrictions on capital movements, and support for a Tobin tax is mixed, certain so-called **macroprudential measures** applied at the national level to keep financial stability, e.g. capital requirement for banks, can contribute to a prudential management of international capital flows (Forbes, Fratzscher & Straub, 2015).

For developing and emerging economies, the IMF recommends a very cautious opening of capital accounts only. This new 'institutional view' of the IMF (2012) is now guiding its policy advice, recommending that opening up to international finance should be informed by the level of economic and financial development of the country.

An alternative route to address dollar dominance and its consequences for national policy autonomy is to develop the IMFS towards a multipolar one, with a larger role for other currencies. Two pathways are discussed:

- The first way is based on national or regional currencies, graduating to global currencies, and thus challenging the primacy of the dollar. As argued by Eichengreen, Mehl and Chitu (2019), the global economy may well be compatible with more than one global currency, and the IMFS may thus converge into a multipolar one. This, however, depends on the intrinsic strength of the dollar contenders. Especially for the Euro this means overcoming the weaknesses revealed in the Euro crisis, and to become a fully developed currency with deep financial markets and a single Eurozone safe asset.
- Second, a global synthetic currency could become the key global means of payments. This idea harks back on the Keynes plan, that was proposed by the British delegation at the Bretton-Woods conference in 1944. Keynes proposed a global currency, named 'bancor', in which countries settle their cross-border payments. In fact, the IMF's *Special Drawing Rights* (SDRs) are such a currency, yet its use is restricted to central banks. Some scholars argue the case of revisiting the Keynes plan, maybe in a digital version, in which a global synthetic currency may become a global means of payments, created and managed by a global monetary authority (see Chapter 6).

In sum, the IMFS will have to come to terms with an emerging multipolar world in a way that finds a sustainable balance between national self-determination, global responsibility, and financial, economic, and political stability.

5 Epilogue: governance and the wealth of nations

Governance should ultimately be geared in the broadest sense to increase the 'wealth of the nations and people'. Globalisation is a means and not an end in itself, and whenever it becomes dysfunctional, corrective action should be taken.

In this sense, there are clear cases for global governance, from governing global commons, such as global climate and pandemics, avoidance of beggar-thy-neighbour policies, including tax havens, multilateral cooperation in all areas where it is mutually beneficial, and last but not least, ensuring basic labour and human rights.

Moreover, global governance of world trade, money, and finance must ensure that all rules and regulations are indeed favourable to all countries. This is especially relevant in terms of creating a development-friendly global trading system, which allows fast diffusion of technology and knowledge to spur latecomer development and overcome poverty.

Regional integration can be beneficial also to non-members, yet there is no guarantee. The compatibility of regional integration schemes with a non-discriminatory multilateral system cannot be taken for granted, but needs to be actively pursued.

What, then, is the role of nation states? They are still at the heart of political decision-making, and will in all likelihood continue to do so. In general, not everything needs to be regulated at the global level. It is therefore important to reserve global governance for those activities where it is needed, while the rest could be allocated by the principle of subsidiarity and regulated at a level nearest to the people.

Yet, nation states have responsibilities to both their citizens and the world. With respect to citizens they have to care about well-being "beyond GDP", to paraphrase an OECD initiative to develop metrics to monitor well-being (Stiglitz, Fitoussi & Durand, 2018).

With respect to global responsibility, the United Nations Sustainable Development Goals (SDGs) ask nation states to work towards achieving these goals. Global responsibility starts with the first SDG, which asks to aim at ending poverty in all its forms everywhere, to SDG 10 (reduce inequality within and among countries), listing responsible migration policies, special and differential treatment for developing countries, as well as development assistance, to SDG 17 (Global Partnership for Sustainable Development), e.g. requesting the sharing of knowledge and for cooperation for access to science, technology, and innovations.

In sum, governance in the NGE should be designed – and if need be, rebalanced – to ultimately make globalisation work for people.

Recommended readings

For a more detailed coverage of international economic institutions, the world trading system, and the international monetary and financial system, the reader may consult standard texts like Daniels and Hoose (2017) or Krugman, Obstfeld and Melitz (2018).

For a discussion of governance in the global economy in the light of the political trilemma see Rodrik (2011). Eichengreen (2018) provides an in-depth analysis of the rise of populism with a special attention to Europe. In Evenett and Baldwin (2020a), leading experts discuss the future of the WTO.

For up-to-date information and analyses the reader may consult the WTO website (wto.org) and the IMF website (imf.org).

Notes

1 These are the findings of a study on global income distribution by Lakner and Milanovic (2013), which have been graphically summarised by the 'elephant curve'. In a recent update, Milanovic (2020) shows that the rise of a global middle class in emerging countries and its relative demise in advanced countries has continued, though the "elephant has lost its trunk", i.e., after the GFC the income of the richest 1% of the global population has increased less now than the global average.
2 By contrast, in emerging markets, participation in GVCs accounts for the lion's share in the almost 6% point reduction of the labour share, while technology played only a minor role. One should, however, note that we are talking here about income shares and not absolute income. As income has been growing rapidly in several emerging economies, particularly in China, labour incomes are still rising, but just less than capital income.
3 This is the optimal tariff argument discussed in Chapter 3.
4 Eichengreen and Sachs (1986) have contested this view. They argue that the competitive devaluations in the 1930s had the additional effect of lowering the value of a country's money against gold. This allowed to print more money and stimulate recovery.
5 See European Perspective 4.3 in Chapter 4 for a discussion of tax havens in the EU.
6 The MFN principle has been used earlier in international diplomacy to facilitate bilateral agreements by guaranteeing that – in case another country receives a better treatment at a later point in time – the now negotiating country will receive the same treatment. Otherwise, countries would have an incentive to continue negotiating until all other agreements are concluded, which would ultimately postpone agreements endlessly.
7 For an analysis of these trade policy instruments, see Chapter 3.
8 In the official language of the WTO, the term preferential agreement is reserved for agreements that provide unilateral trade preference without demanding (full) reciprocity. The most prominent example is the Generalised System of Preferences under which developed countries grant developing countries tariffs below the MFN level. We use the term preferential agreement in the broader sense of discriminatory agreement.
9 Article 24 of the GATT, Article 5 of the General Agreement on Trade in Services (GATS), and the Enabling Clause (Paragraph 2(c)) allow WTO members to form RTAs, provided a number of specified criteria are met. The discussion of these criteria is beyond the scope of this book.
10 It should also be noted that the WTO criteria for accepting an RTA are at best loosely related to the trade creation-trade diversion argument.
11 For a detailed discussion of this argument, see Agénor and Pereira da Silva (2018).
12 These points have been raised and discussed in detail by Frankel (2016).
13 For an analysis of the impact of national differences in deposit insurance schemes of global banking, see Qi, Kleimeier and Sander (2020).

References

Acemoglu, D., & Restrepo, P. (2018). The race between man and machine: implications of technology for growth, factor shares, and employment. *American Economic Review*, *108*(6), 1488–1542.

Agénor, P., & Pereira, L. A. (2018). Financial spillovers, spillbacks, and the scope for international macroprudential policy coordination. *BIS Papers* (Issue 97). Bank for international Settlements. https://www.bis.org/publ/bppdf/bispap97.htm.

Alesina, A., & Spolaore, E. (1997). On the number and size of nations. *The Quarterly Journal of Economics*, *112*(4), 1027–1056.

Alesina, A., & Spolaore, E. (2005). *The size of nations*. MIT Press.

Alesina, A., Tabellini, G., & Trebbi, F. (2017). Is Europe an optimal political area? *Brookings Papers on Economic Activity*, *2017*(1), 169–214.

Algan, Y., Guriev, S., Papaioannou, E., & Passari, E. (2017). The European trust crisis and the rise of populism. *Brookings Papers on Economic Activity*, *2017*(2), 309–400.

Autor, D. H., Dorn, D., & Hanson, G. H. (2016). The China shock: learning from labor-market adjustment to large changes in trade. *Annual Review of Economics*, *8*, 205–240.

Daniels, J. P., & Hoose, D. D. (2017). *Global economic issues and policies* (4th ed.). Routledge.

Eichengreen, B. (2018). *The populist temptation: Economic grievance and political reaction in the modern era*. Oxford University Press.

Eichengreen, B., Mehl, A., & Chitu, L. (2019). *How global currencies work: Past, present, and future*. Princeton University Press.

Eichengreen, B., & Sachs, J. (1986). Competitive devaluation and the great depression: a theoretical reassessment. *Economics Letters*, *22*(1), 67–71.

Evenett, S. J., & Baldwin, R. (Eds.) (2020a). *Revitalising multilateralism: Pragmatic ideas for the new WTO director-general*. Centre for Economic Policy Research.

Evenett, S. J., & Baldwin, R. (2020b). Revitalising multilateral trade cooperation: why? why now? and how? In S. J. Evenett, & R. Baldwin (Eds.), *Revitalising multilateralism: Pragmatic ideas for the new WTO director-general* (pp. 9–53). Centre for Economic Policy Research.

Forbes, K., Fratzscher, M., & Straub, R. (2015). Capital-flow management measures: what are they good for? *Journal of International Economics*, *96*, S76–S97.

Frankel, J. A. (2016). *International coordination*. Working Paper 21878, January. National Bureau of Economic Research.

Funke, M., Schularick, M., & Trebesch, C. (2016). Going to extremes: politics after financial crises, 1870–2014. *European Economic Review*, *88*, 227–260.

Guiso, L., Herrera, H., Morelli, M., & Sonno, T. (2019). Global crises and populism: the role of Eurozone institutions. *Economic Policy*, *34*(97), 95–139.

International Monetary Fund (2012). The Liberalization and Management of Capital Flows: An Institutional View, Washington: International Monetary Fund, 14 November. https://www.imf.org/external/np/pp/eng/2012/111412.pdf.

IMF (2017). *World economic outlook*, April. International Monetary Fund.

IMF (2020). G-20 Surveillance Note, November. International Monetary Fund. https://www.imf.org/external/np/g20/pdf/2020/111920.pdf.

Krugman, P. R., Obstfeld, M., & Melitz, M. (2018). *International economics. Theory and policy* (11th ed.). Prentice Hall.

Lakner, C., & Milanovic, B. (2013). *Global income distribution: From the fall of the Berlin wall to the great recession*. World Bank Working Paper 6719, December.

Lamy, P. (2020). Foreword. In: Mattoo, A., Rocha, N., & Ruta, M. (Eds.), *Handbook of deep trade agreements* (pp. ix–xi). World Bank.

Mattoo, A., Rocha, N., & Ruta, M. (Eds.). (2020). *Handbook of deep trade agreements.* World Bank.

Milanovic, B. (2020). *After the financial crisis: The evolution of the global income distribution between 2008 and 2013.* City University of New York: Stone Center on Socio-Economic Inequality. Working Paper Series 18, July.

Qi, S., Kleimeier, S., & Sander, H. (2020). The travels of a bank deposit in turbulent times: the importance of deposit insurance design for cross-border deposits. *Economic Inquiry, 58*(2), 980–997.

Rey, H. (2015). *Dilemma not trilemma: The global financial cycle and monetary policy independence.* National Bureau of Economic Research. Working Paper 21162, May, Revised February 2018.

Rodrik, D. (2011). *The globalization paradox: Democracy and the future of the world economy.* WW Norton & Company.

Rodrik, D. (2017). *Straight talk on trade: Ideas for a sane world economy.* Princeton University Press.

Rodrik, D. (2020). Putting global governance in its place. *The World Bank Research Observer, 35*(1), 1–18.

Schoenmaker, D. (2011). The financial trilemma. *Economics Letters, 111*(1), 57–59.

Stiglitz, J., Fitoussi, J., & Durand, M. (2018). *Beyond GDP: Measuring what counts for economic and social performance.* OECD Publishing.

INDEX

Note: **Bold** page numbers refer to tables and *italic* page numbers refer to figures.

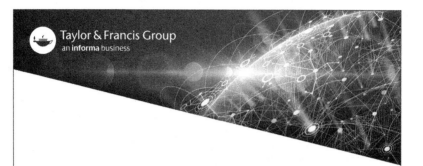

Printed in the United States
by Baker & Taylor Publisher Services